A SORCERER'S APPRENTICE

A SKEPTIC'S JOURNEY INTO THE CIA'S PROJECT STAR GATE

JOHN HERLOSKY

SORCERER'S APPRENTICE

A Skeptic's Journey into the
CIA's Project Star Gate and
Remote Viewing

John Herlosky

A Sorcerer's Apprentice: A Skeptic's Journey into the CIA's Project Star Gate and Remote Viewing
Copyright © 2015 John Herlosky. All Rights Reserved.

Published by: Trine Day LLC
PO Box 577
Walterville, OR 97489
1-800-556-2012
www.TrineDay.com
publisher@TrineDay.net

Library of Congress Control Number: 2015934568

Herlosky, John.
A Sorcerer's Apprentice—1st ed.
p. cm.
Includes index and references.
Epub (ISBN-13) 978-1-63424-001-7
Mobi (ISBN-13) 978-1-63424-002-4
Print (ISBN-13) 978-1-63424-000-0
1. Spiritual biography -- United States. 2. Remote viewing (Parapsychology) -- Research. 3. Remote viewing (Parapsychology) -- United States -- History. I. Herlosky, John. II. Title

First Edition
10 9 8 7 6 5 4 3 2 1

Printed in the USA
Distribution to the Trade by:
Independent Publishers Group (IPG)
814 North Franklin Street
Chicago, Illinois 60610
312.337.0747
www.ipgbook.com

The future depends on what you do today.

— Mahatma Gandhi

Ester asked why people are sad.
"That's simple," says the old man. "They are the prisoners of their personal history. Everyone believes that the main aim in life is to follow a plan. They never ask if that plan is theirs or if it was created by another person. They accumulate experiences, memories, things, other people's ideas, and it is more than they can possibly cope with. And that is why they forget their dreams."

— Paulo Coelho, *The Zahir*

No one saves us but ourselves. No one can and no one may. We ourselves must walk the path.

— Gautama Buddha, *Sayings Of Buddha*

For millions of years, mankind lived just like the animals. Then something happened which unleashed the power of our imagination. We learned to talk and we learned to listen. Speech has allowed the communication of ideas, enabling human beings to work together to build the impossible. Mankind's greatest achievements have come about by talking, and its greatest failures by not talking. It doesn't have to be like this. Our greatest hopes could become reality in the future. With the technology at our disposal, the possibilities are unbounded. All we need to do is make sure we keep talking.

— Stephen Hawking

Contents

AUTHOR'S NOTE

It will never work. The bomb will never work. I know explosives and that's why I know it won't work.

— Admiral Leahy: head of the Bureau of Ordinance during the Manhattan project

I have used only the first names of my classmates to protect their anonymity. I have used the real names and identities of the military remote viewers who were my teachers, friends, and mentors. Although they are integral to the narrative, this is my story. Due to editing and space considerations, it was not possible to put everything that occurred either in the classes I took or the conferences I attended, in the narrative. All conversations are as I remember them, as well as from my notes and journal, and are as accurate as I could make them. It was of course not possible to record every word verbatim, and some conversations and meetings were combined or edited in order to keep the continuity of the narrative.

In that spirit, the remote viewing sessions were depicted as seamless experiences. They generally are not. The remote viewer cycles in and out of "The Zone" as one's brain wave state changes, and so the information comes in a cyclic manner. They were depicted as seamless to keep the continuity of the story. The intensity and vividness of the sessions is as it was experienced. I ask the reader's indulgence.

Foreword

"Nothing is impossible" (Luke 1:37)

There are some things that happen to us in our lives that not only change us but also those around us in ways we never could have imaged. John Herlosky came to a major crossroad in his own life – where he began to question who he was and even what he thought reality was. His belief systems did not match what he was discovering from his inner journeys. John, by his own admission a non-psychic skeptic, was now experiencing on a personal level something that was much deeper, more spiritual and stranger than anything he believed in, or thought possible. He discovered that life may be filled with parallel universes, multi-realities and even psychic abilities.

It all began for John when he took an active interest in "remote viewing" as taught by David Morehouse, the author of "Psychic Warrior". That led him to taking classes taught by Morehouse and eventually becoming an assistant instructor in those classes.

Those of us who were "gifted" at birth with certain psychic abilities and talents have had a whole lifetime to adjust to this phenomenon of out-of-body-experiences, ESP, time travel, reality shifting and knowing things that are outside the normal experiences of most people. I personally have had to learn how to handle what I sensed and knew. Those who do not live life on that edge of reality might not understand the burden that it adds to your life. If you know something 'bad' is going to happen to someone, is it your responsibility to prevent it from happening? More importantly, should you alter another's fate and karma? If you change the future for someone you also change their life lesson as well. For someone like John who is thrust into this psychic world mid-life it can be a great emotional and spiritual learning curve. It could even cause one to question their sanity.

John's world was changed and his whole sense of himself was altered in a few short years by his personal explorations within. He was sensing and learning things that were not a part of his old belief systems. He was diving deep into this never-never land of "remote viewing" and was trying to deal rationally with what he was discovering. This great inner conflict and growth is what makes his personal journey a reading adventure. His story could easily be that of the average man or woman; I think readers will feel that they are personally taking this journey with him.

At some point in all of our lives, events will occur and people will come to us to help us find that next road ahead; like the old Yogi once said, "When the student is ready, the teacher will come." In this case, John's teacher was David Morehouse.

It is not important to understand quantum mechanics or why "remote viewing" works – all that is needed is an open mind. I believe that people can be taught to develop and use their own latent psychic abilities. I have personally witnessed too many strange and supernatural events in my own life, not to believe that everyone has that divine seed within them. John found a path and method and began his inner spiritual quest. That journey is what his book is about.

John is a 'spiritual adventurer' who is taking his own path in search of truth. Where will these roads take him in the next decade or two, or better yet, after you read his book, where will your roads take you? I am betting that you will also be altered and changed just by reading his story and being exposed to his life experiences. Just as with the famous "butterfly effect", so it is with all of us, and the way we live our lives. We each have an impact on everyone else to some degree. David Morehouse had an impact on John's life. John has also impacted people and they will impact others. Our whole reality and future has already been altered and changed at some level for the better.

I do not claim to know how or even why all these things work, but if what John discovered piques your interest investigate for yourself and take your own inner journey of discovery. May God bless your quest!

W. H. "Bill" McDonald Jr.
mapamcdonald@yahoo.com

Former president of The Military Writer's Society of America. Author of *The Spiritual Warrior's Journey: The Inspiring Life Story of a Mystical Warrior, Purple Hearts: Poetry of the Vietnam War, Sacred Eye: Poetry in Search of the Divine, Journey of the Heart: A Near Death Experience in India,* and other books.

The Vietnam Experience website: http://www.vietnamexp.com"
Military Writer's Society of America: http://www.militarywriters.com

96 Hours

Learn to be silent. Let your quiet mind listen and absorb.

— Pythagoras

It was a typically beautiful Southern California day, warm and sunny, as I walked into the Katy Geissert Library in Torrance, California. It was Friday and for the past several months, I had been coming here regularly to use the computer lab.

I was in the library working on an experiment in associative remote viewing (ARV) for a company called Physics Intuition Applications. The president of the company, a congenial man named Marty Rosenblatt, was doing research into remote viewing. A mathematical physicist by trade, Marty and I had met while attending a coordinate remote viewing (CRV) conference in El Paso, Texas that previous June. His presentation at the conference was on using remote viewing to predict the stock market. At that conference, we had a chance to discuss ideas and begin a strong friendship and working relationship that would lead to a startling event that would one day come back to haunt me.

Associative remote viewing isn't a viewing technique, but rather a targeting protocol. It allows a remote viewer to access information that might normally be difficult to perceive using standard remote viewing methodologies.

Marty's program was set up to forecast the movement of a particular stock index two days in advance. The computer chooses two pictures at random from a photo pool. One photo is assigned to an outcome of 'stock index up at the end of the trading day' versus the previous day's closing price. The other photo is assigned to a no-movement or down outcome.

For example, the computer would choose a picture of a mountain and assign it to the outcome-stock index moving up. The computer would then choose a photo of a waterfall and assign it to the index not moving or moving down. A remote viewer would look forward in time two trading days to see what picture the computer would show him as feedback based on what the market did. In two days, depending on the outcome of that trading day, the program would show one of the pictures to the viewer. If the index was up, the program would show the photo of the mountain, if down, the picture of the waterfall. Marty had numerous viewers using the protocol. The computer showed how many viewers had chosen each outcome and if one choice was an overwhelming favorite, he would put in a trade.

Today's session happened to be a Friday, and since there was no trading on the weekend, I would get my results on Tuesday.

So on that Friday afternoon I chose a console away from the other library patrons in order to minimize noise and distractions. Sitting down with pen and paper handy, I wondered what the people here in the library would think if they knew what I was doing.

I logged on to the computer and went to Marty's web site. Typing quickly, I pulled up the P5 protocol prediction and scoring program. After logging on to Marty's website, I began the cool-down process. After so many CRV sessions, it only took me several deep breaths to enter an alpha state. I no longer used the cool-down CD that I had trained on to achieve it. Now I needed to quiet the inner turmoil. The signal I would be tuning in to could be lost with as little as a stray thought.

Once relaxed, I opened my eyes and wrote down the heading at the top of the first page of the paper that I would use to record my impressions during the session. Once the session was complete, I would enter the data in the computer. I would allow myself only ten minutes for each viewing session.

Looking at the computer screen to see the coordinates or the first target, I took a deep breath and prepared to enter the Matrix. Like the fabled Kwisatz Haderach from the science fiction masterpiece *Dune,* who could be many places at once, I prepared to leap ahead in time and space.

The Matrix was the name that the creator of Coordinate Remote Viewing, Ingo Swann, coined for this level of reality. It wasn't a physical reality but rather a storehouse of all knowledge. Technically it could be described, in the words of physicist Dr. Elizabeth

Rauscher, as part of an 8th-dimensional complex Minkowski manifold; our regular 4 dimensional space-time plus a complex component in 4 dimensional space-time contiguous to it.[1]

The doorway to this M4 manifold in imaginary time and space, called the Matrix, is the unconscious. The problem is, the unconscious doesn't understand words and numbers. It understands pictures and feelings. It understands allegory. So how do you pull the information from the Matrix? That was the genius behind the work done by Ingo Swann, under the direction of the CIA, at the Stanford Research Institute. He set up a multi-stage methodology to access the Matrix and bring back usable data. It was a two-part process, one part detect, the other part decode. To enter the Matrix, the remote viewer entered an altered state of consciousness known as an alpha state; a state of relaxed alertness. It is here that the remote viewer detects data floating up from his unconscious mind, and then decodes it using the multi-stage methodology.[2]

Following that methodology, I wrote the six-digit number assigned to this session across the top of the page. The numbers represent a notional set of coordinates in the Matrix that are randomly generated. Their significance is for record keeping and as a point of focus for the remote viewer. They have no other significance.

Writing the last digit on the page, I allowed the first kinesthetic contact with the target to pull my pen across the paper. The resulting scrawl was the ideogram, the first graphic representation of the gestalt of the target. What the scrawl looked like was unimportant. It was the feeling that you felt as the pen moved across the paper that was important, what Swann called the 'feeling motion'.

Touching my pen to the ideogram, I entered the first stage of the Matrix. From the sharp right angle and hard flat feel of the ideogram, I knew I would be looking at something man-made, most likely a structure or structures. I wrote down the information on my paper. Then, again, I touched the tip of my pen to the center of the page and closed my eyes. The pen acted like an antenna for the signal line, the hypothetical conduit of data from the unconscious mind. The afterimage of the white paper faded and the twilight world of the Matrix appeared.

Every remote viewer experiences the Matrix differently. For me, it was like standing in a dark room surrounded by dense mists or fog. The fog was colored purple, magenta, gray, and black. It swirled around me like clouds. Sometimes there would be a flash of light deep in the background, like heat lightning on a summer's evening. The fog was the canvas that my unconscious mind would weave into pictures.

As I sat there quiescent, I knew that Stage two sensory impressions would be next. Stage twos are colors, sounds, smells, tastes, textures, and dimensionals. Dimensionals are the physical aspects of the target: its height, width, and mass.

Ill-defined forms that moved and morphed began to seep into my visual field. They seemed to float up behind my closed eyelids. I mentally tried to move with the image, focusing on it and trying to get a clearer picture. I wasn't trying to analyze what I was seeing as I struggled to increase the quality of the signal line. It wasn't my job to analyze; my job was to simply record data. I took a few moments to get a section of data, then stopped and described on my paper what I experienced. Then I touched pen to paper again and recorded another section of data.

I had the feeling of height; a sense of a sheer drop. The shapes were taking on the form of structures. What I was seeing seemed to be an urban scene. There was water, because I sensed a boat nearby. The dimensional aspect of the target was strongly vertical.

OK, I thought. My feedback picture is going to be some sort of cityscape. I was only halfway through the session and I was thinking I might have enough, but just to make sure, I continued into stage three.

Stage three is where the viewer finds that the information he is receiving in the form of sensory verbal data begins to diminish and sketches became dominant. The sketches are usually crude at that point of the process but it doesn't matter. Stage three sketches of the target gave me an advantage in deciding which picture was the correct one.

A shape swam up from the depths of the Matrix. It was long, cylindrical in form, and had a row of small windows along the side. It reminded me at first of a train because the front end was flat. Its dimensionals were curved, smooth, and elongated.

Strangely, there were no wheels or tracks. I sketched it on the page and first labeled it as an AOL, or analytical overlay, of a train. Analytic overlay is simply the mind's attempt to place a label on what one is seeing. However, there was no guarantee that the shape actually was a train. It could be something entirely different that was similar to a train. There was only one way to find out. I took my pen and probed the sketch, trying to gain more insight into what it might be. The thought came to me that it could be the fuselage of a commercial jet, although it had no wings or tail, and of course, the strangely flat nose.

Again, I turned inward with several deep breaths. Detect and decode. View and write. I followed the mantra of the coordinate remote viewer. However, the images that materialized in the visual field behind my eyelids seemed to have no connection to what I had just seen.

I reminded myself it wasn't my job to analyze data; my job was to observe and record. Dealing with results was the job of the analyst.

These first images resolved into a crater; no ... two craters. They reminded me of craters on the moon, except for the spired, jagged edges around the rim. I took a slow, measured breath and held it. Touching my pen to the paper again to pick up the signal line, I waited expectantly for the next images to form.

And they did.

Dogs, lots of dogs. German Shepherds, or wolves, and Labs and dogs I didn't recognize. Dogs. Jeez Louise. Dogs!

Dutifully, I wrote the information down, but frustration was beginning to seep in. These images seemed totally unrelated to what had preceded them. I took a quick glance at my chronometer. The countdown timer showed 90 seconds remaining of the original ten minutes. Just as well, I sighed. I thought some dirty words and then surprisingly, something in the back of my mind said, one more time.

There was a time when I would have ignored that little voice. A time when I would have laughed even at the suggestion that any of this was even possible. That time was four years and a dozen miracles in the past. I took one last deep breath, held it on a four count. Then I exhaled and touched pen to paper for one last college try.

Now I saw great clouds of billowing white snow or maybe dust or ash. I couldn't tell which. It reminded me of the near whiteouts of upstate New York winters I lived through as a teenager.

With a start, I realized that my chronometer alarm had gone off, signaling the end of the time I had allotted for the session. I wrote "end session" at the bottom of the page and the time in the heading on the first page.

Well, I'll see what the computer shows me before I get too disappointed, I thought. I might still be able to salvage this session depending on what I'm shown.

I typed the results into the computer and then went to the judgment page. Here, the computer would show me the two pictures chosen at random. Based on what I had just experienced, I would choose one of the two pictures as the feedback I would be shown on Tuesday.

The computer flashed the first picture up on the screen. It was a rural wooded scene. It had no correspondence to anything I had seen. Whew, I thought with relief. No lunar landscape. No billowing clouds.

I hit the key for the other choice and smiled when I saw what flashed up on the screen. It was a city skyline, seen from across a river. There was a large suspension bridge in the foreground. In the background was the skyline of a large metro area. Two monolithic skyscrapers dominated the skyline, one with a tall radio tower on the roof. It looked vaguely familiar, maybe Chicago or New York. There were boats on the river in the background. The water and boats I had seen in the ether.

This was so obviously the photo I would be shown in the future that I didn't hesitate. I keyed it into the computer as my choice.

The computer accepted my choice and the graphics flashing across the screen read: YOU HAVE CHOSEN PHOTO X AS YOUR CHOICE FOR TARGET COORDINATES 535 645. Then the computer continued: FEEDBACK FOR THIS SESSION WILL BE AVAILABLE AFTER 2PM, TUESDAY – I looked at the date the computer displayed, blissfully unaware of how devastatingly clear the mysteries of this session would become in 96 hours … on Tuesday, September 11, 2001.

J. HELLOSKY

9/7/01

ST: 1330

ET:

$$\frac{AV}{10}$$

$$\frac{P1}{428 - HUNGARY}$$

535

645

A) SLOPING DOWN,
ABRUPT ANGLE UP TO
PEAK AND CURVE

B) MAN MADE

C) STRUCTURE

$$\underline{S_2}$$

VERTICALS

CURVES

SMOOTH

SHEAR

AOL: BUILDINGS

AOL: BOAT

You will notice that the session lacks a lot of detail compared to a regular CRV session. This is not unusual as I was in session for only 10 minutes versus 60 to 90 for a CRV session. These were just notes that were only there to help me identify the correct photo. Thus the lack of detail and no session summary at the end.

S2

LONG
SMOOTH
CYLINDRICAL
ELABORATE
DESIGNER   AOL: ~~TRAIN~~

AOL: CARVED
     WOODWORK

LIFEFORM   AOL: WOLF

LIFEFORM   AOL: DOG
      BREAK
      RESUME

ROUND
JAGGED
POKED

AOL: CRATERS

AOL: SEA URCHINS

③

S₂

WHITE

LIFEFORMS

AOL: SNOW

AOL: DOG

AOL: WOMAN

BREAK

END SESSION

Target Feedback, john_herlosky

MyNotes   CoolDown

TargetID = 535645

CHAPTER ONE

Beginnings

I'm not a "natural" psychic. I know that sounds strange given the title of this book. But I've never had a premonition, seen a ghost or UFO, or had a prophetic dream. As far as I knew, I had the psychic ability of a sack of hammers.

What I am, is a very pragmatic and determined person who doesn't like to accept a rationale unless it's backed up by facts. If you say that a proposition is truth, then you had better be able to back up your assertion with research and conclusions that can be corroborated.

My schooling had been in the tradition of the scientific method. In college, I majored in mathematics with minors in engineering and philosophy. From college, I went on to law enforcement. I worked for two large metropolitan police departments and earned a degree in criminal justice. I was trained in observation and investigation. I learned how to weed out the facts from the fiction.

My feelings at that time regarding ESP were that if it did exist, it was a rare phenomenon, virtually uncontrollable and not replicable in the lab. I wasn't the only one who thought so as a large contingent of famous scientists shared my position.

In the early 70's, though, a paradigm shift was gaining momentum. Although, it happened first in the scientific community, its greatest impact would be on organizations shrouded in secrecy and intrigue.

Events were soon to illustrate the well-known saying that when a famous scientist says something is possible, he is probably right; when he says something is impossible, he is invariably wrong.

In the early 1970s, the Soviets were heavily involved in psychic research. Unable to keep up technologically with the West, the Soviets were desperate to find a way to close the gap. Psi research seemed plausible to Soviet leaders. They began looking into ways of turning psychic ability into not only an intelligence-gathering tool, but also into a weapon. They began research into what became known as "psychotronic weapons"; infernal devices that use electromagnetic energy tuned to the same frequency as a person's brain waves to disrupt cognitive activity or even to kill. Alarming reports came in that the KGB was beaming microwave energy into American embassies, causing a number of disturbing symptoms.[3]

As these reports came in to U.S. intelligence services, two laser physicists working for the second largest think tank in the U.S., the Stanford Research Institute, began a series of experiments under CIA auspices that were to demonstrate certain "psychic abilities". The men tasked with this assignment were Dr. Hal Puthoff and Dr. Russell Targ, working with a noted New York artist and psychic Ingo Swann and a retired police officer, Pat Price.

In 1975, the Air Force Foreign Technology Office, under the direction of Dr. Dale Graff, took over the program from the CIA and became the primary funder of the SRI program.

In 1975, the U.S. Army's Assistant Chief of Staff for Intelligence, Maj. General Edmund Thompson, learning of the experiments run by SRI, began his own program code-named Gondola Wish.[4]

Thus was started one of the most controversial and highly classified programs in U.S. intelligence history. Funded with over $20 million dollars, the program lasted for over two decades under the auspices of the Defense Intelligence Agency, the Central Intelligence Agency, the National Security Agency, the U.S. Army and Air Force. It was also under yearly congressional oversight and review. The project was variously known by the code names Gondola Wish, Grill Flame, Center Lane, Sun Streak, and finally Star Gate.[5]

With the Stanford Research Institute in charge of further research and the intelligence services and military handling the operational aspect, there was an uneasy alliance.[6]

The members of the remote viewing program never felt as if those they worked for appreciated their efforts. Many times information that the viewers provided, information that proved correct, was not utilized. The common belief at that time was that if you were a military officer on the fast track to promotion, assignment to the remote viewing program was career suicide. Many in the intelligence community sneered at the program members, saying that they were nothing more than charlatans, or worse, in league with the devil.

Several general officers of the command staff of these intelligence services who tasked the viewers and utilized their results, were uncomfortable with the implications of the remote viewing program. Many of these officers had strongly fundamentalist religious views and felt that even if the program wasn't exactly evil; it wasn't exactly 'kosher' either. The fact that the viewer's data was accurate repeatedly in situations where no other intelligence asset could retrieve such data reinforced their religious prejudice.[7]

These general officers decided to cancel the program. The CIA was the first of the intelligence agencies to do so, surprising, since they were the progenitors of the program. The remote viewing program however had some strong support in congressional committees, committees that controlled the purse strings of these agencies. These friends found a new home for the program with the DIA, the Defense Intelligence Agency.

Again, the people in the project found themselves ostracized, even as the program's friends in Congress continued the funding.

It wasn't long before the program's enemies and the inevitable internal conflicts generated by the stress that the viewers themselves were under, caused the program to suffer once again. The Defense Intelligence Agency no longer wanted the program. In 1986 the congressional friends found another home for the project, now christened Sunstreak, with the Air Force Office of Science and Technology Directorate, code-named OTS-D. More and more, however, the congressional representatives who were once friends with the program began to drift away. The controversy was becoming too dangerous for their political careers. Then in 1995, disaster struck. The remote viewing project had been reassigned back to the CIA, under a new congressional budget, now christened Star Gate. The same organization that had been trying to eliminate the program for the past ten years now had their chance. Under a Congressional mandate to provide an evaluation of the remote viewing program, the CIA commissioned a private research firm, the American Institute of Research, or AIR, to conduct the investigation. The CIA only allowed the investigators two percent of the thousands of remote viewing sessions to be reviewed and only sessions after

1993 were allowed. This was at a time when there were only three remote viewers available and few sessions were done. It wasn't a surprise then that the AIR conclusion was a negative one and the CIA had their recommendation that the program be disbanded. So ended the remote viewing program; a program that despite all odds had produced some of the most amazing intelligence coups in the history of American spying.[8]

Some of the findings of the Ft. Meade Unit, where the remote viewers were primarily based, have been declassified. These files read like something out of the "The X Files", and are absolutely amazing and incontrovertible. In many of the cases, the data gleaned from the remote viewers was deemed so sensitive that the remote viewers received no feedback on their target. It would have been impossible for the viewers to fake the information.[9]

Example one, a remote viewer targeting an unusually large structure spotted by satellite, found it housed under construction a huge submarine. The CIA was initially skeptical since the building was not near the water. The viewer, asked to look ahead in time, said that a rail line would be built within six months, from the building to the water in an attempt to circumvent American spy satellites. Within six months the rail was built and the existence of the Typhoon class ballistic missile submarine was confirmed.[10]

Example two, the US Air Force tasked the Ft. Meade viewers with an unknown target with the intention of finding out if the "spooks" could ascertain any information about one of their most highly classified programs. The viewers took up the challenge. The remote viewer who did the session described a large bat-winged aircraft with no tail. The viewer also reported that there were light beams in the wiring of the plane, rather than electricity. When the Air Force received the report, they were aghast. The remote viewers were told they were forbidden to access that target again under penalty of court-martial. The aircraft was the B-2 Stealth Bomber. These are just two examples of the amazing abilities of these unsung American heroes.[11]

Consider that the remote viewing program was under the scrutiny of not just one congressional oversight committee, but several. If it had been found to be non-viable, the program would not have lasted twenty years. Until recently, most of the program's files remained classified. Many still are.

The body of evidence supporting the existence of psychic phe-nomena is overwhelming. The debunkers and skeptics are in the minority now. I should know; I was one of them.

My association with remote viewing was a purely fortuitous one and began as the result of a project failure. Fortuitous is the polite term; it was purely a fluke, a shot in the dark.

"Synchronicity," Dr. Jung would say," Synchronicity."

Synchronicity, indeed.[12]

CHAPTER TWO

Background

Just begin and the mind grows heated
– continue, and the task is completed!

– Goethe.

In late 1992, I initiated a project to resurrect a formerly classified US Army program from the mid-80's code-named Trojan Warrior. This multi-disciplinary program was an outgrowth of the US Army's Task Force Delta. Task Force Delta, under a concept then known as Golden Sphere, was asked to find alternative "force multipliers" for the future battlefield. Since the U.S. military would never match the Soviet Union's huge army in numbers, they needed these force multipliers to make up the difference.

The primary force multiplier was the use of advanced technology. Developing superior equipment, however, did not address the human element. The U.S. Army wanted a technology that would make more capable soldiers. Trojan Warrior was one of the programs that were a result of the conclusions of Task Force Delta.

Trojan Warrior's concept was to teach a group of US Army Special Forces soldiers a carefully integrated set of mind-body integration techniques. I learned about the project just after the Rodney King riots had torn apart Los Angeles. It occurred to me that with some modifications, this program could address the deficiencies in training that had been at the heart of the King debacle. By that time, Trojan Warrior had been declassified. One of the instructors involved was Dr. Richard Heckler, a psychologist and Aikido instructor. He wrote about his experiences with the project in a book called *In Search of the Warrior's Spirit*. I had read the book and contacted Dr. Heckler to see if he would be interested in my idea. Dr. Heckler was intrigued and said that, coincidentally, a crime analyst in Colorado Springs had independently come up with the same idea. He suggested that I contact her to work together on the project. Dru, the crime analyst, was delighted with the idea and agreed we should work together to create Trojan Warrior II.[13]

That started a four-year odyssey that was to end in disappointment. Although successful in putting together a multi-disciplinary team as talented as the original, with Dr. Heckler heading the instructors, we were unable to overcome the bureaucracy involved in getting the project funded. But the time I spent trying to get the project going was not in vain, as I received training in a number of the disciplines taught in the program. I also got a chance to work with several members of SEAL Team's One and Three, who had been chosen as guinea pigs for the project. Working out with these highly trained individuals gave me much more appreciation for the profoundly dedicated men and women of our armed forces.

The training I received in advanced EEG biofeedback enabled the success that I found in learning remote viewing. I still hope to recreate Trojan Warrior, but that remains for the future.

The failure to get the program funded hit me hard. My long-term relationship with the woman I was engaged to marry had also recently ended badly, in deceit and betrayal. Another blow came from one of my closest friends, who turned away from me when I needed support the most. These betrayals were devastating. I was forced to re-evaluate where I was, and even more importantly, where I was going. The sudden sense of urgency filled me with apprehension.

It was a very difficult time in my life. I was spiritually and emotionally bankrupt. It would be a stroke of fate that would send me in a new direction.

One afternoon, I happened into a local bookstore in Torrance, California. As I walked in the door, I noticed one of the books on the table of newly published hardbacks. It had a striking blue and black cover and the intriguing title of *Psychic Warrior*. As I looked at the cover, I thought this might be good for an entertaining read. The subtitle said that the book was about the CIA's Star Gate program. I was not familiar with it, but I was a fan of good science fiction, so I opened the book to read the inside flap. It was then that I realized this was not a work of fiction. It was a true story of an Army officer's involvement in the Pentagon's psychic spy program, detailing how he had become a "remote viewer" with the ability to extend his consciousness to other places across space and time and accurately report on what he experienced.[14]

To say that I was shocked is an understatement. It wasn't the US government's involvement in psychic espionage, with a capital E-S-P, which surprised me the most. Nor was it that the CIA was giving new meaning to the word "spooks". It was the fact that the author, David A. Morehouse, not a natural psychic but a pragmatic special operations soldier, had been *trained* to be psychic. This went against everything that I believed about ESP. How could you train someone to be psychic when ESP didn't exist?

I bought the book and read it that night cover to cover. What I found was stunning: its implications would have very personal repercussions for me. The book detailed the adventures of Morehouse when he was assigned to the Star Gate program as a remote viewer. I was determined to learn more and to locate the author. I hoped to persuade him to teach me remote viewing. I did not know then that I would be undertaking the greatest adventure of my life.

It took almost two years to reach Dave Morehouse, as he was living in Europe. During that time I settled for researching everything I could on remote viewing. I read numerous articles and books on the subject, including some written by the military remote viewers themselves. The more I read about their exploits, the more intrigued I was with the subject.

In the spring of 1999, I spied an advertisement in a newspaper for a class on remote viewing taught at UCLA. I was delighted to discover that the instructor was none other than Dr. David Morehouse. I immediately called the number and signed up.

The five weeks before the class started finally meandered by and I found myself driving up the road to Kovel Commons on the beautiful tree-lined campus at UCLA. Arriving early, I parked my car and walked to the location of the classroom. I took my time, wanting to see the campus as well as enjoy the beautiful morning. There's almost never a shortage of sunshine in Los Angeles.

I considered what I was getting myself into as I walked along the tree-shaded sidewalk. I wanted to see for myself what remote viewing was all about. I wanted to know if it was real or, as the debunkers clamored, a fake or a delusion. If it *was* real, was it a useful tool, or just an amusement?

Everything I had discovered after reading Morehouse's book told me that remote viewing was a genuine phenomenon. I had studied the research done by Dr. Robert Jahn and his associate Brenda Dunne with the Princeton Engineering Anomalies Research group (PEAR). They had set up extremely tight controls in their tests to explore the question, does ESP exist? They chose precognitive remote viewing in which a double-blind study examined whether or not subjects could describe a single target from a pool of targets. Neither the subject nor the researcher chosen to work with them had any idea what targets would be in the pool. A random number generator selected a target from a pool of ten. An independent judge would choose the correct one based on the description that the viewer provided. However, the target would not be chosen until after the viewing.[15]

In other words, the viewer had to look ahead in time to see the correct target. In the dry words of the scientists, the results categorically were statistically significant. Jahn and Dunne did not select for subjects that appeared to do the best. They simply asked for volunteers for an experiment in extrasensory perception. They did not want psychics; they wanted people who were motivated.

The implication was that the ability was innate. Jahn and Dunne found that the ESP ability exhibited by their subjects varied over a binomial distribution, the famed bell-shaped curve. Some at the one extreme were very, very good. Those at the opposite end of the spectrum were not so very good. However, the majority showed an ability that was considered significant. Ergo, even I should be able to do this. I was realistic enough to know that I could fall anywhere in that spectrum. I just hoped it wouldn't be on the not-so-very-good end.

Chapter Three

CRV

Structure! Content be damned!

—Captain F. "Skip" Atwater
Exclamation during a training exercise
with the creator of CRV, Ingo Swann

As I entered the classroom, I was still a little early so I introduced myself to one of my fellow classmates, who had also arrived early. Val is a tall, pleasant woman with short brown hair and an easy-going personality. As we sat chatting, I heard an angry voice coming from the adjacent stairwell. When the man appeared I recognized Dr. Morehouse from the pictures in his book. Dressed in an open-necked shirt and sweatpants, he was of medium height and stocky build with a thatch of graying hair. His face was drawn with fatigue and fury flashed in his eyes.

I turned to Val and said, "Doesn't look too happy about something." Some of the excitement dimmed. As we settled into the classroom, I watched Dr. Morehouse as he set up his lecture equipment. There was nothing fancy, just an overhead projector, a VCR, and a boom box.

I walked over to him as he was grabbing what appeared to be handouts for the class. I said, "Dr. Morehouse, why don't you let me hand those out for you?" He turned to me and smiled, surprised but pleased by the offer, "Thanks, I'd appreciate it."

I grinned back at him, "No problem; glad to help." I didn't know it then, but that simple exchange was the seed that would grow over the next five years into a close friendship.

Dave Morehouse and Author

As he took his chair at the podium, Dr. Morehouse underwent a surprising transformation. A big grin lit up his face and the fatigue I saw earlier seemed to melt away.

"First of all, I apologize for being late. We had a late start up from Orange County and got caught in some traffic. I would like to welcome you to this class in coordinate remote viewing. I am honored and humbled to see all of you here, and I'm proud to be your teacher.

"Today we'll start the lecture after the class intros. My plan is to get through phase three by Saturday afternoon and your first target that evening. Sunday we'll start the lecture for phase four and finish the following weekend."

Our teacher chuckled, "Be forewarned! I'm going to force-feed you guys. This stuff is going to come at you like a fire-hose. Stick with it though; it'll be intense, but I think you'll enjoy this week. I've got some good targets that you'll enjoy."

Dave turned more serious and continued, "Please ask questions if you have any, regardless of what your concerns are. You will always get an honest answer from me. That includes any questions regarding my past." He paused a moment to emphasize the point.

After giving us a short bio on himself, Dr. Morehouse said, "What I'd like to do now is to have you all, one by one, stand and introduce yourselves." Most of us had read his book, so we already had a working knowledge of his past. Each member of the class gave a short talk on who we were, what we did, and why we wanted to learn remote viewing. We ranged the spectrum from homemaker to deep-sea diver. Some had previous psychic experiences; some had not.

When it was my turn, I stood up, slightly embarrassed like everyone else, "My name is John Herlosky and I'm a former police officer. I've never had a psychic event occur in my life and I'm a little dubious about all this but I read Dr. Morehouse's book and was very impressed. So I thought I'd try the class and see if my mind could be changed." It wasn't until the introductions were finished that I realized I was the only member of the class who had voiced any skepticism. This was going to be interesting.

After a video about Dr. Morehouse's experience in assisting a Baltimore County Police Department find a murder victim, we had a short break. Back in class Dr. Morehouse talked about the importance of remote viewing to the human race. This was to be a constant theme throughout his seminars.

"Does anyone know what the single greatest enterprise is on this planet?" Dr. Morehouse asked. "It's war! Our country alone outspends all others in defense-related spending. Do you know what country has the largest weapons sales in the world?"

I spoke up. This answer I knew, "The US."

Dave pointed to me, "That's right. We do. Yet we're the ones deploring third world nations for trying to do the same. A little bit of hypocrisy showing, don't you think?"

His hands went to his hips as he shook his head with a slight frown, "I've worked for the military for half of my life and I'm telling you that you shouldn't take everything the government tells you at face value. If you do then you're liable to be disappointed. You need to check things out, investigate and come to your own conclusions."

He continued, "It's not just us; some of the poorest countries in the world have huge armed forces. They may not be able to afford the basic needs of their people, but they can bomb their next-door neighbors back to the Stone Age. Moreover, this has been going on since recorded history. At any one time, there are up to thirty conflicts going on in the world."

As a student of military history, I knew that he was right. I have had numerous conversations with my friends over beer and pizza on this very subject.

"Societies follow a well-defined path called the Four Turnings, according to researchers William Strauss and Neil Howe. Each phase takes roughly 20 to 30 years. The Four Turnings are, first: the building phase. Society builds up in complexity and ability. Then comes the sustainment phase, where the society prospers. Following is the unraveling phase where, whatever the faults of the society are, they reach a critical stage with enough momentum to cause the final phase: destruction. The society collapses and returns to the build-up stage. The upheaval can be gradual, as in the fall of the Roman Empire; or rapid, as in the fall of the Mayan Indian civilization."[16]

Dr. Morehouse looked around the room and asked, "Where do you think we are now as a global society?"

One of the students offered the 'critical stage'. Dr. Morehouse nodded soberly. He continued, "What we have to do as remote viewers is to help our society get through the fourth turning. We do that by helping people to understand that they are co-creators; that they are wondrous beings with the power to transcend space and time; that they have the ability to know truth, and that no truth however disguised or camouflaged can be hidden from a remote viewer."

Looking at his watch some 60 minutes later, Dr. Morehouse stopped the lecture, "Okay. Let's take a 15-minute break and we'll start into the Stage One lecture of coordinate remote viewing."

I caught up with Val as she was going out the door. "So how did you get into all this?" I asked her. "You were a little vague in the intro."

"Well, as I said, I'm retired and I just like to do interesting things. When I see something that piques my interest, I get involved with it. I love traveling to new adventures. Like you, I read *Psychic Warrior*, and I've always had an interest in the paranormal. I had a couple of weeks free before my next trip so I signed up." She looked at me curiously, "You sound like you're in a bit of a quandary. Part of you sounds like you believe in ESP, but your words tend to take a skeptic's viewpoint."

"Yeah, that's my dilemma," I admitted. "When I was a kid I read sci-fi books about people with psychic powers and always wanted to be psychic. I even used to try and send telepathic messages to my high school sweetheart after we had broken up, to try and get her back. However, that didn't seem to have much success. As a kid I had never had a prophetic dream or anything like that. I played around with Zener cards, you know, the cards with the five different symbols on the back. They have a star, a set of wavy lines, a circle, a square, and a cross. You shuffle up the deck and then take the cards one at a time and try and see in your mind what symbol is on the back."

She nodded her understanding.

"The problem was that in the beginning I was pretty good, but then I'd start missing and get bored. So my scores never really got overall very good. I figured that ESP was just for good sci-fi."

Val sighed, "But that's just the novice effect. That's why Zener cards aren't used that much any more. People get too bored with stacks of just guessing cards. I think you'll find remote viewing will change your mind."

I shrugged, "I guess we'll find out."

Most of the remainder of the evening was spent with the mechanics of Stage One. This included the ideogram and the A, B, and C components, which are the first elements in the CRV protocol. At the end of the class, with an admonition to drive safely, Dr. Morehouse bid us good night. To the chagrin of some of the class, who hadn't attended in a while at the university level, he gave us homework. Tomorrow would be the lecture on the second and third stages of coordinate remote viewing.

Saturday morning found me in the classroom once again bright and early. I had gone over the workbook for the first stages in coordinate remote viewing the previous evening. I knew that after the lecture and dinner, we would be doing our first training target. I hoped for an exciting day. I should have remembered the saying, "Be careful what you wish for." It would certainly prove to be exciting, but not the kind of excitement I wanted.

Prior to the lecture I got into several conversations with others in the class. 'Wings', the deep-sea diver, had taken not only the CRV course, but had also just finished the Extended Remote Viewing course in Carmel.

I had to ask him about the ERV class, "Wings, what was the ERV class like?"

Wings rocked back in his chair, slapping his leg, "You guys aren't going to believe that class. It was so outrageous that it just blew us away."

His friend Marc, who had taken the class with him, added, "If you think this class is great, wait till you take Extended Remote Viewing. It's nothing like Coordinate Remote Viewing. It's total immersion in the Matrix. It's as close to an out-of-body experience as you can get."

Several of the others nodded as I said, "I'd like to try that class if I do well in CRV. Ever since I read *Psychic Warrior*, I've wanted to learn ERV. Dave's description of an ERV session really was the reason I signed up for his remote viewing class." From my investigations prior to this class, I knew that Dr. Morehouse was one of the few remote viewers that taught ERV.

Marc nodded knowingly, "You are going to love that class."

Sitting with us were three others, two women and a man. They introduced themselves as Jill, Saundra, and John. They knew each other from their association with MUFON, the Mutual UFO Network. After the introductions, I tell them that I've never seen a UFO and frankly have not seen any evidence that extraterrestrials have ever visited this planet.

"You mean with all of the photos and eyewitness accounts, the testimony of thousands of people, some of whom are acknowledged experts in their fields, you still don't believe in UFOs," Jill exclaimed.

Jill was short and intense and apparently had some strong opinions on this subject. Evidently, I had touched a nerve.

I glanced over at the woman named Saundra. She was tall, slim, and beautiful, with dark hair and dark expressive eyes. I replied as diplomatically as possible, "I didn't say that I don't believe in UFOs; I said that I don't believe we've been visited by alien spacecraft. I believe that people have seen something, but to jump to the conclusion that ET's are here is a leap that I'm not prepared to make."

Saundra came to my rescue as Jill started to reply. Putting her hand on my arm in a friendly manner, she said in a light voice tinged with humor, "Well, he has an open mind, Jill. We'll give him time. After all, he didn't originally believe in remote viewing either, but he's here."

The day went quickly, divided between Dr. Morehouse's lectures and breaks for lunch and dinner. The lectures were excellent, with just the right amount of science blended with the occasional war story from the Star Gate Unit to spice things up.

"Remember, don't get too caught up with Stage One. Get in and get out. Don't waste time asking, "Do I have an ideogram or not?" You are beginning coordinate remote viewers. I don't expect all of you will feel your ideogram the first time. That comes with practice. What is important to remember is the structure. Keep to the structure; it won't let you down."

Dr. Morehouse paused with a memory from his past. Smiling, he said, "Those of you who have read *Psychic Warrior* know of Mel Riley. Mel was a natural psychic who got even better after he had trained in remote viewing. He knew the structure like the back of his hand and was one of the best coordinate remote viewers we had in the Unit. Before Mel came to the Unit, he was a photo interpreter. He had an artist's talent when it came to sketches and renderings. His session drawings had perspective and shadings, depth and texture. They were like black and white photos. Really high quality."

With a grin he continued, "At the opposite end of the spectrum, artist-wise, was Lyn Buchanan. He was another natural psychic that reveled in coordinate remote viewing. Lyn was quite a character. At Fort Meade, he liked to walk around in his stocking feet. Well, Lyn's drawings were stick figures. Half the time he would drive the analysts crazy as they tried to decipher his chicken scratching. Lyn was also unusual in that he was a warrior with a pacifist's soul when it came to remote viewing. You see, Lyn couldn't see weapons. On a training target that happened to be a museum at a Civil War battlefield, all Lyn saw were rows of empty glass cases. He couldn't see the muskets or bayonets. Yet Lyn had a special affinity for getting into people's minds. He was very good at pulling information from a human target. That was one of his specialties. He was also the one who codified the protocols for remote influencing."

I had read about remote influencing in Dave's book. I wondered if I would ever have the chance to learn it and meet these two fascinating military remote viewers. I could imagine the conversations we might have.

The talk was lively at the lunch and dinner tables that day, with heated discussions tinged with laughter. Again, Jill tried to convert me to her view on UFOs, while I took the stand of the character Dana Scully from the X-Files; that of skeptical interest. The exchange of viewpoints and opinions, spiced with lighthearted banter from some of the other classmates, made for an entertaining evening.

Later that night our first practice target was scheduled. I was excited but concerned about whether or not I could do an ideogram. I had read about the difficulty every beginning remote viewer experiences when trying to form one. Ideograms are the first big hurdle that new students have to overcome in coordinate remote viewing.

The creation of an ideogram is a purely kinesthetic response. It occurs after a remote viewer quiets their mind and listens to the randomly generated numbers that stand for the concept of the target. When the viewer hears the last digit, his pen is supposed to move across the paper. The line or curve generated by unconsciously controlled muscle movements is related to the gestalt, or overall aspect, of the target. Then the remote viewer decodes the ideogram based on how it felt to him when he drew it. The viewer does not decode the ideogram by the way it looks, only how it feels.

I put aside my anxiety and took a more positive attitude. As we cleared our desks of everything but a stack of drawing paper and a pen, I looked over at Val. She smiled encouragingly, and whispered good luck. I smiled back.

Moments later Dr. Morehouse started the cool-down tape of breathing exercises to help quiet the mind. As he did so, one of his assistants dimmed the lights. I voluntarily slowed my breathing and pulse rate. This part was easy for me, because of the techniques that I learned in the Trojan Warrior II program.

When the tape ended, Dr. Morehouse announced quietly, "Alright, class. When you have completed your heading and are ready to accept your coordinates, place your pens on the paper in the ready position." I wrote the heading and then placed my pen on the paper. The lecture had taught that the pen acted as an antenna for the data that would begin streaming from the Matrix, and as a prompt to the unconscious that a request for information was coming. It was part of the ritual of CRV; the way you trained the unconscious to communicate. It took only moments for the rustling of paper to end, signaling that the class was ready.

"Your coordinates are, one-nine-nine-nine." Then he paused for a brief moment and in a measured cadence that duplicated the first set of numbers, he read off the second set, "Zero-seven-seven-en-one."

As Dr. Morehouse read off the numbers, I wrote them on the paper. As we got to the last digit, I anticipated the ideogram. I heard the last digit and wrote it on the page and... nothing, just a flat line straight across the paper.

This is not good, I thought. I pushed down the rising panic and forced myself to relax. Okay, I thought, no problem. I know that Dr. Morehouse will read off the coordinates two more times for this very reason. I'll just try again. Two minutes later, he repeats the numbers. The result is the same, a flat line. Two more minutes of agonized waiting and once again a flat line.

"You have received your coordinates. Access the target and describe what you see." Then in a lighter tone he encouraged the class. "Have fun with this! You all can do this. Trust the structure. Please continue working until I tell you to stop."

I glanced around the room to see how the class was doing. Everyone was writing down something. Out of the entire class, I was the only one who had failed.

Biting my lip in frustration, I sat there thinking my fear of the ideogram was now justified. Nevertheless, I decided to continue to give myself the coordinates and keep trying. After all, I thought, I seemed to have some time on my hands.

So I did. I gave myself the coordinates repeatedly. I got over twenty pages of flat lines. Appropriate, I thought, as I slumped back in my seat. They looked like the flat lines a heart monitor traces on a dead patient.

My first try at CRV was DOA.

Fifty minutes from the end of the cool-down tape Dr. Morehouse came back into the room. As the lights came up he said, "Okay, let's end the session. I'd like you to write your session summaries as I take a look at what you've got."

The summaries are a written narrative of what the viewer experienced while at the target. As I sat slumped in my seat, I ruefully considered the fact that my summary was going to be more like a post mortem.

I watched as Dr. Morehouse moved around the room, chatting amiably with the students and looking at their results. Occasionally he would transfer a student's drawing onto a transparency.

Watching them sent my spirits and my ego even lower. Everybody else was apparently successful, except yours truly. I just shook my head and thought, "Well, this sucks."

Finally, Dr. Morehouse made his way to my table. I sat slumped in my seat as he asked, "How did it go, John?"

"It didn't, Dr. Morehouse. I couldn't get past the ideogram," I said miserably. "Let's see what you've got," he said simply. He reached down and flipped through the pages, seeing rows and rows of neat straight lines. Putting his hand on my shoulder sympathetically, he said, "Listen, I'm proud that you didn't quit. You could have, you know. You could have just said, "The hell with it," but you kept trying. Moreover, you only made a simple error here, that's all. When you got the first straight line and felt correctly that it wasn't the ideogram, you started again. However, at that point, you were out of structure; you needed to declare a missed break. Just remember that for tomorrow's target. You'll do just fine." He smiled reassuringly and moved on to the next student.

I looked over at Val. She had a questioning look in her eye. I just frowned and rolled my eyes, shaking my head.

She leaned over and whispered, "You'll get it tomorrow."

While the class took a break, Dr. Morehouse finished taking data from the student's papers and transferred it to the transparencies. Outside I spoke to Jill and Saundra. "Damn, I can't believe that out of the entire class, I'm the only one who failed!"

"Don't take it so hard; you'll do better tomorrow," Saundra replied, trying to reassure me.

Val walked up as Jill asked, "What happened?"

"I screwed up. I didn't get an ideogram the first time so I kept trying. Twenty pages of straight lines and no ideograms."

"Wow! And you didn't get at least one ideogram?" Val asked.

"No, apparently, like a dummy, I forgot to declare a missed break," I said shaking my head ruefully.

"Well, Dave seemed pretty impressed that you didn't quit. That's a good sign. I don't think he would have said anything if it hadn't been," Val replied. At that moment, one of the assistants stuck her head out the door and said the class was about to start.

"Maybe it didn't go that well this time, but you know what you did wrong. Next time you won't forget," Saundra said, as we walked to the door. She was right about that. I wouldn't forget again.

Once the class was seated, Dr. Morehouse began, "I want each of you to read off just your session summary. Then we'll go through the data I collected off your sheets with the overhead to give you all an idea how well you did."

I squirmed in my seat, thinking oh boy, this is going to be fun. Hi everyone, I'm John and I'm the only one who screwed up and got nothing.

When my turn finally came I said I had made a mistake in the beginning phase and was unsuccessful. I could feel the hot burn of embarrassment on my face. I thought to myself, oh yes, it doesn't get any better than this.

It was Dr. Morehouse that saved what little pride I had left at that point, "John made a minor error in structure. It's not unusual considering all that you have to learn so quickly. My first time wasn't much better. It took months for me to learn this. You've had two days. What I was most impressed with was that he didn't give up. He had twenty-plus pages of attempted ideograms with dozens of attempts on each page. I'm proud of your effort, John."

The class looked at me with respect. Well, maybe it could get better after all. Thank you Dr. M, I thought to myself with feeling.

After everyone had a chance to read their summaries and Dr. Morehouse had shown the transparencies, he asked if the class wanted the feedback. There was a resounding yes. I wondered what the target had been. The data suggested something big and massive. Several people had described large castles of stone surrounded by water.

When the overhead projector was switched on and the target flashed on the screen, everyone started talking excitedly. Dr. Morehouse spoke out over the class din, "Your target was Ball's Pyramid." The photos on the screen showed a large steep rock that juts some 1800 feet from the water like the fin of a huge shark.

"Some of the class saw castles surrounded by water. That's not unusual for this target with new remote viewers. Remember what we talked about with AOL–analytical overlay. Don't take anything for granted from your conscious mind. If it's a postcard-like image that is static, then it's AOL. Challenge that image, probe it, and find out what's underneath. If the image becomes fluid, morphs, and changes, then you know you have good data. Your conscious mind always wants to put a label on any data, even if it isn't clear what you are seeing."

Then, with a mischievous grin, he pantomimed pulling cards out of a Rolodex. "Is it this? Is it this?"

The class laughed, as Dr. Morehouse continued, "Right now you are seeing in stage two and three. The conduits are not fully open yet, as they will be in the later stages. Your visuals in these stages will be primitive. Don't worry. They're supposed to be. They'll get clearer and more detailed as you get further into the structure. Have patience and trust the structure. It won't let you down." With that, the class ended for Saturday. I was in no mood to share the excited conversations that were going on. I was still devastated that I had failed. I begged off going out for a drink with Jill and Saundra. They, like Val, commiserated with me for a moment. But I had to get out of there. Val asked if I was up to some ideogram practice. I think she knew how badly I was feeling. I declined, saying, "Thanks, anyway."

When I got home, I spent two hours doing ideogram drills until I was too tired to continue. I could only hope that tomorrow would be better. I considered dropping out of the class. Another failed session would be hard to stomach. As I lay in bed, the memory of another choice from my past tugged at my soul. My mind wandered back to the time when I was involved with Trojan Warrior II. I remembered how close I had come to a failure of a different sort.

Chapter Four

The SEALs

The only easy day is yesterday.

—Sign posted over the entrance to BUD/S: U.S. Navy SEAL
training school.

It was the early 1990's. At that time, the difficulties in funding the Trojan Warrior II project were beginning to be felt; it was a constant drag on me. I was to meet the SEALs chosen for the program for a run at Will Rogers State beach that Saturday and frankly I was a bit intimidated by the course; a grueling twelve-mile run up into the Santa Monica Mountains. The daily grind of trying to locate funding was wearing me down and I hadn't trained that week as much as I had wanted. I had never run anything longer than half that distance at any one time, and that had been in the police academy fifteen years ago. The beginning of this run would be up the side of the foothills, 1500 feet to the summit.

I thought sarcastically to myself as we walked to the beginning of the trail, my teammates laughing and joking amongst themselves, that a half-marathon in the hills was just what I needed to take my mind off of the funding problems. Right.

I knew I was in trouble when we reached the beginning of the trail at the foot of the mountains. One of the SEALs, Shawn, yelled out, "Let's go!" and sprinted up the trail. He wasn't jogging; he wasn't running. He was sprinting. I followed as fast as I could but as we got higher up, the trail became clogged with brush and was so steep that when you reached straight out from your body, you touched the ground. In less than five minutes my thighs were burning so badly that I fully expected my shorts to catch on fire! I was also falling behind, something I didn't want to happen. My legs kept a constant conversation with my brain stating they were going to explode if I didn't stop. My heaving lungs seconded the motion. But I remembered the look on the SEAL's faces after the last run that we had completed down at Torrey Pines State Beach where I had not done so well. I was determined not to quit.

Suddenly there was a rush of gravel as Shawn pulled up beside me, almost knocking me over on the narrow trail barely big enough for one. With a smile of doom, he got behind me and with a roar yelled, "GET YOUR ASS IN GEAR! MOVE IT HERLOSKY!"

That sent a shock of adrenaline racing through my body and I could feel my thighs and lungs snap to attention as I leaped up the slope. Shawn chased me the rest of the way to the summit where I collapsed in a heap, lungs heaving, as if I was sucking vacuum. Here was the make or break point. I could see it in their faces. Keith said, "You want to rest a little, John?"

Keith was saying anything but that. I could almost hear the plea from his heart to get up, GET UP! My body was literally shaking with fatigue. I had never run like that in my life. Even the most difficult runs or exercises in the Police Academy could have matched the intensity of that climb.

And I had eleven and a half miles to go.

Every part of me pleaded yes, just a little break. To make it worse, my mind went along with the subterfuge; only a little while, it cunningly appealed, just to catch your breath.

At that moment, when every part of my body screamed for relief, a line from the cadence tape that I usually ran with came to mind. The tape played the cadence calls of the SEAL trainees during their passage through BUD/S, the basic training program for SEALs. The line went, "Gotta keep runnin', for to stop is to die!"

Only in this case it would be the death of any hope to continue with these men. So with the complimentary thought that echoed in my mind of the legend displayed at the entrance to BUD/S, "The only easy day is yesterday", I slowly got to my feet, my body screaming with disbelief, and stated, "No, if I stop now, I'll never get going again."

Keith grinned as Shawn yelled out exuberantly, "All right! Let's run." I finished with those guys that day. Twelve miles – the longest, most intense run I have ever done. It was one of the proudest days of my life.

The following week the project was over. My partner Dru and I had put our time, money, and effort into getting the program funded, only to have it pulled out at the last minute. We were totally exhausted.

But I remembered the lesson of that bright Saturday morning when I went for a simple run up the side of a mountain.

I'd be there in class next morning.

Before I dropped off to sleep, I remembered what Dr. Morehouse said just before we had the break prior to our first target: "Put aside ego and self-doubt. Trust the structure. It will not let you down."

God, I hoped so, but my desires were taking a back seat to my beliefs.

The next day, there was more lecture from Dr. Morehouse on Stage 4, and our second target. I was psyched; my heart was racing and I was sick to my stomach. Talk about performance anxiety. As we cleared off our desks, I quickly reviewed my exemplar. I sure as hell wouldn't forget to declare a missed break if that happened again.

Listening to the cool-down tape, I tried to concentrate on Dr. Morehouse's voice and doing the breathing exercises. It was more difficult this time because of the anxiety I was experiencing, but finally my training took hold and I found myself calmly waiting for the coordinates. This time, I told myself that I didn't care about the outcome. I was going to concentrate solely on the structure of CRV.

As Dr. Morehouse read off the last digit, my pen traced a wave-form shape. My first ideogram! Damn, it really works, I thought to myself exultantly.

Okay, so don't get cocky.

Quickly I moved through the components of first stage. From there, I moved on to Stage Two sensory impressions. It was here that I entered the Matrix for the first time.

Behind my closed eyelids, my visual field was at first dark. I remained patient but I wondered, how could I see anything with my eyes closed? How would the information present itself? Somehow, I didn't think it was going to be like a movie screen. I really didn't know what the hell I was looking for.

A strange thing happened as I sat there quietly, expectantly, breathing a slow, measured cadence. Slowly a swirl of, well, the only way I can describe it is as if a fog or mist flowed up into my visual field. It was colored violet, magenta, gray, and purple. As I watched in amazement it seemed to flow up around me. Surprised, I opened my eyes, blinking in confusion. No fog, only the darkened room. Well, well, well, I thought. Is this supposed to happen? I didn't know. This was my first time. I mentally shrugged. All I could do was go back and see what developed. I closed my eyes again and continued with my pen on the paper, breathing slowly and quietly. And, damned if the fog didn't return. This time I just waited to see what would happen next. As I watched, the fog began to take on ill-defined shapes. I struggled to figure out what I was looking at as the shapes formed and then dissolved. I couldn't identify anything recognizable.

I thought for a moment, and then remembered what Dr. Morehouse had said in lecture earlier. If you don't get something right away, then prime the pump. He had said to write on the page the color black. Almost always there would be black at a target, so use this fact to tell your unconscious that you want information on colors.

I thought, why not?

Immediately the fog disappeared and a color flashed across my vision. It was a light tan color, like sand. More colors flashed across my field of view-tans, a dull red. Then textures…rough then smooth. I realized that I was warm and it wasn't the room, which was cool from the air conditioning.

This is so unreal, I thought to myself. I heard voices, a loud yell. I opened my eyes but the room was quiet except for an occasional rustle of paper as a student wrote down some data. Shaking my head in disbelief, I wrote the impression down on the page. I wondered, is this really happening or is it a delusion? For all I knew this was just my imagination and had nothing to do with my target. What could I do but continue and see where it led?

So I closed my eyes once again and waited uneasily for my next impressions. They came, and came rapidly. This time my unconscious seemed to want to show me a shape or picture. The fog suddenly morphed into a wavy line, then was gone. I chased after it mentally and it rematerialized in front of me. It reminded me of the low hills I had seen outside of Las Vegas where my parents now lived. More shapes and sensory data streamed past my vision and I rapidly wrote that down. Then dimensionals began to show, vertical and horizontal lines, then diagonals. Box shapes inside of other box shapes, simple at first but rapidly becoming more intense and complex. I drew them as fast as I could; I could barely keep up. It was like riding a runaway train. The images were flashing past me, giving the impression of great speed. I should have called a 'too much' break at this point, but I was terrified that if I tried to slow down, I'd lose the images.

First time a drought, now a flood.

I was getting aesthetics now; it felt like I was standing in the Old West. I started drawing more detailed sketches as I moved into Stage Three imagery. I was dancing between verbal data and visuals. Verbal data like descriptors of colors, textures, temperatures, and smells. Visuals like simple box, circular, and domed drawings. More kinesthetics made their way to my attention. I felt that the terrain here was semi-arid, low hills with sparse vegetation. It was hot and dusty, and I was thirsty. I heard the sounds of lots of people, voices. It was chaotic, almost like a war. I saw buildings that reminded me of the Alamo, but somehow I knew this was not that famous battle. I felt confusion, strong emotions with a purpose to it all.

I didn't realize that Dr. Morehouse was next to me until he said, "Wow, lots of images now!" He sketched some of my drawings on a transparency and moved on.

After he made the rounds of the class, Dr. Morehouse called an end to the session. "Complete your session summary and then you're free to take a break. Be back to class by 7pm."

Saundra and Val looked over at me to see how I was doing. I flashed a quick grin of triumph and a thumbs-up sign. By their wide smiles, I could see that they were jubilant that I had overcome my first failure.

"Well, I don't know if I got the target, but I at least I got an ideogram," I remarked to Saundra as we walked outside.

"I'll bet you did better than you think," she replied. I looked around as we stood outside in the coolness of the approaching evening. The sun was beginning to set and the birds were voicing the coming of night. This is my favorite time of day, when the twilight mutes the colors with the anticipation of darkness.

Suddenly it hit me. Everything around me looked more, I don't know, more alive, more intense. The sounds, the colors, the smells, even the fact that the light was fading seemed to have the opposite effect, that of making everything more, well … more.

I turned to Saundra even as she turned to me. The look on her face said volumes. We said almost simultaneously, "You see it too!" We both laughed as Jill and John walked up on us, quizzical looks on their faces.

"What's so funny?" Jill asked, looking at the two of us.

"I don't know about anyone else, but does everything around us look really sharp and alive to you?" I replied. Saundra added, "And do you feel a little spacey, almost like a high?"

John and Jill looked at each other. "Like you're in La-La land?" John asked.

I nodded.

"Come to think about it, yeah, I do kind of feel a little spacey." With a giggle, Saundra said, "Now we're really Space Cadets!" The four of us shared the laugh. I looked at my chronograph, "It's time to head back to class." Looking toward the door to the classroom the four of us realized everyone else had already gone inside.

Dr. Morehouse had already collected the data from the class and put it on transparencies that he placed on the overhead projector. "As you can see from the data up on the screen, we have what is called congruence. Everyone is seeing similar impressions. Hills, arid climate, buildings, lots of people, et cetera. Many of you had the impression that the site was the scene of a battle. That's not unusual for this target. You all have done really well on this session. I'm very pleased and proud of all of you."

I looked over at Val with a grin; she flashed a smile back. It felt good, real good.

"OK, let's have each of you give a brief — that's brief, people — summary of your session," Dr. Morehouse requested, gently reminding some of the more loquacious students to keep the narrative short. It was fascinating listening to each of my classmate's description of the target. I had seen many of the same things they had.

When it was my turn, as I stood up to recount my experience, Dr. Morehouse exclaimed, "John had a terrific session tonight. Much better than yesterday, wouldn't you say John?"

The kind congratulatory applause the class gave me on my success was embarrassing as all hell and it was appreciated as all hell.

When the picture of the target was flashed up on the overhead projector, it was obvious that I had a session as good as Dr. Morehouse said I had.

9945 0419 – The target: Mecca during Ramadan.

I had been there … seen, felt, smelled, tasted, and heard. I sat there, stunned.

Dr. Morehouse continued, "That's the reason many of you thought it was like a battlefield. Mecca at this time of the year is as close to a battlefield without being one as you can get. It's over-crowded, hot, dusty and chaotic. Millions make their pilgrimage there on a yearly basis."

I felt overwhelmed with what had happened. I savored the feeling, like a fine glass of wine. It was a very special moment.

Saundra raised her hand. Dr. Morehouse acknowledged her.

"Dr. Morehouse, when John and I were outside during the break we noticed two things. One; that the colors, sounds, and smells all seemed more vivid."

Vivid. That's the word I had been looking for, I thought.

"Two; we both seemed to be a little spacey, like a high."

Dr. Morehouse replied, "That feeling comes from the fact that you just spent over an hour in an altered state. It gets even more pronounced in extended remote viewing because the brain state that you work in is so much deeper than in CRV."

Dr. Morehouse paused a moment then continued with a memory from the past. "At Ft. Meade one day, my friend Mel Riley had a really tiring session where he had experienced a very strong bi-location. We'll talk more about those in ERV class, but anyway, Mel came out of the session totally loopy. He walked outside in a daze, went over to the dumpster, and to the amazement of the rest of us who were outside watching, took his car keys out and dropped them in the dumpster."

Dr. Morehouse shook his head, laughing, and continued, "Mel turned around and walked over to us as if nothing had happened. One of us asked, "Hey Mel. Do you know what you just did?" And Mel had no clue. He was so spacey he didn't realize that his unconscious mind had brought him to the dumpster to drop his keys in because it was trying to keep him from driving."

I laughed with the others; I could understand where Mel had been.

"When you finish a session you need to ground yourself. That means getting together with others and doing things; go for a walk or get something to eat. Do not go stand around gazing at the tree bark thinking to yourself how wonderful it is." The class giggled. "Get together with others in the class and go do something. And remember Mel; don't go driving until you come down from the high," Dr. Morehouse cautioned, then sent us off with congratulations. He was pleased with the results. As we left, everyone was talking happily together. It was nice to be among them.

When the class reconvened the following weekend for the second phase it was just as exciting, as I expanded my abilities. I took the CRV class many times in the future, first as refresher training, then as an assistant instructor and group leader. Each time I took these classes, I learned something new. I would never have a problem again with a CRV session.

The great conversations with my new friends, Jill, Saundra, and John, continued long after the class was over. They all lived only a short drive away and we saw each other again in September for the ERV class in Carmel. I would go on to meet new friends and have new and more fantastic adventures. But this first experience would always be a special treasure.

I was very proud of the simple diploma that I received at the end of the final day. It wasn't as fancy as the ones that his classes get now. It sounds silly, but that plain "vanilla flavor" diploma meant more to me than any of the others I have received from his courses. As I said good-bye to my new friends, I thought about the previous two weeks. The entire experience had been so incredible that it was hard to put into words.

It was like thinking that magic carpets were the stuff of mythology, and then getting a ride on one. But I wasn't sure what it all meant yet. I was still trying hard to reconcile my previous beliefs with this newfound ability. Later, it was hard to believe that this hadn't all been just coincidence or luck.

In the ensuing months before the upcoming ERV class, I practiced CRV on targets that I had friends make up for me. I would struggle just before the session started to remember that I could do this, that I *had* done this. And on successfully completing the session, there would be a part of me that was over-joyed, yet also a part that rebelled at the significance of what I had accomplished.

I didn't realize then that I was beginning a change that would have important consequences for my future in remote viewing. It was too much to assimilate all at once. It would take time. I wasn't yet ready.

In the following five years, spending over 1100 hours with him in the classroom, as well as many hours together on a personal basis, I have never seen him deviate from what I first observed in the CRV class. He remains a humble and thoughtful individual that shuns the limelight. Perhaps the review of his book on Amazon by a former member of his Ranger battalion said it best. He said his men would follow him anywhere. I could understand why. Hell, I would too.[17]

I have never heard him publicly say anything about his detractors; he has only kind words for them in his class. That, more than anything, is a testament to his integrity.

I looked forward to seeing him again up in Carmel at the next stage, the ERV class.

ERV ... Extended Remote Viewing. Dr. Morehouse's book depicts it as an almost mystical experience. Among the military remote viewers, ERV was considered the "sexy sister" of coordinate remote viewing. In the Ft. Meade unit, it was the preferred method used by Dr. Morehouse. However, it would prove to be, for me, a double-edged sword.

J. HELLOSKY
5/20/99
ST: 1720
ET: 1815

AV
——
MO
——
PI
——
YES — TIRED

9945
0410

A) SLOPING UP, THEN
SLOPING GENTLY
DOWN, SOFT

B) NATURAL

C) NO C

9945
0419

A) SLOPING DOWN,
THEN GENTLY SLOP.
UP — SOFT

B) NATURAL

C) LAND

S₂

BLACK
BROWN
GRAY
TAN

This is a typical beginners session. Notice how the sketches are small and rough with little detail versus the narrative, which is much more rich. The sketches become renderings in Stage 6, which are much more detailed and in perspective. This being my first successful beginners session, we only went through Stage 3. The successive stages 4 through 6 were covered in the following class a week later

RED
ROUGH
SMOOTH
WARM
BLUE
WHITE
HARD

SOUND

AOL: YELLS

AOL: HILL

SPECKLED

HUMPED

AOL: HORSE

BLACK
BLUE
ROUND
RED
TAN
DAPPLED
VERTICAL

TAN

ROUND

AOL: BYCYCLE
TIRE

S₂

SQUARE
BLOCK
HOLLOW

AOL: BUILDING

[TURN 180°]

BLUE
BLACK

AOL: HILLS

GREEN
LT GREEN
RED
BROWN
TAN
YELLOW
SQUARE
HORIZONTAL
VERTICAL

DIAGONALS
HEAVY

AOL: ALAMO

BRIGHT
SUNNY
DRY

S_2

HOT
SUNNY
SWEATY
ROUGH
WOODEN

A1: MAKES ME
FEEL HOT &
THIRSTY

SOFT
MOUNDS
BLUE

AOL: HILLS

BREAK

$$S_3$$

AOL: BUILDING

END SESSION

SESSION SUMMARY

SOFT ROLLING HILLS SLOPING UP AND DOWN
NATURAL AREA BUT SEMI ARID. BLACKS, BROWNS
SUNNY, DAYLIGHT. BROWNS, TANS, SOFT DIRT. HAD
THE FEELING OF THE OLD WEST.

HEARD VOICES AND SHOUTS OR YELLS —
LOUD AND ENERGETIC —. A LAND SETTING
W/ BLUE SKY — STRONG AOL's OF RIDERS AND
HORSES, STAFFS WITH FLAGS

SOME SORT OF BUILDING, LIKE A FORT
FELT LIKE I WAS SWEATING AND TIRED AND
THIRSTY. SAW LOTS OF RED, SOME LT GREEN
SO MAYBE SOME VEGETATION BUT NOT MUCH

AS FOR THE BUILDING, SEEMED HEAVY, ANGULAR
AND HAD SOME OPENINGS.

SCENE SEEMED MARTIAL IN CHARACTER

MECCA

The ancient Moslem holy city where each year a pilgrimage is made by hundreds of thousands of devotees to worship in this holiest of Moslem places.

TARGET ATTRIBUTES

1. MANMADE

2. STRUCTURE

3. DIMENSIONALS: ARCHES, COLUMNS, FLAT, OPEN CIRCULAR, PEAKED OR SPIKED, TOWERS.

4. ENERGETICS: POWERFUL, BUSY

5. STAGE II: COLORS: (AS DEPICTED OR PER-CEIVED), TEXTURES: (AS DEPICTED OR PER-CEIVED), SOUNDS: MUSIC, VOICES, ANIMAL SOUNDS, SMELLS: FOOD, HUMAN, ANIMAL, WASTE, TASTES, TEMPERATURE,

6. AESTHETICS: ORNATE, BEAUTIFUL, VAST, ETC.

7. EMOTIONALS: SOLEMN, VARIOUS – HUMAN

8. TANGIBLES: STONE, CLOTH, GOLD, CEMENT

9. INTANGIBLES: RELIGION, POLITICAL, PRAYER

Chapter Five

ERV

What you set your heart upon, surely shall be yours.
                    – Ralph Waldo Emerson

September arrived with the promise of new adventures. I drove up to John's house in Pasadena to meet him for the drive, as we were carpooling to Carmel. He greeted me as I got to the door.

"Good to see you again, John. How have you been since UCLA?" I asked him amiably.

"Been busy; I'm afraid that I haven't done much remote viewing since then," he replied, shaking my hand.

John worked for a large government facility as a security officer. He was big, at six feet and well over two hundred pounds. His size belied a friendly and relaxed manner.

John went back inside to say good-by to his wife and kids as I transferred my gear to his car. It was another beautiful Southern California day, perfect for the eight-hour drive to Carmel. I had a surprise for John as we drove away. "I talked to Jill and told her about the deal we got at the motel. She called and got a reservation for both her and Saundra there too," I said with a smile. "I think this is going to be one hell of a class."

"Hey, that's great! We'll definitely have to have a party this time. At UCLA, we didn't have the time since the class was broken into two weekends," John replied.

He looked over at me as I reached into my rucksack in the backseat. His eyes grew wide as I pulled out a bottle of Jack Daniel's. I grinned and said, "I was prepared for that possibility." We both laughed.

The eight hours passed quickly and we checked in to the motel just outside Carmel. I had only been this far north in the state once, during Trojan Warrior II. I had gone up to Willets, California, about ninety minutes north of San Francisco. It was there I met my friend Jeff, who introduced me to Geshe Gyltsin, a Tibetan Buddhist monk, one of the delegation to the U.S. I met Jeff through our mutual interest in Shaolin Kung-fu. Jeff was the only American ever to be ordained as a Shaolin monk at that time, and I had spent eight years learning it from my university chemistry professor, Dr. Shie-Ming Hwang. Jeff was one of the advisors to Trojan Warrior II and our intent was to learn two of the specialized Tibetan meditations, Tumo and Lung-gom. Tumo is the meditation for heat and Lung-gom the meditation for long-distance running. The Willets trip had been an eye-opener.

We had just finished unpacking when a female voice said from the open front door, "We're here!" John and I looked and there stood Jill and Saundra.

"Hey you two," I replied, as John and I exchanged hugs of greeting with them. After unpacking, the four of us walked to a local restaurant near the motel and sat down to a nice dinner.

On the way back to the motel, I nudged John and said to the women, "Okay, time for a party at our room. I've got a bottle of Jack Daniel's best. We have to start off this adventure the right way."

Jill piped up, "Sounds like a plan to us. I brought a bottle of Southern Comfort, and I think we could all use a drink."

Never underestimate a woman, I thought, shaking my head. John must have read my mind because he slapped me on the back with a grin. We all met in our room, made ourselves comfortable and broke out the bottles. After pouring a healthy glass for John and me, Saundra and Jill surprised me by asking for the straight bourbon. They poured glasses just as tall as ours. When everyone was settled I asked Saundra a question that had been tugging at my mind ever since I had first met her. She was an admitted UFO abductee. I had always felt that such beliefs were, well, speculative at best, and delusional on closer inspection.

Treading carefully, I asked, "Saundra, how do you know that you were abducted? Please don't misunderstand, but you have to realize that it's hard for someone like me to actually believe that extraterrestrials came 90 bazillion light years to Earth to perform experiments on humans." I looked at her, hoping she wasn't going to get angry. "I mean is it possible that it was a very vivid dream?"

Saundra looked thoughtful for a moment before she replied, choosing her words carefully. "I don't think it was a dream. It's happened several times and although it's possible it might have been, I don't think it was. It was too vivid. If you're skeptical, I don't blame you, but think about how we treat experimental animals. What makes you believe that E.T.s would treat us any differently?"

I thought about that for a moment as I sipped my drink. I had to admit that she had a point. Maybe we would be just lab rats to an advanced civilization. I hoped not. Having been brought up on the optimism of *Close Encounters of the Third Kind*, I'd hoped that if any E.T.s did exist they would be benevolent.

But I had also read what scientist Charles Pellegrino said about how an alien civilization might react to us.

He said that if it came down to Us vs. Them, they wouldn't choose us. No species survives by self-sacrifice. This, of course, makes perfect sense. He also said that wimps don't become top dogs. They might see us as a threat, because they would assume that the above attitude would apply to us as well. Look at our history. How often has a technologically advanced civilization contacted a more primitive society without a disastrous outcome for the latter. If you think advanced intelligence implies benevolence you might get an argument from the Aztecs and the American Indians.[18]

I said as much to Saundra. Jill, who had been listening, pounced. "So you *do* think that they exist!"

We all laughed for a moment, then I replied, "They probably do exist, Jill. But if they do, they're nowhere near here. We have been studying the local neighborhood of stars for any sign of intelligent life and found nothing. Remember, we've been sending out radio waves for 100 years now, which have been traveling at the speed of light. That means that any civilization of equal or greater technological background within 50 light years would have had time to send us back signals which we would have picked up by now. Yet we've heard nothing. If they exist, they are probably thousands of light years away. The technology necessary to travel that distance in any reasonable time is enormous. And they would still have to find us, a far less technologically advanced society," I finished.

"I've seen vehicles over Area 51 that defy our technology. And after that occurred I had black helicopters following me for days afterwards. How do you account for that?" Saundra questioned. Jill nodded her head in agreement.

This sounded too much like something made up. But Saundra seemed completely sincere. She had nothing to prove or any need to impress me. She was intelligent and articulate.

I asked Saundra what these helicopters looked like. I wanted to see what she drew. If she described an ordinary police helicopter then her credibility might be suspect.

"Here, let me draw it." She took a piece of paper and began to sketch. Then she said, "It was colored black and had small ramps or winglets on the side like this." She drew more shapes on the sketch, then handed me the drawing when she was finished.

When I saw what she had drawn I caught my breath. I looked up at her sharply. When Saundra saw the look on my face, she exclaimed," What? You know something?"

Yes, I knew something, but it seemed so implausible. She had drawn a teardrop-shaped body with a thin tail boom. It wasn't your everyday ordinary Bell Jetranger, Robinson R44, or Aerostar that most departments use. I recognized it right away. I should have – I've flown them.

It was a drawing of a McDonald-Douglas 500 D. The 500's are used all over; a popular helicopter. It's my favorite, as a matter of fact. Several police departments use them.

But not where she lived. Police helicopters aren't painted black either, nor do they have winglets or planks. The helicopter she described was known as the MH-6 "Little Bird," the military version of the 500 D, and was used by only one unit in the Department of Defense that I knew of: the 160th SOAR unit in the US Army. SOAR stands for Special Operations Aviation Regiment. Few people would have known about this highly secretive unit at that time.

It seemed unlikely that they would be assigned to domestic spying. But, of course, that wouldn't stop some machinery in the US government. I had personal knowledge of US Army Intelligence spying domestically during the Vietnam War. If the Little Bird 500's were used by the 160th, then it wouldn't surprise me to learn that some other black ops unit might be using them as well. I told Saundra this.

"So you think that some government organization could be following me?" She asked.

I said I didn't know, shrugging my shoulders. "You probably saw some classified vehicle when you were near Area 51, and they might have been watching just to keep tabs on you."

The three of them shook their heads. John said, "Well, I don't think you're going to change his mind." He smiled and held out his glass for more Jack Daniel's.

I poured, saying, "Until they come down and I see one, I'm going to be a skeptic. I just need more evidence than what I've seen so far."

We moved on to other subjects, most highly speculative but interesting, including our upcoming class in ERV.

I shared my experiences during the development of Trojan Warrior II. They were fascinated, agreeing that the training would give me an advantage in obtaining the deep theta states necessary to do ERV successfully.

Finally, fatigue and alcohol took its toll, and we called it a night. As the women left for their room, I thought this was starting off to be a great week. Tomorrow beckoned with the promise of new adventure.

The next morning, after a quick breakfast, the four of us drove to the meeting hall near the center of town where the class was to be held. This was the first time I had ever been to Carmel so I watched the scenery with interest.

Just after our arrival, Dr. Morehouse drove up and parked. Several other students had arrived by that time as well. I recognized a few. All of us joined the doctor as he unloaded his equipment.

"Jill, Saundra, good to see you again," Dave greeted the two women. He gave each of them a cordial hug. He shared greetings with John and the others. Then he turned to me and said with a generous smile and a hug, "John, glad to see you made it."

"So am I, Dr. Morehouse. It's good to see you, too," I said, feeling a little awkward. I tend to be a bit reserved on greetings until I get to know someone. Its a holdover from my police days. There was no denying the warmth in his gesture, though, and I was impressed that he remembered my name. We hadn't seen each other since we had first met almost five months ago.

The pleasure and genuine enthusiasm that showed on his face as he greeted each of the students was heartwarming. It was clear by the way the students responded that they were just as happy to see him.

In a short time, with the extra hands available, we unloaded his equipment and got it set up.

By this time the rest of the students had arrived. I recognized some of them from my CRV class at UCLA. Most were strangers. This was a much larger class, over twenty people.

After a short break, Dr. Morehouse began the class with introductions. There were people from all across the country. It impressed me that someone would take the time off from their job, pay for the course and then fly cross-country to attend his class. Dr. Morehouse obviously engendered a great deal of trust, as well as interest.

Then, taking his laser pointer, Dr. Morehouse started his lecture. "Remember from the CRV class that the same rules apply to ERV as well," he began, placing a transparency on the overhead projector.

"First, despite what some of my colleagues have said, remote viewing is not 100% accurate. Never was, and probably never will be."

He put down his pointer, and turned to the class, his voice dead serious, "Remember this. Don't do remote viewing, your colleagues, and yourself a disservice by embellishing accuracy just for personal gain. This is a wonderful gift, brought to you by dedicated people at no small personal sacrifice. Don't dishonor it."

He turned back to his presentation, picking up his laser pointer, "Second, never trust the results of a remote viewing session to just one viewer. Remote viewing is a process, not an event. Each remote viewer brings a piece of information back that will be fitted into the jigsaw puzzle. So you see, it doesn't matter whether you come back with seventeen percent correct information or seventy. Remote viewing is always done in support of an operational model," he explained.

Dr. Morehouse paused, a memory from Fort Meade coming to mind. "At Ft. Meade, the remote viewing unit was housed in two small barracks that dated back to World War II. There were several rooms where training was conducted, one of them being the Garden Room. It was called that because it was the only room in the two buildings where plants would grow. It was in this room that my friend Mel Riley conducted my training. Those of you who read *Psychic Warrior* know that Mel was one of several instructors who trained me. One of the important lessons that he taught me was to forget the outcome. Don't get wound around the axle over results. When Mel Riley finished his session, he would bring his results and session summary to the unit's project manager's office. Mel would walk into the office, drop his work on the desk and say, "Time for coffee." No equivocating over the results. As far as Mel was concerned, he had done his best. Whatever results were produced, then that's what they got. You need to have that kind of detachment to be a successful remote viewer."

He turned back to the overhead projection. "Finally, remote viewing is not a stand alone endeavor. It was designed as part of an overall intelligence gathering strategy. Remote viewing provides one piece of the puzzle. Other pieces come in the form of signal intelligence, human intelligence, satellite photographs and so on. And that goes for police work, scientific research, medical discoveries and any other model you care to name."

At this point in the lecture, our instructor answered several questions from the class.

I had a question I had wanted to ask for quite some time, "Dr. Morehouse, have remote viewers ever targeted previous lives in order to see if reincarnation is real?"

With a self deprecating gesture, Dr. Morehouse replied, "You guys don't have to call me Dr. Morehouse. If you've put up with me this long, just call me Dave. When remote viewers targeted their past, or for that matter their future, they found that they've lived countless lives in countless dimensions. It was like looking into a mirror reflecting into another mirror, an endless series of reflections. However, it wasn't just forward and backward in time. Their lives were lived sideways in time as well. The remote viewers believed that they were living different lives in different dimensions, and at the same time.

"Now, would you return to this dimension after your life had ended here? Possibly. But it would be much more likely that you would end up in some other existence. You might not even have a human form."

Another dimension, I mused. That was food for thought. Dave answered some more questions then continued with the last section of lecture. This was on the theory and application of extended remote viewing.

Much more free flowing than CRV, extended remote viewing is a hybrid form. The two methods are as far apart in technique as you could possibly make them. CRV is difficult to learn, with its multi-stage protocol and arcane terminology. However, once learned, it's relatively easy to apply. It was designed that way in order to teach anyone the technique. CRV is done in a state of relaxed alertness, a brain state characterized by a preponderance of alpha waves.

ERV is exactly the opposite. Easy to learn in theory, it is much more difficult to achieve in practice. It requires the viewer to move deeper into the meditative or hypnagogic state. Typically, ERV is achieved in a deep theta state, right on the edge of dreams and sleep. But if a viewer can hold that edge, the data is free of AOL (analytic overlay). Analytic overlay is the tendency of the mind to identify what the viewer is seeing, even if that label is incorrect. ERV is a state of pure viewing. It is in ERV that bi-locations usually occurred. A bi location is a situation where the viewer so strongly identifies with the target that they have the impression of actually being at the target site, experiencing everything as if they really were there.

However, ERV is not for everyone, as Dr. Morehouse would tell us. It is virtually devoid of the structure of CRV. It is also very difficult for untrained individuals to get down to a deep theta state without some sort of biofeedback or meditation training. There were also other implications in using ERV, as I would find out. Some people never make the transition, finding that CRV is more their style.

Each had advantages and disadvantages, so, in the unit, both techniques were used in a complementary fashion. CRV was good at generating pages and pages of data. Of course there was lots of AOL to deal with, but then that's what the analysts were for.

ERV didn't produce as much data, but it was good for entering into the mind of the target. If you wanted data, let's say, on what a Soviet test pilot knew about the performance of the latest MiG fighter, ERV was the preferred mode.

One of the big differences was that the ERV class would utilize makeshift beds: inflatable mattresses and sleeping bags. Extended remote viewing is done lying down, with eye shields and earplugs to mask outside disturbances. This assists the viewers to achieve a brain state in the deep theta level where ERV is conducted.

At the completion of the first and only day of lecture, Dave ended the class by telling us, "Okay, now you know the basics of ERV. But don't let that lull you into a false sense of security. Just because ERV is easy to learn, doesn't mean it's easy to do. I want you to stay up late; do the homework questions. I need you to come in tired tomorrow."

Dave's voice took on a more serious tone, "If you get eight hours of sleep and come in here tomorrow fully rested, you're going to find out just how long 90 to 120 minutes is. I guarantee that you will not achieve a deep enough state and you will be lying there bored stiff.

"Have fun tonight and I'll see you in the morning."

I met John, Saundra, Jill and several others from the class, and went out for dinner. Carmel boasts several outstanding restaurants and we were hungry.

As I sat next to Saundra listening to the conversations around me, I found my mind drifting back to my first class in remote viewing at UCLA five months ago. I started the course as an interested skeptic, wondering if remote viewing was a viable technology or a pseudo-science. I had successfully completed the course and had done well as a beginner. In the intervening months before this ERV class, I had worked hard at practicing CRV, but I found myself second-guessing my ability. Part of me was elated if I did well, which became the norm after numerous practice sessions, but that elation was blunted by the suspicion that I had just been lucky. Tomorrow's sessions in ERV would have to be more than noteworthy to supplant that skepticism. They would have to be spectacular. I knew my belief system wouldn't settle for anything less.

Next day, the class started with Dave going over some of the issues we might face on our first foray into ERV. "We talked about dimensional issues yesterday, but I want to touch on that one more time. We believe there are countless dimensions without end, like the pages of an infinite book. This is a basic tenet of quantum physics. We also believe that some of these realms are inhabited by various entities, just like our own.

However, we also know that there are discarnate beings that inhabit the Matrix as well. They range from the benevolent to the malevolent. There is both good and evil in the Matrix. Normally, the only ones that will actively seek you out will be the Tricksters. They are harmless as long as you remember your training. Do not engage them. They will do everything to keep you misdirected."

Dave pantomimed opening a long coat and with a grin, whispered, "Hey, buddy, have I got a deal for you." I cracked up with the rest of the class.

Dave laughed too, but he said with a serious tone, "They'll be just like that, the huckster on the corner looking for his next score. They will promise you anything to keep you engaged. They will weave you a story based on what you want to hear. I assure you, it will have nothing to do with your mission. They have had millennia to practice their craft, so don't think you're going to outsmart them. It is not your mission to get bogged down with an entity who wants nothing more than to keep itself entertained at your expense."

A hand was raised by Bob, one of the older men in the class, "Why do these tricksters do this, what's their motive?"

Dave shrugged his shoulders saying, "They feed off of negative emotions, like fear. If they can engage you in some manner, then they can get you to fixate on them, instead of your mission. Then you are feeding them, entertaining them.

"Don't let it happen. It's not your mission. I can't emphasize this enough. But I know some of you will disregard what I say and you'll go out there in the Matrix and get wound around the axle with some entity that does not have your best interest in mind. You'll come back with a fanciful story and how your pet trickster was so helpful. And your data will have nothing to do with the target."

With that now familiar grin, Dave once again pantomimed opening the coat, emphasizing the point he made with a raised eyebrow, "You were taught the tools to use to get to the target. Use them. Remember the mission.

Just as there is a spectrum of good and evil in this world, so it is in the Matrix. We have dealt with the minor bad boys but there are those much worse."

Dave paused as he walked over to his director's chair and sat down. "You were taught two weapons that will keep you safe: the resonant energy balloon and your strict adherence to the mission objectives. Concentrate on what you are there for and you will not have a problem."

Another hand, this one from a young woman named Sandy, "Dave, can these really bad ones physically hurt me?"

I thought that was a good question.

"No, not physically. But they can cause some psychological trauma, if you give them the power. Once again, don't give them the power.

Trust in the training and the mission," Dave said, as he looked around the class. With a broad smile at the memory, he recalled,

"I'll tell you about Bo, one of my Swedish students. Bo is this big Scandinavian who looks like a throwback to his Viking ancestors. Before Bo entered the ether, he would imagine himself putting on a Viking helmet and arm himself with an imaginary Viking sword and armor. He'd tell everyone that he would slay any demons that would show themselves. Can you imagine what this guy looked like in the ether, doing battle with the tricksters with this big helmet with horns sticking out of the sides? But that's Bo. He was a real character."

Looking at his watch, Dave announced, "Okay. Let's go to lunch. Be back here in an hour and a half for your first target briefing."

As I sat with my friends at lunch, I thought about the upcoming session. I was feeling a rising excitement countered by the specter of my thoughts at dinner last night. I hoped that the upcoming session would be as powerful as the one Dave described in *Psychic Warrior*. Dave had given me my eyes in the CRV class. Now I hoped to earn my wings.

On our return, after the class had settled down, Dave handed out our tasking sheets. These sheets had the coordinates of the target, plus focus questions to concentrate on while at the target site. These were very general questions, carefully worded so that they gave no hint of the target. As usual, the only description of the target was the ubiquitous two sets of four random numbers, and the admonition that the target was to be viewed in present time. Then the lights were turned down low and the sounds of the cool-down tape came over the speakers: a specially configured monologue of breathing exercises and wave sounds. The ERV tape was much longer than the CRV tape. It had everything that the CRV tape had as well as the ERV format designed to assist the students to drift down to that elusive mind state where ERV takes place.

This first session did not go well. Most of the class finished with more than half of the time still remaining. I felt like I had been dreaming, rather than viewing. In Sanctuary, I had only a brief appearance of the Vortex. My excitement at its emergence caused me to lose the edge and I drifted out of the ultra-deep state. My frustration and anxiety got the better of me and I wound up floundering in the Matrix. There were no handholds here – no structure to fall back on. I saw some imagery float up in the darkness but the experience did not match the description that I had read in Dave's book. My three friends were equally disappointed. Our instructor echoed our disappointment. Dave was upset at our class's lack of resolve, and he did not mince words about our performance. The reprimand was sharp.

I felt embarrassed, and looking around, I thought I wasn't the only one.

After the stinging rebuke, Dave sighed and said simply, "Okay, let's put this behind us. Let's take a twenty-minute break. When you come back, we'll try it again. This time I'll join you at the target and do something to help guide you to it."

There was a flurry of questions but Dave would not elaborate. It didn't seem possible that our second attempt at the target could possibly generate any more excitement, suspense or anxiety then the first. But it did. Added was the tension of Dave's announcement that he would join us. During the break, speculation ran high, but there was no real consensus as to what action Dave would take. As we returned and got into our workstations, I looked over at Saundra and Jill on the other side of the room. Saundra caught my glance and waved. I returned it with a slight smile, but I was anything but relaxed. I still didn't know how to get into ERV. I knew the ritual but I had no handholds. There was no signpost up ahead saying "ERV'ers enter here!"

I pulled the blanket up to my neck and slid my eyeshield down to block out all light as the cool-down tape started and the lights dimmed. All I could do was follow the instructions on the tape like last time and hope that something happened.

Ninety minutes later, something had happened, all right. I experienced my first bi location, a mind numbing but exhilarating experience. This ERV session went exactly as I had dreamed. A magic carpet ride! The rest of the class did well also. Dave was much more satisfied with our second effort.

"First, I want to tell you that I'm proud of your second effort. It was what I had expected of this most talented of classes. Take a look at all the data that the class as a whole has generated. And remember, all of that from two sets of randomly generated numbers, that's all." Then Dave allowed each of the class a chance to give a short summary of their experience again as he did after the first session. The differences were remarkable; the data that the class spoke of suggested a sunken ship, possibly the Titanic.

Then Dave put up the feedback on the overhead projector, "OK, let's take a look at how you did. Your target was..." The gasp that followed the pictures appearing on the screen made the extra effort on this session very satisfying.

It *was* the Titanic! The pictures had been taken from the Ballard mission to explore the famous relic. I felt a chill that ran through my body like an electric shock as I looked at the photos up on the screen; a chill that matched the bi location that I had experienced at the wreck. The bi location had been so strong that it nearly ended my session early. I had started the session nice and snug in my sleeping bag. Once at the target however, that warm comfort had been replaced not only by a mind-numbing chill, but also a frightening sensation of being crushed. The sensations had become so uncomfortable that I was on the verge of ending my session when something totally unexpected happened. My friend John, lying next to me, had fallen asleep and begun to snore. The loud guttural snort had abruptly pulled me out of my session, and caused a massive case of vertigo. Dave came over and gently woke John up, while I fought back the nauseating sensations.

After John's somewhat nonplussed apology, both of us slid our eye shields back down to head back to the target. It was not without some trepidation that I attempted to return, fearing that the intensely unpleasant sensations of the bi location would reappear. Before I could complete the ERV ritual though, the time allotted for the session had expired.

After a number of questions and further explanations from Dave, the class ended for the day. The four of us decided to get some dinner and talk over the day's events.

As we were eating, my mind wandered back to the session. It had been a powerful but frightening experience. I felt like I had actually been there at the Titanic, wrapped in the cold and the suffocating pressure on the bottom of the North Atlantic three miles down. It had been an eerie feeling, floating in the gloom next to the remains of that once-great ship's hull. And what Dave had done to guide us had blown the class away with amazement.

Suddenly I felt uncomfortable, as if someone was watching me. Someone was. It was Saundra. She had noticed that I was rather quiet. When I saw her looking at me, I realized I had drifted away for a moment.

"You're kind of quiet, John, what's up?" She asked.

I looked out the window of the restaurant. I saw the familiar sights of Carmel at night from a new and vaguely unsettling perspective.

It took me a moment to collect my thoughts, and then I turned back to Saundra. "I'm still reeling from today's session. Not just the bi location, but also when we found out what Dave did to guide us to the target. It's so fantastic I wouldn't have believed it, if I hadn't been there," I said with feeling. What Dave had done was impossible. Yet I was there; I saw it happen with my own ERV eyes. Saundra, John and Jill were listening intently. "That bi location was so real, it was as if I was floating alongside the wreck. I felt the cold and the crushing pressure. It was nothing like CRV. It was like what Dave described in his book. Then, to have Dave guide us to the target in the manner that he did, left me feeling dislocated, like I was no longer a part of my old familiar world." I looked at the three of them watching me. All three had ever so slight smiles on their faces.

"OK, I know what you're thinking," I said, feeling a little angry at their smugness. "There are more things between Heaven and Earth than are dreamt of in your philosophy, Horatio."

Saundra said warmly, "John, you've taken a huge step. Look at how far you've come since the CRV class at UCLA. From an interested skeptic with no previous paranormal experience, to where you are now. We aren't laughing at you; we're happy for you."

That caught me off guard. "Well, I bet Alice felt the same way in Wonderland," I replied, feeling better. It was true; I had come a long way. My world was no longer the same familiar place, fitting me like an old favorite shirt. "I wonder what Uncle Dave has in store for us tomorrow?" I said, thinking out loud.

That day that will live forever in my mind, for, unknowingly, Dave's choice of target would fulfill a long-standing childhood dream of mine. It should have been the day where the last vestiges of my Old World would fall away, and I would face my New World transformed. *Should* have been. Instead, I found myself erecting new doubts to replace the old ones. It would take much, much more to break down my resistance to the implications of the session. The inability to accept the truths that I had witnessed would have dire consequences in the months to come. More and more I would find myself at odds with myself, trapped between the world of my past and the world of my future.

CHAPTER SIX

God of War

Look beneath the surface; let not the several
quality of a thing nor its worth escape thee.

— Marcus Aurelius Antoninus

When I returned to the motel, I talked for a bit with Saundra, Jill, and John about the day's events. Then the four of us returned to our rooms to review our notes for tomorrow. I wanted to make sure I had the protocols memorized so I could concentrate on the sessions. After midnight, I put away the materials and went to bed. As I lay there, I thought about the answer that Dave had given to my question on reincarnation. Multiple lives lived in the past, present, and future. Not only that, the remote viewers had seen the same phenomenon going off in every direction they looked. They interpreted that observation as living different lives in different circumstances from the one in this existence, all at the same time.

It struck a cord.

I've never been a religious person, although I do consider myself a spiritual one. I did not believe in much of the standard religious dogma. It seemed too arbitrary and too many excesses and atrocities had been committed under the guise of "God wills it."

If you live a good life, standard dogma says you go to heaven for eternity or paradise where all your wishes come true, or some variation of those themes. Eternity is a long time. Even paradise would become boring. The truth must be more sublime than that. I have always thought religious knowledge has lagged behind scientific advances because of the dogma of religious canon. There was no 'evolution' of religious thought. Fundamentalist views say if the science does not match the dogma, then science must be wrong.

I didn't have to think very hard to find examples of the above.

The thought occurred to me that there was a scientific theory that might explain the observations of the military remote viewers and would satisfy religious beliefs. The theory is quantum mechanics and it is the cornerstone of today's technology. Quantum mechanics is a kind of Alice in Wonderland world where particles and waves are complimentary aspects of all energy and matter. This bizarre situation is further complicated by the fact that a particle's position is indeterminate until an observation is performed on it. This indeterminacy means that during the time when a particle is traveling from one position to another, it has no specific location. Only when a particle interacts with something does it establish a physical reality to an observer.

Quantum mechanics also forbids a single history of a particle, since, if a particle can take any number of paths in an interaction, then it must take *all* paths. Originally, physicists thought that the observer established reality through an observation, which caused the collapse of the wave function of that particle to a single real history. The rest of the 'other' histories were ignored. However, many physicists were uncomfortable with giving the observer and a single history such special status. In 1957 a brilliant university student named Hugh Everett proposed in his doctoral thesis that all the possible histories had to be considered as real. These possible histories had to be considered in relation to each other as separate real histories. He called his paper the "Relative State Formulation of Quantum Mechanics."[19]

Just as in the theory of Relativity, where there is no special frame of measurement, Everett's formulation gave no special status to one particle history over another. All possibilities existed, each in its own dimension or universe! In this view, the wave equation never collapses. It continues to describe the system history as it evolves deterministically through all histories.

Now physicists started to accept the reality of multiple universes, each with a slightly different history. That would explain why the military remote viewers saw multiple lives when looking at a persons life history. We all exist simultaneously in multiple universes.

Then the thought intruded that perhaps, when you die, you snap to a different universe that is slightly different from the one you "previously" inhabited. Since quantum mechanics forbids a single history, then you must have been living multiple lives in the past, the future, as well as multiple lives at each moment of your life. You would not know of or be aware of all these histories because quantum mechanics forbids communication across these different worlds. Each of your selves would never be consciously aware of any of the others. In quantum mechanics the only thing that can cross the boundaries are interference effects. If this is true, then death is just a door to another existence. As to the ultimate destiny of each person, the remote viewers involved in this series of sessions were never able to establish an answer.

It was an intriguing idea but it was late and so I put away my ruminations and tried to go to sleep.

I slept fitfully that night, tossing and turning, dreaming of the cold and the nightmarish feeling of suffocation. I awoke the following morning drenched in sweat and exhausted. I figured I wouldn't have any trouble getting down to the Zone today. The problem was, did I want to? I realized that remote viewing wasn't all fun and games anymore. I admitted reluctantly to myself that I was apprehensive about the upcoming session and the possibility of another terrifying bi location.

Hell, I was scared.

I arrived at the classroom with John, meeting Jill and Saundra as the morning started with Dave taking questions and reviewing the previous day. After yesterday's experience, the entire class was rapt with attention.

"All right, now you know from yesterday's session that ERV isn't like its detractors say it is. It's hard work. And don't let anyone tell you it's just guided imagery. I think what you experienced yesterday was proof positive of the power of ERV," Dave stated in his lecture.

There was no way that what I experienced yesterday was just a form of guided imagery. That session was as powerful in its impact on me as the iceberg that shattered the Titanic.

I was both excited and nervous, hoping for another bi location and yet fearing it. Bi-locations are extraordinary experiences. They're the reason that ERV is known as "the sexy sister of CRV." They weren't always welcome, either from an operational standpoint or a personal one. Operationally, they could have a negative impact on the session because they tended to focus the viewer's attention on the experience rather than strictly on information gathering. Personally, last night's turmoil was a testimony to the result of a bi location. This time though, I knew that I wouldn't be going back to the wreck of the Titanic. My target would be different. I just hoped it wouldn't be another ordeal.

I could tell the class was nervous about the next target session, as the questions were all about, "What if this happens," or, "What if that occurs."

Finally Dave exclaimed in exasperation that if we kept obsessing with the outcome, we were going to blow it. "This class can do this! Let go of the outcome and have fun with it. I've picked out a special target that you're really going to like. So let's take ten minutes to set up and clear for action. Go to the bathroom; get a drink of water, whatever else you need to do, and we'll launch in ten."

I looked over at Saundra and Jill. They smiled and waved as we started to get into our sleeping bags on the inflatable mattresses. I grinned back and gave them the thumbs up sign. I heard John say to me, "Good hunting!"

"Lock and load!" I replied, snuggling down in my sleeping bag. I put in the earplugs and slid down the eye shield. The roar of ocean surf from the cool-down tape filled the room and I started the ritual for ERV. I listened to the sounds of crashing waves on a remote beach in Santa Cruz, recorded during a violent night storm. This faded and Dave's voice took its place in quiet, measured tones, hypnotic in intensity, beginning the breathing rituals. It wasn't long before I was sitting expectantly in my Sanctuary.

I sat in the quiet twilight of the Matrix, in the center of a small circle of soft blue light.

Sanctuary is the launch point and return venue for extended remote viewers. It is one of several techniques classified as delivery mechanisms. These mechanisms are designed to launch the viewer into the Matrix and drop them into the target area.

My body felt numb and heavy. The sounds of the room faded away, replaced by the ethereal fog. Cat's paws of purple, magenta, gray, and black swirled in the background, lit by an occasional flash of light, like heat lightning on a summer night. It was unearthly, surreal.

As I watched, a spot of violet light suddenly appeared. I knew it was the beginning of the Vortex, the wormhole-like structure that a remote viewer travels through to get to the target. Tendrils of violet color spun off from the center as the Vortex formed. I watched as the mouth of the wormhole widened until it was large enough to enter. With the parting thought that this was just like a sci-fi movie, I was off.

Once again, the ride was exhilarating; the walls of the Vortex flashing past at high speed. I almost expected to hear a roaring sound because of the velocity at which I was moving, but there was only an incongruous silence.

Up ahead, the event horizon of the Membrane approached. The Membrane is simply the terminus of the signal line. On the other side lay the target. This time I was ready and went through it easily. It had no more substance than a breath of fresh air.

I found myself down on one knee, the darkness of the mists once again surrounding me. I took several deep breaths to steady myself and drop farther into the ultra-deep state. As I did so, I had that familiar uncomfortable feeling of falling.

Then, as my stomach settled down, the fog cleared away and I found myself standing on a flat expanse of land. The plain stretched out to a horizon that appeared strangely close. It was flat, arid and the ground was strewn with rocks of various sizes. Desolate and empty, it reminded me of Death Valley. I realized that once again, just as in the first bi location, I was short of breath. I thought to myself that if this continues, I'd better bring along an oxygen mask next time.

There was no feeling of being crushed, as there had been when I was at the Titanic; just that there wasn't any oxygen. It was uncomfortable and I looked at the sky to take my mind off the feeling of being smothered.

This was weird. The sky was a salmon color close to the horizon but quickly gave way to blackness as I looked toward the zenith. There were stars clearly visible even though it was daylight.

I was still having trouble breathing, when it occurred to me that this wasn't Earth. I heard a soft, high-pitched humming sound and turned to look off to my right. Spinning nearby was what looked to me like a dust devil. I could see the dust motes whirling inside the tall tornado-like phenomenon. There appeared to be an energy associated with the dust motes. What kind of energy I didn't know, but the motes reminded me of a cloud of glittering fireflies.

There didn't appear to be anything else around this desolate landscape. No sounds of animals. No sign of human habitation. No vegetation. No sign of water. Nothing.

A hissing sound caught my attention. I quickly looked up and saw what appeared to be a meteor flash across the sky and disappear over the too-close horizon.

My consternation grew, as there didn't appear to be anything of interest to see. It seemed to be a boring desert tableau, except for the weird foreshortened horizon.

I started to get angry, thinking maybe I missed the target or I was dreaming. But as I looked around, I knew it wasn't a dream. I was somewhere, but somewhere was getting boring, boring, boring. I angrily thought about Dave saying this was going to be a special target and the only thing I got was a giant rock garden. The anger brought me out of the Zone and the surroundings dissolved back to the twilight world of the Matrix.

Lamenting the fact that I hadn't remained calm, I put aside the anger and concentrated on returning to the target. I would have to use my breathing techniques to try and get back down to the zone of ultra-deep theta. There had to be more here. Starting the deep-breathing sequence all over again was time-consuming. Finally, the familiar but uncomfortable feeling of falling returned. The twilight of the Matrix dissolved and I found myself back in the giant rock garden. There was no change. It was the same boring montage.

As a last resort, I turned completely around, trying to see if there was something that I had missed. I caught a glint of light at my feet as I turned. Looking down, I saw that I was almost standing on a flat, rectangular shape about two feet long. The surface was covered with a reddish-blue glass that appeared to have electronic circuitry inside. Curious, I stepped back to focus on it.

Once again, John's timing was impeccable. He had fallen asleep again and started to snore. That explosive guttural snort blasted into my deeply meditative state like a bomb.

The effect was the same: like being on the end of a stretched-out rubber band that suddenly snapped back. With a groan, I rolled over on my side, fighting the instant vertigo and nausea.

I reached over to grip John's shoulder. As he came back to consciousness, I smiled wryly and whispered, "We've got to stop meeting like this. People are going to talk."

John flushed with embarrassment. He started to apologize but I cut him off, saying, "Hey, don't worry about it, I was almost finished anyway. We'll just have to find a position for you that reduces the risk of snoring."

I discovered I wasn't going to have time to get back to wherever I had been. Dave was walking up to the front of the room to announce the return to 'reality'. During the break, after everybody finished writing up their summaries, I took the time to go outside with Saundra.

"Well, it was a great ride getting there, but then things went downhill fast," I commented.

"Did you bi-locate this time too?" Saundra inquired.

"Yeah, for what it was worth. I don't understand. Dave said it was an interesting target. But all I saw was desert and rocks. Except for the dust devil with the glowing particles and the electronic panel, it was pretty boring. Vivid, but boring."

"What do you mean by dust devil and what kind of panel?"

"Well, there was a dust devil whirling nearby, like a tornado, but the dust inside glowed like fireflies. And I saw a flat, rectangular panel a couple of feet long that appeared to be covered by reddish-blue glass. It looked like some kind of electronic panel or a solar cell. I couldn't tell because John started snoring again."

Before Saundra could reply, I heard a voice behind me. "He got you again?" Smirked Jill, and pretending to hide behind her was John. Trying to hide behind her was like trying to hide the Queen Mary behind a cabin cruiser.

I slid around Jill and playfully grabbed John by the arm.

"I'm sorry, I'm sorry," he said smiling and feigning a cringe. We all laughed as I said to John, "Well if nothing else, you keep *me* from falling asleep." We talked for a bit then walked back into class.

I thought about what I had seen. It seemed so real, so vivid, as if I had really been at the target. The bi location had been that strong. But was it real? I had no confidence in what I had seen, partly because it just didn't appear to be the exciting target that Dave had said he had chosen for us.

However, there was an even more compelling reason. Yesterday's session had such an unreal aspect about it that I found myself wondering if it had been an illusion. Part of me believed; part of me still wanted to return to the familiar world of the status quo. As I sat down, I wondered how I was going to feel if I blew this target. Following the previous pattern, we all had a chance to talk for a short time about our experiences. Then, Dave strode up to the podium and said, "Okay, your target is an interesting and difficult one to get this early in the class. However, yesterday you showed how far you've come in just two days. This target is difficult not for what's there, but what's not. There isn't a lot to look for at this site, with the exception of two objects. That's why this is such a fun target because it's always interesting to see what the viewers discover," Dave said as he turned to put up the transparency of the target.

There appeared on the screen the block letters of the target feedback.

9922 –
1030.
TARGET, MARS:
TWIN PEAKS SECTOR

Below the title were pictures of the rocky plain of the Red Planet taken by the Mars Sojourner Rover. The same plain I had stood on. And there, on top of the rover itself was the solar panel. It was a rectangle about two feet in length, topped by the reddish-blue of the solar cells, exactly what I had seen.

I felt a shock race up my spine. I had only felt that twice before in my life. The first time was when I had heard President John F. Kennedy had been assassinated; the second when I saw the Space Shuttle *Challenger* explode.

For a moment I felt suspended over an abyss, caught between my past and the future. I turned slowly to Saundra; she was looking at me with her mouth open, her eyes wide.

I smiled weakly, "Gee ... was I close?"

Dave commented further on the target. "The two objects are, first, the Mars Sojourner Rover, the small cart-shaped vehicle with the solar panel on top. The second object is the lander vehicle that contained the rover and other science equipment. The lander looks like a triangular platform with each side having a ramp folded down to the Martian surface. That's why some of you reported a flower or flowers."

Over the next few days after class, as I sat in my motel room, I would pull out the session summary for the Mars target. The wonder of it had not worn off. It still sent chills down my spine, thinking about how it felt to be standing on the surface of another world; the moment when John inadvertently snored and yanked me back some 50 million miles. It had been one hell of a trip: Mars to Earth in the space of a heartbeat.

When I was a child, I dreamed of being an astronaut. I wanted to be on the first manned mission to Mars, but life's twists and turns led elsewhere. I never would have made it without Dave and the extended remote viewing class.

It was a wonderful gift and I would treasure that session. It also, however, brought up issues that ultimately caused me a great deal of anguish. I had a great time during the following week, with more mind-bending bi-locations. I was no longer apprehensive about them; the fear had been replaced by wonder. The ERV class turned out to be the most fun of all of Dave's classes, but I had a conflict brewing.

My skepticism was making it hard for me to accept the spiritual aspects of what I had experienced. The events of the past week weren't enough to overcome my prejudices. Coordinate remote viewing was just barely within my comfort sphere. Now my belief system was on the verge of a melt-down.

To avoid dealing with this conflict I took the easy road; I ignored it, compartmentalized it. I rolled it into an unwieldy ball and hid it in an empty recess in the corner of my soul. It was easy for me; cops do it all the time. It's one of the defense mechanisms you learn to survive the everyday outrages you deal with as a police officer. My failure to deal with these implications, however, would come back to haunt me.

That remained for the future. Now I set my sights on the Master level class. Dave had held such a class only once before, for a group of law enforcement officials, and was in the process of modifying it for civilian attendance. It sounded exciting. I signed up for it immediately.

ERV TARGET-5
THE PLANET MARS

MARS—TWIN PEAKS SECTOR. THE TERRAIN SEEN IN THE TOP PHOTO IS TAKEN AT A (272 DEGREE) AZIMUTH FROM THE ROVER SEEN IN THE PHOTO BELOW. STUDENTS ACCESSING THIS TARGET OFTEN COMPLAIN OF DIFFICULTY BREATHING IN THE ALIEN ATMOSPHERE— A "BI-LOCATION" EFFECT. THE TERRAIN IS INSIGNIFICANT AND BORING—WHICH IS WHY THIS IS PREDOMINANTLY A STAGE V TARGET, DESIGNED FOR THE VIEWER TO SEE TO LEVEL TWO. WHAT IS HERE THAT WE CANNOT SEE? THE VEHICLE ABOVE IS THE "ROVER" A SMALL, TRACKED, VEHICLE THAT SCOUTS AROUND THE LANDING AREA WHERE THE "LANDER" (THE MAIN VEHICLE) SETTLED INTO THE MARTIAN SOIL. FOR ADDITIONAL RESEARCH INFORMATION—LOOK TO SEVERAL "MARS" WEB SITES HOSTED BY NASA AND OTHERS.

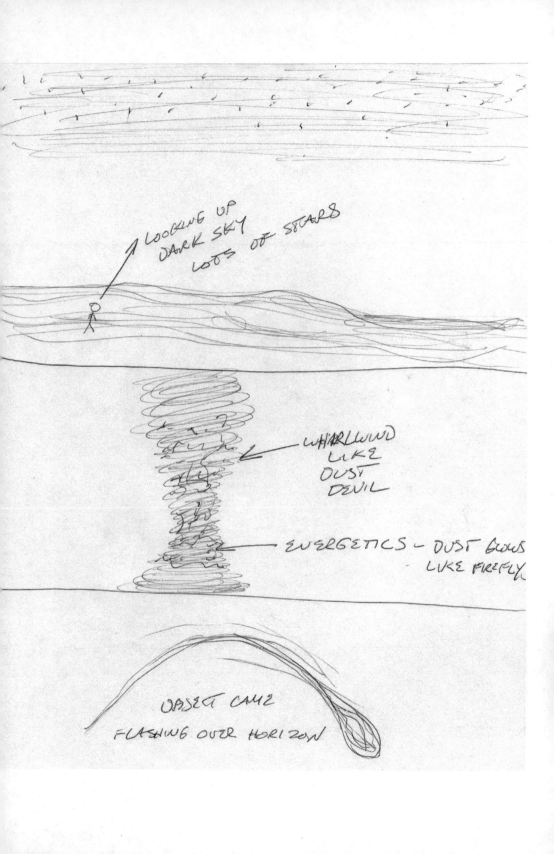

LOOKING UP
DARK SKY
LOTS OF STARS

WHIRLWIND
LIKE
DUST
DEVIL

ENERGETICS - DUST GLOWS
- LIKE FIREFLY

SUNSET CAME
FLASHING OVER HORIZON

GLASS LIKE
TOP — REDDISH
GLUE

STRANDS OF WIRE
ON TABLE TOP

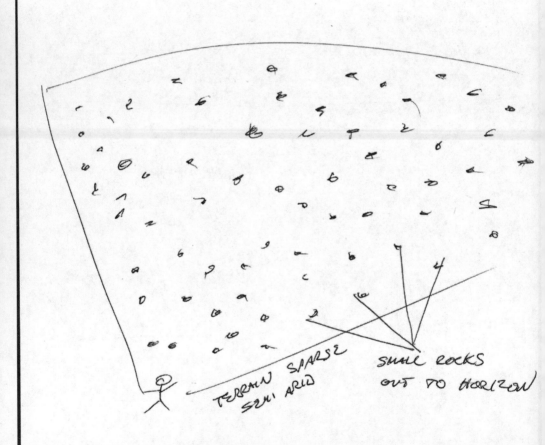

TERRAIN SPARSE
SEMI ARID

SMALL ROCKS
OUT TO HORIZON

SESSION SUMMARY

OBSERVED FLAT PLAIN — LOTS OF ROCKS
SEMI ARID OR DESERT — NO SENSE OF
WATER NEARBY. STARS BRIGHT OVERHEAD
HIGH PITCHED SOUND NEARBY AND FLICKERING
LIGHT. SAW VERY ENERGETIC DUST MOTES WHIRLING
AROUND IN A DUST DEVIL LIKE WHIRLWIND.
REMINDED ME OF GLOWING LOCUSTS OR FIREFLYS
HARD TO BREATH — TENSE ATMOSPHERE.
SAW METEOR OR METEOR LIKE OBJECT
FLASH OVER HORIZON.

HIGH PITCHED SOUND ASSOCIATED WITH
SOME ENERGETIC — MAY HAVE BEEN THE
DUST MOTES.

SAW FLAT ELECTRONIC TABLE TOP
WITH REDDISH BLUE GLASS OR TRANSPARENCY
ON TOP. WIRES OR CIRCUITRY IN THE GLASS.

CHAPTER SEVEN

Blindness

To see what is in front of one's nose requires a constant struggle.

−George Orwell

I was looking forward to the Master class, but due to extensive overseas commitments and a lack of time to polish the finishing touches, Dave had decided to wait until the following year. Although we were all disappointed, it would turn out to be not only a wise decision, but also one especially fortuitous for me.

In the meantime, I decided to take the two courses, CRV and ERV again, to review and hone my skills for the upcoming Master class. I wanted to be completely at home with these new abilities that I had acquired. In the spring of 2000 I met John, Saundra, and Jill at Saddleback College in Orange County to retake the CRV class.

"Hi Jill. How's the leg?" I inquired.

"Better and better. I'll be off the cane after a few more weeks of physical therapy."

John walked through the door as I was about to ask Jill if he had made it. "That's good news. Hi John. Nice to see you again." I shook John's hand and asked, "Well, three out of four so far. Where's Saundra?"

"She'll be up momentarily. She was right behind me." Jill replied. I nodded and as I looked up at the front of the room I saw Dave talking to a couple of students. I was about to walk up and say hello when Saundra walked in.

"Saundra, you're looking great," I remarked.

"Hi John. I'm happy to see you made it," she said graciously, with a warm hug.

"Come on. Let's all say hi to Uncle Dave," I replied. The four of us walked up to Dave as he finished answering a student's question.

"Jill, Saundra, John, and John," he welcomed, giving each of us a friendly embrace. After exchanging some pleasantries, he excused himself to get handouts for the class. The four of us chose seats next to each other and sat down.

I was especially happy to see Saundra. We had started a strong friendship that an event during the last days of the Carmel ERV class reinforced. I thought back to that amazing weekend of wonders.

As part of the search for a personal mythology, Dave had the class do a target session on a very special set of coordinates.

The room seemed to fade away as my thoughts drifted back.

"Okay, class. You have your tasking sheets. Take a look at the focus questions. For this target it's important to concentrate on getting the answers to those questions, so take special note," Dave had cautioned. "I'll start the cool-down in five minutes."

I was buttoned up in my sleeping bag when the lights dimmed and the heavy sounds of surf invaded the room. Following the ERV protocols brought me quickly to Sanctuary, and before the tape had finished I was off to the target. I didn't know what to expect. The focus questions were so vague that they gave no clue to the target's identity. As the mists of the Matrix dissipated, I found myself in a dark tunnel. It was claustrophobic; the walls were close on either side.

This place is creeping me out, I thought, as I tried not to panic. It reminded me of the time I had been inside an MRI machine prior to arthroscopic surgery. When I was a kid, tight places never bothered me. Nothing scares kids because they have no preconceived notions. When the tray I was on began to slide into the tight confines of the magnet, I had thought that there would be no problem. Once inside with the walls of the magnet almost touching my nose, panic reared its ugly head and I told the technician to get me out, *now*! I had to shut my eyes and think of something else to keep my attention focused away from the stifling closeness.

Now I found myself in the same claustrophobic circumstances. I tried to keep my attention focused on my surroundings, hoping that would hold the rising panic at bay. The tunnel rock around me appeared to be a hard igneous type colored a uniform black. It had numerous passages that snaked off into the distance. There didn't seem to be anything else to look at. No smells or sounds intruded on my senses.

I was confused, but, remembering the experiences of the previous targets, I knew that I shouldn't take anything for granted. I flipped a mental coin and chose a passageway at random. As I moved through the darkness, following the labyrinth, I noticed that there were flickering lights in the passageways that I passed, like low fires in the background. It was surreal. The surroundings reminded me of a target that I had been given by Saundra. We had agreed to make practice targets for each other after the UCLA class. One of those targets had been Jewel Cave National Park. But I had done that target in CRV, not ERV. As I continued working my way through passageway after passageway, I realized that there was no chance this could be Jewel Cave. The claustrophobia was missing at that target and there was no feeling of restrictive suffocating closeness. There were no crystalline formations or stalactites and stalagmites here, no water. There was just the endless series of narrow passageways curving through the rock, occasionally lit by the flickering lights in the background. I tried finding the source of the flickering lights but they seemed to move away as I attempted to approach them.

The claustrophobia closed in around me. The feeling was uncomfortable and made it difficult to concentrate. Jeez Louise, I thought resignedly, when do I get an easy target?

As I stood there confused, the sounds of music intruded. The fog of the Matrix closed in and a disembodied voice said quietly, "All right, viewers. Please end your session and return to Sanctuary. When you are ready and only when you are ready, complete your session summary. When you have finished you are free to go to lunch. Be back by two thirty for feedback." It was Dave ending the session.

I returned to the peace of Sanctuary and lay there for a minute letting the tension subside. Then I took a deep breath, stretched my muscles and rolled over. I lifted my eye shield and removed my earplugs. It didn't take long to write my summary. I wondered where we had been sent. Remembering the Mars ERV session, I knew I could take nothing for granted. That session had also started out boring, but what a target! Even though this had been an unusual session I thought Dave would have a reason for such a target. I'd probably missed something. I shrugged my shoulders with a sigh. In any case, I'd find out shortly. I hoped I hadn't blown it too badly. When I had finished the summary, I walked outside and joined the others in the sunshine.

"So how was it?" I asked Saundra, curious to see what she would say.

Saundra uncharacteristically paused. For a moment I had the feeling that she was going to break down and cry, but she replied, "I'm not sure. My mind kept wandering over personal issues and I'm afraid I didn't get much data."

"Me too!" Jill exclaimed. She turned to me. "How about you?"

"Tell you the truth, I have no clue where I was. I was in a labyrinth of tunnels. It was dark and there were so many tunnels I couldn't explore them all. It was intensely claustrophobic and I nearly panicked. There was a flickering light in the background but I never saw any light sources. I tried to find the source but the lights always seemed to be moving away as I tried to get closer. I trudged around trying to find something interesting but there was nothing else. I thought I might be in a cave complex but there were no stalactites or anything you might associate with a cave. I don't know where I might have been. For all I know, I was on some other planet." That comment would hit closer to home than I wanted to admit. It wasn't another planet, but it *was* another world.

John offered to drive us to lunch, so we piled into his car and went over to the main street in Carmel. After eating we drove back and walked around, stretching our legs. Twenty minutes later it was time for the class to reconvene. We walked back, wondering what our target might have been. Dave took the podium.

"This target may have confused some of you. Those of you who compared notes may find that your data doesn't seem to match. There's a reason for that." Dave then took on a different tone of voice, more diffident. "Some of you might have had a difficult trip on this target, so I will tell you that participation in the group feedback is voluntary. You can share as much or as little as you want."

I thought that seemed a bit cautious for a target that was about as interesting as watching concrete dry.

I was wrong. As the students began sharing their experiences it didn't take me long to realize I must have missed the target. Not one of the students had seen what I had. My composure began to slip at that unwelcome discovery. When it was my turn, I muttered "crap" under my breath and stood. It was tempting to lie and say my session was too traumatic, but I had already told Saundra and the others what really happened. Besides, I would have been too uncomfortable with the deception. So I bit the bullet and repeated what I'd said to my friends.

Surprisingly, I saw several people nod their heads as I spoke. When I sat down all I could think was, how strange could this target be? How could all of these pieces of data be pieced together?

When it was Saundra's turn, she stood and strangely did not look at the class but instead looked down at her paper with an unusual intensity. "My session had a lot of issues that I've been dealing with lately. I can't talk about most of it because it's very personal." She stopped and tears began to fill her eyes. She quickly wiped them away before she continued, her voice quivering, "I just want to say that it has to do with changes that I should make in my life and I'm so very grateful for Dave and his classes which helped me to realize it." She quickly sat down, continuing to wipe tears away, Jill comforting her. Dave thanked her for her candidness and the compliment. It was the perfect touch. Saundra returned a wan smile and her tears ceased.

I felt helpless watching her. Jill, as well as John and I, knew what she was talking about. The other students didn't. The first night of the Carmel ERV class we had spent drinking and talking. First, the conversation centered on UFOs. Later, the liquor and camaraderie had led us to talk openly about ourselves to each other. Each of us had shared some really personal information. It had deepened our relationship since the first time we met at UCLA.

Whatever the target was, it had elicited some very unusual responses, and not just from Saundra. I really began to wonder, considering what I had experienced, what the target was.

"I know everyone is wondering about the nature of this target so let's show the class the feedback," Dave said, directing his comments to his assistants. The projector snapped on and the reason for the confusion became clear.

2000 –
0482:
THE TARGET IS...YOU!
THIS IS AN OPEN SEARCH INWARD.

"An open search inward is a journey to somewhere on the time-line of your soul," Dave explained. "It's part and parcel of your quest for a personal mythology. You have to figure out what the Matrix is telling you and its import to you; what it means, where on the timeline of your soul you were, is for you to discover." He paused to let the significance of his words sink in.

"I urge you to go back and further explore those coordinates. They are yours. You can go there anytime. There is more informa-tion waiting there if you take the time to return to the Source. That choice is yours."

I didn't know what to think. This was, well, too *something* for me. I had no clue what my session had been telling me. And I really didn't care. I had better things to do than open searches inward. I wanted real targets, not metaphysical mumbo-jumbo. I wanted to increase my skill level. What did tunnels in the dark have to do with my personal mythology? This touchy-feely stuff didn't interest me. I could worry about that later. For now all I wanted to do was to concentrate on targets and improve my skill.

That immature outlook would come back to haunt me again and again. Had I taken the wisdom in Dave's words to heart, my future in remote viewing might not have been so traumatic.

Dave cut us loose for a break. We were scheduled for an early evening target, then dinner. My thoughts, though, were on Saun-dra. My heart went out to her; obviously this session had affected her deeply. I walked over to her as she started to gather her things.

"Hey you, are you okay?" I asked carefully, putting my hand on her arm. She suddenly turned and embraced me, her arms around me, her face buried in my shoulders, sobbing. She caught me off guard and I didn't know what to do other than just stroke her hair, hold her and say. "Hey now, you're with friends. It'll be okay. I'm here for you, baby." I kept repeating those words as she cried, until she had calmed down.

The class filed out, not saying a word or compromising the mo-ment. Dave glanced at me with a wordless acknowledgment and left the room, leaving the two of us alone. Finally the tears subsided and she gave me a quick kiss on the cheek and stepped back.

"Thanks for being here, John. There's so much going on in my life. It's been so hard."

"Hey now. I'll always be there for you, Saundra. If you need to talk or anything, you've got my number. Anytime, anywhere."

I meant it. "Besides, it's good karma. I'll probably need even more help than you one day," I grinned, lightening the tension. Her smile was shy, vulnerable. It made her very attractive right then. I didn't know how prophetic a statement I had just made. I would find out in the upcoming months just how accurate that assessment was.

The recollection of the Carmel class faded, and I put aside the memory as Dave started the CRV lecture.

Dave had revised the CRV course, upgrading it to take into account the addition of viewers that had taken his course before, as well as another phenomenon that was starting to manifest itself. Dave had noticed that his current classes were advancing faster than the earlier ones. The famed physicist Dr. Rupert Sheldrake coined a term to describe this non-linear effect. He called it morphic resonance. Many scientists, including Dr. Sheldrake and English quantum physicist Dr. David Bolm believe that our existence has two expressions of reality. There is the existence of sense perceptions that we all experience in everyday life. This reality is what Dr. Bolm characterizes as the explicate order. It is an illusion of sorts, because it is characterized by our sense perceptions and therefore has only the weakest correspondence with true reality.

Then there is the true expression of reality which underlies our perceptions, known as the implicate order. Implicate order is just another term for the Matrix of all Creation of the remote viewer.

Implicit in the definition of these terms is a non-local correlation between objects that have interacted. This correlation has been demonstrated in quantum physics experiments. Dr. Sheldrake characterized these correlations as a morphogenic field, a field that connects all matter on a very fundamental level.

Like the *Star Wars* mythology of 'The Force', morphogenic fields connect everyone on the level of the collective unconscious, a term made famous by the psychiatrist Dr. Carl Jung.

Sheldrake postulated that these fields interact in a non-linear fashion such that they reinforce each other. This effect means that each new class gains the experience of all those that went before, on the unconscious level. New classes would learn faster and view better than previous classes.[20]

Each year Dave had to revise his courses to take advantage of this effect. The CRV class at Saddleback College would be tasked with targets that I had when I was in the advanced ERV class. It was one of the reasons he hadn't had the time for the Master class in this year. He had to devote too much time catching up with morphic resonance.

This CRV class brought out my ability. My sessions were becoming more accurate with less noise. Dave commented that I had excellent structure and results, something he had expected of one of his advanced students. I was secretly pleased by his praise. However, I was getting too caught up in results.

The two biggest hurdles that a remote viewer faces are ego and self-doubt. Each can have an effect on the other.

I was forgetting one of the most important lessons of remote viewing – letting go of the outcome. Don't get ego driven, because the first disappointing session will cause an immediate downward perception of your abilities. It could lead you to doubt the whole skill-learning process.

I was heading for disaster, letting ego drive my sessions. I was intoxicated with my success; the praise and admiration of my fellow classmates was seductive. I began to lose perspective, and was more concerned with praise than growth.

I had forgotten the reason I had taken the remote viewing classes to begin with. I had forgotten the message that Dave teaches at the beginning of each of his classes. I had even put aside the message that his book had taught me when I first read it over three years earlier.

The message of the wonderful gift that is remote viewing, the promise it holds for the fulfillment of human destiny, was lost in the selfishness of ego gratification.

The only thing that I can say in my defense is that the bundle hidden away in a dark corner of my soul was still unresolved. Filled with disbelief and skepticism, I had suppressed it rather than deal with the issues it represented. Not dealing with those issues would generate some highly unpleasant repercussions. I couldn't commit to what I had supposedly committed.

After finishing the CRV class at Saddleback, I said good-by to my friends. It would be the last time I saw them in one of Dave's classes.

Jill and Saundra went on to take advanced training in CRV with former military remote viewer Lyn Buchanan. They found that this form of remote viewing worked better for them than ERV. John went back to the demands of his family and job. He too, found CRV better suited to his style, due to his affliction of sleep apnea. But each, in his or her way, learned something precious in Dave's classes.

I gradually lost touch with John and Jill as I would of many of the acquaintances made in Dave's class. There were just too many to keep track of and, after all, we all had our own lives. Not everyone went on to the more advanced classes or made remote viewing a priority in their lives as I did. But Saundra and I remained very close friends.

Several months in the future, I took the ERV class again to get ready for the Master class. It brought about some radical changes in my thinking.

There were changes going on with Dave's operation as well. Several months after the Saddleback College CRV class, Jill and I attended a lecture on remote viewing that Dave was doing for the Learning Annex, a company that sponsored lecture series and workshops on various subjects. He liked to see his students show up at these workshops for moral support as well as to talk with members of the audience about our experiences. Dave had added a new assistant by the name of Patty, an attractive curly haired brunette with a bright smile and a flair for organization; as well as a whole new set of multimedia presentations. I had met Patty several months before when Dave introduced us during another Learning Annex presentation that Jill and I attended.

This time, Dave's operation had professional sound systems, computer generated video presentations, and all sorts of marketing materials to enhance his classes. I could see Patty's hand in this. It was a quantum leap for him, and a definite step up professionally. But the hallmark of his classes, his dedication to the students, remained as intense as always.

October rolled around and I found myself down in San Diego. My destination was the Marina Village complex adjacent to Sea World, right on the oceanfront, to audit the ERV course. I was looking forward to it for several reasons. First, it would be the first time that I would see the revamped ERV course with the new computer and video equipment. These promised a new and exciting presentation. But I had an even more pressing reason for taking this course again. I had noticed since Saddleback that I had been having trouble seeing in ERV mode. For some reason I couldn't access targets. I hadn't given it much thought after my performance at Saddleback. My CRV sessions had been great. But afterwards my attempts at ERV were fruitless. I attributed it to stress in my job or something silly like sunspots, but inwardly I was getting concerned. The problem had already generated turmoil in my life. I had joined a number of fellow students meeting every couple of weekends to chat and do a practice target. I had the same problem there and, not wanting to share it or look like I was less of a viewer to my peers, I stopped going. I had heard second hand that some of them thought I was trying to hide something. I was too proud to share my predicament.

The Master class was fast approaching and it was conducted in ERV. I hoped that this class would be just what I needed to get back into the ERV groove.

I would be right about half of that.

One of the large meeting rooms was the venue for the ERV class that I was auditing. I had called Dave and told him that if he needed help setting up the rooms in the building, I'd be glad to assist. He had readily accepted the offer. It took half a dozen people several hours to set up all the equipment and to prepare the rooms, so my offer was much appreciated.

I entered the Sunset room, where the class was to be held. Dave was there with several people I was unfamiliar with. Seeing me, his face broke into his familiar boyish grin. I couldn't help it; I had to smile back — it was that infectious. After a warm welcome he said, "Come on, I want you to meet Jason and my daughter Danielle."

He waved over a teenage girl and a tall, slim man.

"This is my daughter Danielle. Danielle, this is John Herlosky. He was in the Carmel ERV class." Danielle had long brown hair, a pretty face, and the shy smile typical of an awkward teenager. I had read about Danielle in Dave's book. Although on first impression she seemed shy, it didn't take long for her to shed her reserve.

"And this is Jason. Jason is a recent addition to RVT. I met him at the Omega Institute, while teaching a class in remote viewing. He was looking for a job since the Institute is closed during the winter so we brought him on board. He's an expert in yoga and audio-visual presentations, so he's a welcome addition."

Jason had an open smile and a thatch of unruly dark curly hair. We spent the next few hours setting up the room for the class, laughing and catching up on events. By the time we were done, the main lecture hall with the sunny interior, picture windows and airy feeling, was transformed. Now it was a dark, cozy, womb-like place ideal for our journeys of the mind.

Dave turned to me, his hands on his hips, "Oh yeah. This is perfect. Nice and dark, lots of room for the students. ERV Heaven."

I looked around. He was right; it would be perfect. I looked back at him and grinned, "I love ERV class." This was a large class, with over fifty participants, all recent graduates of Dave's CRV course. It was set up differently now that Dave had several able assistants.

After the target sessions, the class would break up into small discussion groups. There, the group leader would discuss the experience and the results with the students. It would allow greater feedback and a more personal touch for the students. Then the class would gather around Dave for a further open discussion.

I was in Patty's group. Jason had a group, as did two other assistants.

The standard format had also changed. Although the first day was devoted to lecture on the theory and application of extended remote viewing, there were additions. To assist the students to relax and put aside any anxiety, Dave added a moving meditation to start each morning.

After the moving meditation, Jason led the class in a series of yoga exercises. That was an instant hit. Jason's aforementioned free spirit emerged and he kept the class amused with his eclectic brand of humor and exercises.

After a break, it was on to the lecture with Dave. The presentation was much more comprehensive than my ERV class had been, with additional explanations and videos to compliment Dave's teaching. It was a definite improvement over the old format.

I listened intently, trying to immerse myself in the lecture. I wanted to make sure that there wouldn't be a failure in procedure, like my first CRV class.

The lecture seemed to go quickly, although the day started at 10am and finished up at 8pm. The class broke up tired but excited about the upcoming adventure. I had already started the beginnings of several new friendships. That was one of the best parts of Dave's courses; you always wound up meeting the most interesting people.

That night, sitting alone in my motel room, I reviewed the day's lecture. I found no mistakes in procedure in my previous sessions.

They should have produced the same incredible results that they had in the past.

But they hadn't.

I mused, what does it matter? I wasn't supposed to be psychic anyway. Maybe this was all just a fluke. What was I supposed to do with this so-called gift? I mean, you couldn't take remote viewing that seriously, could you? Could I? How could this possibly become important to me? What would I do with it? How did I fit in with remote viewing? Why should I get so bent out of shape, over something that I still half didn't believe was possible?

No easy answers.

So, I thought, the hell with it. Tomorrow was a new day.

The following morning, after moving meditation and yoga with Jason, Dave finished up the lecture on the mechanics of ERV. Following a break, the class would be given its first ERV target.

On return from the break, Patty handed out the tasking sheets as Dave addressed the class, "Here is the tasking sheet with the co-ordinates for your first target. This target is to be viewed in present time. Take a look at the focus questions. I want you to consider these questions while you're at the target."

I took a few moments to lock the coordinates in my mind as Dave briefly took questions. I had to smile. The questions from the students just before the launch were much the same as in my earlier class. At first serious, then becoming almost comically repetitive, they reflected more the nervousness of the students then their need for information.

I watched with amusement as Dave put an end to their thinly disguised attempt to postpone the inevitable. "Listen class. You are getting too wound around the axle over the delivery mechanisms. Just go with what you get. Every class seems to worry too much on the mechanics and not enough about having fun with this. You can do this. Just go with whatever shows up in Sanctuary."

The students were like fledgling raptors, nervously flexing their wings before garnering enough courage to launch into space. Been there, done that, I thought. It would be interesting if these students were to have as much trouble on their first attempt as my first ERV class. They were a lot alike in temperament and makeup. I'd find out shortly. Dave announced, "Okay, let's get ready to launch. Go to the bathroom if you need to. Get a drink of water. We'll start the cool-down in five minutes. Have fun, work until you're told to stop."

There was a flurry of movement as the class rushed around, getting their workstations ready. I slid into the familiar sleeping bag on top of an inflatable mattress, put in my earplugs and slid my eye shield in place. Well, I thought, hoping my brain wouldn't vapor lock again, time to find out if I have some sort of problem in ERV. I had the protocols memorized and I knew they worked. I couldn't be better prepared.

The cool-down began. The sound of waves drowned out the ambient noise. I relaxed, moving my breath to the rhythms of the ocean, following the yogic breathing exercises. It didn't take long to be surrounded by the twilight world of the Matrix, waiting in Sanctuary. As the mists of the Matrix writhed and swirled around the soft blue glow surrounding me, I shifted my breathing sequence to bring on the Vortex.

I waited, expectantly at first, then with a growing unease. There was no doubt that I was deep enough in theta to manifest a wormhole. The heavy, almost numb, feeling in my limbs and the silence confirmed it, but Sanctuary remained eerily quiescent. The calm, blue light that surrounded me seemed dimmer, more foreboding than in the past. Or was it just my past that haunted me right now with the specter of failure?

My anxiety increased with each passing minute, as the Vortex failed to materialize. Trying a different tactic, I used my breathing techniques to drop even deeper, to assure myself that I was in the zone of ultra-deep. I hoped that by dropping deeper I might trigger the formation of the Vortex. After several minutes of trying, it was clear that I had a real problem. The Vortex would not form.

Trying a different tack, I took a break, quietly breathing and putting everything else out of my mind. I lay there relaxing and breathing. Then, after a time, I gave it another shot.

This proved to be just as fruitless as the previous attempts. I knew at this point that I wasn't going anywhere. The remaining time seemed to drag on, mocking me with each passing moment. Mercifully, the warm-up music began to play, and Jason's voice announced the end of the session.

As the other students began writing their session summaries, I lay there thinking something was very wrong. In my first ERV class, Dave had warned us not to expect the "magic carpet ride" on our early forays. First ERV sessions were often subtle affairs, and only after several sessions did the experience ramp up. Each person would experience ERV differently, depending upon the student's primary mode of viewing.

My primary mode was visual. I had gotten the magic carpet ride on my second session. Intense bi-locations seemed to be the norm for me, perhaps because of my training in advanced EEG biofeedback. Whatever the reason, ERV had been easy for me. This should have been a straightforward session.

I didn't want to get into a self-reinforcing failure mode, reminding myself what happened in my first try at remote viewing. Taking a page straight from the remote viewing manual, I chalked it up as just another session. You did your best, that's all you could do. I felt better; I knew we would have another target session later in the day. I'd give it another shot then.

When we returned, each of my group mates talked about their experience. In many ways, this class had a lot in common with my ERV class. Composed of mostly professionals of above average intelligence, their performance in CRV had been admirable, as those in my class had. And like those in my first ERV class, they were finding ERV to be more difficult than they had anticipated.

All of the members of my group had less than stellar results, with only sparse data for their efforts. Several had never made it out of Sanctuary or had problems with the delivery mechanisms.

This class had responded much like our class had, with spoiled petulance. They were bright, competitive individuals comfortable with success. Having had brilliant results with a minimum of effort in CRV, they had expected similar success here. It hadn't happened. In listening to their narratives, it was easy to see the parallels as well as diagnose their failure to achieve results equal to their expectations. Then it was my turn. Patty looked at me expectantly, "John, would you like to share with us?" I didn't have much to offer Patty or the group in the way of results either. So instead, I offered them my experience, little as it was.

"I'm afraid I didn't get much this time. I've been having difficulty lately in ERV for some reason. These are not my usual results. But I can tell you from personal experience that if you put the time and effort into ERV, the rewards are substantial."

I paused for a moment, looking around the room. I didn't know anyone in my group from previous classes; they were all strangers. I felt uncomfortable talking about my failure. I didn't want to appear foolish. Ah, pride. It has caused me so much trouble in my life.

Instead, I took the easier path and explained, "ERV is nothing like coordinate remote viewing. CRV is hard to learn, easy to do. ERV is the opposite, easy to learn, hard to do. But if you put the effort into it, the results can be spectacular. The best sessions I ever had were in ERV.

You can do this. I'm not a natural psychic. Prior to working with Dave, I'd never had a psychic experience. I've never seen E.T. or Elvis. My first time in CRV class, out of the all the students, I was the only one who failed on the first target. True story!"

With a grin I told them, "I'm CVR's poster child for the psychically challenged. So if I can do this, I know you can. Don't get discouraged because this session didn't turn out like you expected. My first ERV session didn't either."

Tina spoke up, "John, tell everyone the story you told us at lunch."

I had told Tina and several others the story of my first ERV target, the Titanic. I looked over at Patty, "Do we have time?"

Tina quickly interjected, "It's a really cool story. You've got to hear it."

Patty shrugged, "OK, well since no one saw that much, I was going to let you go on a break. But if everyone wants to, then go ahead John."

I took a moment to collect my thoughts, "You guys think you did so badly on your first try. You haven't seen anything. Our class was so bad that Dave sent us right back to the same target. We had a num-

Patty leading our small group session.r

ber of the students actually get up after only twenty minutes or so in session. Dave told us in no uncertain terms that he was extremely disappointed; told us that if we were in the Ft. Meade unit the program manager would have sent us right back into the viewing room to do the target again. So that's what he did. He sent us right back to the same target. Not only that, but Dave went to the target with us. He said he was going to do something that would help us get to the target. And he wouldn't say what that would be either. It would turn out to be the single most impressive ERV session I have ever witnessed."

I had everyone's attention now. Even Patty was listening intently. I remembered our Carmel ERV class. I still found the experience almost too fantastic to believe.

"Dave had just finished answering the last questions our class had before the cool-down was to begin. This would be our first session in ERV. We were no different from all of you. We were just as excited and we wound up just as disappointed. That is, until he sent us back," I said, remembering like it was yesterday the sessions that would forever change the way I viewed the world.

And so I told them.

Chapter Eight

Flashback

Our Life Evokes Our Character.

—Joseph Campbell

The memories of my first target during the Carmel ERV course thirteen months ago came flooding back as I recounted the story. Our class had been filled with anticipation and excited at the prospect of our first foray in extended remote viewing. I had stopped off at Saundra and Jill's location across the room as they set up their workstations.

Saundra looked up; I winked and said, "See you in the ether." She returned the sentiment with a bright smile.

Once the class was ready and put on their opaque eye-shields and earplugs, Dave started the cool-down tape and said, "Okay, have fun with this. Let go of any thought of success or failure, and simply accept what the Matrix has to offer in love and humility."

I listened once more to the sounds of crashing waves. This faded and Dave's voice took its place in quiet, measured tones. It wasn't long before that too faded, and I was in Sanctuary. I sat in the twilight darkness of the Matrix, in the center of a small circle of soft blue light. The maelstrom of the Matrix whirled around me in silent splendor.

In front of me, as I sat there quietly in apparitional form, a spot of light appeared. It was the first manifestation of the Vortex. The spot grew and began to rotate as I watched, transfixed by what I was seeing. Tendrils began to swirl away from the center and the spot began to iris into an opening. The Vortex reminded me of colored water tunneling down an open drain. It expanded until it filled my view.

The beauty of what I saw surprised and entranced me; it was so vivid. I had to restrain my excitement, knowing that it could pull me out of a deep theta state, destroying the nascent wormhole.

But as hard as I tried, the excitement got away from me and the Vortex faded.

Damn, I thought, I was afraid that would happen. Here we go again, CRV class revisited. Okay, we can do this, I thought to myself. My breathing slowed as I felt myself slide back down. I had, at least, gotten the Vortex to form, if only briefly. The Vortex, as I knew from Dave's lecture, was simply the manifestation of the signal line – the conduit of information from the Matrix to the viewer.

I concentrated on getting deeper into the theta state, using the techniques that I had been taught. And as I did so, I began to see pictures form in front of me. They were vague, dream like in quality. They were of a man and woman, dressed in early 20th century garb. Then, a car of the same vintage.

It was strange, more like a dream then my previous experiences in remote viewing. In fact, I couldn't tell if this was a dream or extended remote viewing. Where was the Vortex?

I felt lost, unable to grasp a handhold in the swirl of the Matrix fog. More images appeared, but there was no correlation to the earlier ones. I was getting confused.

Suddenly, I became aware of Dave's voice breaking in, saying, "Alright viewers, return to Sanctuary and when you are ready and only when you are ready, complete your session summaries."

I thought to myself, why was he ending this session so soon? It seemed like I had only been down maybe an hour at best. I couldn't have been more wrong. Looking at my chronometer, I was shocked to see that 90 minutes had elapsed.

It was apparent, as I looked around, that many of the class must have ended their session early. Most of them were already either writing their summaries or had finished. I had a sneaking suspicion that was not a good sign. This suspicion was confirmed when I glanced over at Dave and saw his expression. His countenance was, if not grim, decidedly unhappy.

This didn't look good. I rolled over and wrote a short paragraph on what I experienced and drew a few quick sketches. I hoped that the data I generated was target related, but I had to admit that the session had more in common with a daydream than reality. And based on the look on Dave's face, the rest of the class hadn't done any better.

Dave gave us a fifteen-minute break to allow us to ground our-selves-to return from that deeply meditative state. I don't know about anyone else, but I needed a break. I still felt a little loopy.

I walked out and over to Jill and Saundra, who were already outside, "How'd you girls do?" I asked.

Jill shook her head and said with a tinge of disgust in her voice, "I was just telling Saundra that I didn't go anywhere or see any-thing. I spent most of my time waiting for the Vortex to show."

"I didn't get much of a Vortex, but I saw a few things. Not much though," Saundra echoed.

I told them what had happened to me and mentioned our in-structor's demeanor. They looked at each other. "He did look disap-pointed, now that you bring it up," replied Saundra.

It was time to go back to the classroom. We'd discover the rea-son for Dave's mood soon enough.

We brought our chairs together in a circle in the center of the room. In a carefully neutral voice, Dave asked each of the class to give a quick synopsis of their journey.

As I listened to each of my classmates, it didn't take long to realize that everyone seemed to be describing something differ-ent. That could only mean one thing. Normally, there's a theme to a group of viewers' data, because they're describing different perspectives of the same thing. But here it seemed that we were describing different views of completely different scenes, with no agreement between us. It was like listening to people describing their dreams. There were no similarities or correlations.

After fewer than half of us had a chance to speak, Dave stopped the train. "OK, I'm going to break in here, for a reason. As you can see from the results so far, we have a problem." He paused, lowering his head and running his hand through his hair.

Then, he raised his head and addressed the class, anger beginning to seep into his voice. "This class is one of the most talented I have ever had the privilege to teach. You were some of the best coordinate remote viewers I have ever seen. You got results in CRV that were as good or better than what we ever did in the Unit. But today I saw people getting up after only fifteen or twenty minutes of work. I don't think I've ever felt so disappointed in a class before. If you had come up with these results in the Unit, they would have sent you right back to the viewing room and back to the same target."

Dave's voice got husky as he continued, his eyes intense, "What you are learning here, what all of you represent to the rest of humanity, is important. And it will be a wonderful experience, but you have to do the work. This isn't a movie theatre, where you sit back and watch the entertainment begin, eating your popcorn. This is work. ERV isn't easy. You have to put the effort into it to get results. But if you put that effort into it, you'll find ERV far superior in quality of viewing. It's pure viewing. But you have to do the work."

I could feel Dave's intensity. I quickly glanced around the room, noting the play of emotions across the faces of my fellow students. Most were a combination of chagrin at the rebuke and focus on Dave's words. There was also a hint of some resistance and ego in a few of the students. I wondered how that would play out over the next week.

One thing for certain, I was glad that I had stayed down and worked the target. But could I succeed? My positive mind said yes! I could do anything if I applied it. CRV had taught me that. But there was still an undercurrent of uncertainty, like an elusive shadow in the background. I looked back as Dave's voice changed in intensity. He became once more the engaging teacher.

"Alright, let's take a break. Put aside this first session and take the lessons with you. When you come back, we'll get serious. I'm sending you back to the same target. Only this time I'm going with you."

There was a collective gasp from the class. I thought, how can he "go with" us? It's not like we're all taking the same bus! How can he occupy the same mental space as a dozen or two people?

"I'm going to the target with you and I'm going to do something at the target site to help you find the way." With that, Dave let our class go.

As we stood together outside, of course the talk was about what our instructor was planning. Ideas passed back and forth, but we finally admitted that this was something outside our experience.

It was time to go, so our little intrepid group of otherworldly explorers walked back to the class. The excitement was rising. People were speculating on this next session. We waited in anticipation so strong you could almost touch it.

As Dave walked up to the podium, he looked around with a wide grin, "You guys look like you're about to explode. This is how we'll do it. We'll go back to the same target using the ERV protocols. I'll join you on the mission. I will go to the target and do something to facilitate your finding it."

Immediately, a number of hands shot up. Our teacher had anticipated that.

"Don't bother to ask what I'm going to do. You'll know it when it happens," Dave said with an evil little grin that morphed into an engaging smile. "Come on! This will be an exciting session. Work hard and don't stop until you are told to. You can do this, all of you. I want you all to put in your best effort.

"One last note, don't get too wound around the axle over the delivery mechanisms. I've touched on this before. Just because they may be subtle or not what you expected, go with whatever you have. Remember, as I've said, ERV is a very personal experience and it will be different for each of you. If your Vortex isn't bright and swirling, don't get upset … trust what you see. Before you know it, you'll be at the target." Dave paused a moment, looking out over the class.

"Alright, five minutes to launch. Do your best and I'll see you at the target," Dave said as we scurried about, getting ready for the session.

I returned to my mattress and put on my eyeshield and earplugs. The roar of the surf filled the room, and I listened intently to the sound of Dave's instructions. I felt disconnected from the rest of my body as my breathing deepened. His voice faded as I turned my mind inward, following the ritual of ERV. I sank deeper and deeper into an altered state. Occasionally my muscles would spasm as the tension left my body. I lost all track of time. It could have taken a heartbeat or an hour. The small intimate circle of blue light that was my chosen Sanctuary suddenly materialized around me.

From the swirl of ethereal fog in front of me, the Vortex opened. This time I managed to keep my excitement under control, now no longer surprised at the appearance of the phenomenon. When it appeared to be large enough to allow me through, I thought, one small step for Man...

I found myself falling in a tunnel of whirling mists. I had the sensation of great speed with the walls of the wormhole flashing past. It was exhilarating. It was incredible.

Holy Wizard of Oz, I thought.

I wondered how long the magic carpet ride would last, when up ahead I saw what appeared to be a translucent wall across the Vortex tunnel. I was heading right for it at a terrifying pace. I barely had time to think, "How do you stop this thing?" When I hit.

I reflexively closed, or rather tried to close my eyes. It was then that I realized two things. One, I had gone through the wall as if it wasn't there. And two, you can't close eyes that are already closed.

My apparitional form was standing, or rather floating, in darkness. As I got my bearings, I remembered a portion of Dave's lecture. That wall was the Membrane or event horizon of the Vortex. It signaled that the viewer had dropped into the target site. I had forgotten that salient point in the excitement of the trip.

Chagrined at the lapse, I took a look around. It struck me that I was not only very cold, but it was getting hard to breath. I was in a nice warm sleeping bag a moment ago. Now I was ice cold. And the pressure; it was as if an elephant was sitting on my chest.

Trying to put aside these unpleasant sensations and thinking how quickly the fun had turned to tension, I moved ahead in the darkness. The atmosphere that I floated through seemed thick and viscous, heavily oppressive. It seemed to almost cling to my skin. There was dust or maybe snow floating in it; I couldn't tell which. I had no idea where I was. It was eerily quiet, like a tomb. For some reason, the phrase from *The Wizard of Oz* came to mind – "Toto, I don't think we're in Kansas anymore."

Something materialized out of the gloom in front of me, shocking me with the speed of its appearance. It was a wall of some sort, extending down and disappearing into the shadows below as well as continuing above me.

Ahead and slightly above me, I could see what might be a fence at the top but it was strangely misshapen. It was as if the fence wire was coated with a thick rough material, not unlike a spray coating of insulation that clumped unevenly. I took a quick glance around but there was nothing else to see.

God, it was hard to breathe. And I was freezing! I was getting increasingly anxious over these sensations. I could only hope that they were unique to this target and not a general response to the ERV state.

Then, startling me with its sudden intensity, a light flashed off to my left. I thought, I'm taking a quick look and then I'm out of here. I was tired of the cold and feeling claustrophobic, and I wasn't even sure I was where I was supposed to be.

Before I could close on the source of the light, something happened and I was yanked back to the classroom in the blink of an eye.

My sleeping bag was right next to John's. While we were deep in the session, he had fallen asleep. This was not an unusual occurrence for ERV; viewers sometimes cycle up and down through sleep in a session. John had fallen asleep, but then he started to snore.

The sudden loud snort had abruptly pulled me back to my sleeping bag. The sensation was not like being awakened from a sound sleep or dream, where the sleeper is mildly disoriented. I was undergoing a phenomenon known as bi location at the time. A bi location happens when the viewer so strongly identifies with the target site that it's as if he is there, experiencing the same physical sensations that your body would feel in that environment.

When I was startled and immediately shifted from the target, it was like being on the end of a stretched out rubber band that had suddenly snapped back. The result was instant nausea and vertigo.

I laid there in my sleeping bag, fighting off the effects of the sudden transition. I rolled over on my side and pushed up my eyeshield. As the sensations faded, I noticed that Dave had come over to John's space.

He placed his hand gently on the shoulder of my friend and squeezing lightly, brought him back to consciousness. When John was fully awake, Dave said, "Sorry to wake you John, but you were snoring."

John was obviously a bit nonplussed and started to apologize, but Dave simply said, with a sympathetic grin, "Hey, don't worry. It's an occupational hazard when you're on the edge of dreams. You might want to get a little bit more sleep tonight and see how that helps tomorrow."

I looked at John and gave him a reassuring thumbs-up. We both slipped our eyeshields back down and tried to relax.

It seemed like I was just getting relaxed enough to return to the target when the soft music of the warm-up tape intruded. I had been apprehensive about returning to the cold and pressure so the fact I would not be returning to this target wasn't that much of a disappointment. I had never experienced that level of contact with a target in CRV. It had been both exciting and shocking. But the cold and pressure as well as the sudden transition back from this target when John had snored had been chillingly intense. It was then that I realized that there was no longer that feeling of being crushed, and the cold was gone. It hit me that I must have experienced my first bi location.

Dave's voice said evenly as the lights came back up enough to see to write, "Viewers, let's return to Sanctuary. When you are ready and only when you are ready, please complete your session summaries. When you are finished, take a break and be back at four-thirty."

Four thirty! We had started at one forty-five. The cool down tape was 45 minutes long, which meant that we had been at the target site for 90 minutes. It had seemed like less than fifteen.

When the music started, I had questioned why he ended the session early again. Although I hadn't been crazy about returning, I did want to see what the source of that light was. The realization that we had been down for a full ninety minutes was sobering. The time dilation effect was far more pronounced than in CRV.

I went outside, feeling a little unsteady. I saw Saundra and John over in the courtyard and walked over to them. They looked as loopy as I did.

John spoke up, "John, hey I'm sorry, man. I didn't mean to spoil your session."

I knew he felt bad and tried to assuage his feelings, "Hey, don't worry about it. To tell you the truth, it was so uncomfortable at the target that I was about to leave anyway." I didn't mention that he had kept me from finding out where the strange light had come from or its source.

Saundra, evidently intrigued by my admission asked, "What made it uncomfortable? Were you cold too?"

"Cold? I was freezing! I don't know what the target was, but I think I had my first bi location," I exclaimed excitedly to Saundra. I relayed my experience to her and John about the cold and difficulty breathing.

Jill came up as I was talking and listened to my description. Both women had experienced similar sensations albeit not to the extreme that I had.

"The class must have done much better this time. Uncle Dave looked a lot happier," Jill pointed out. I hadn't noticed, being lost in my own little world.

Jill looked over at me, "Well, you seemed to have no trouble this time, from what you said."

"I'll tell you, this time it was an E-ticket at Disneyland, a magic-carpet ride! The Vortex was incredible. It was like being inside the funnel of the tornado from the movie *The Wizard of Oz*. The target site wasn't so much fun because of the bi location. In fact it was downright scary. It'll be interesting to see whether or not anything I saw and felt was accurate. It seemed like a valid session but we won't know for sure until we get the feedback."

When we were back in the class, Dave had us circle our chairs. His demeanor was completely different. A smile replaced the earlier frown. Each of the students had a chance to speak this time. Dave didn't interrupt. After the last student finished, he addressed the class.

"First, I want to tell you that I'm proud of your second effort. It was what I had expected of this most talented of classes. You worked hard and the results showed.

"Some of you had the magic-carpet ride." He looked at me as he said this. "Others had a more subtle trip."

"Those of you who had trouble getting out of Sanctuary or other difficulties shouldn't get discouraged. It will come, I assure you. Remember what I told you. ERV is going to be a different experience for each of you. This is only your second time. We have eight more targets to work on. Right now just get comfortable with the mechanisms. The trip is the least important part."

Knowing how anxious we were, Dave asked, "Okay, so who wants to know what the target was?"

Immediately a chorus of voices rose from our class with a resounding, "We do!"

With that, he turned on the overhead projector and placed a transparency on it. As the class realized what the target was, there was a chorus of gasps and exclamations. A cold chill ran down my spine and an involuntary "Oh my God!" Escaped from my lips. Now the sensations of where I had been fell into place. The cold, the crushing pressure, the wall with the misshapen fence on top. It all made sense now.

9910
0932
TARGET: THE WRECK OF THE TITANIC.

The pictures were of the famous hulk, resting three miles down at the bottom of the North Atlantic Ocean. The wall had been the hull; the misshapen fence was the barnacle encrusted railing at the top. Had John not inadvertently ended my trip, I probably would have recognized more aspects and realized where I was.

But that left one question unanswered; what was the source of the light that I had seen piercing the gloom?

As the initial shock wore off, the conversations among the students increased in intensity. When it was clear that a number of us were asking the same question, Dave broke in.

"Alright, as you can see, most of your descriptions of the target were correct. Take a look at all the data the class as a whole has generated. Now, does anyone really think that extended remote viewing doesn't work, or is just guided imagery?" Dave asked rhetorically.

He had been saving a surprise for last, "Most of you reported a light source at the target. Well, at that depth, there are no sources of light. That ship is forever shrouded in darkness.

"This brings up an important point. Even though there's no light at the Titanic, you were able to see and describe it. Remember that you are seeing the target through non-physical eyes from a higher dimensional viewpoint. These eyes do not have the same limitations that physical eyes have. You can see in total darkness or see forms of radiation that normally are invisible."

Dave stopped a moment to let that sink in, and then he reminisced, "Mel Riley and Joe McMoneagle were able to detect radiation from nuclear sources like bombs or reactors. They said that the radiation appeared to them as a green glow, as though it came from kryptonite.[21]

"You have this same ability."

I sat there, letting it all sink in. This entire session had been so totally mind bending that it was almost overwhelming. But Dave wasn't finished. A student raised her hand.

"If there wasn't any light at the Titanic, Why did a number of us see some sort of light there. Were we mistaken?" She asked quizzically.

I had almost forgotten the light that I had seen just before John had snored and yanked me back to the classroom. A beam of light had come from somewhere in the darkness near the target.

That's when Dave dropped the bomb.

"I said that there's no light down that deep." He waited a moment before a sly grin crossed his face, "Remember I said that I would accompany you to the target and do something to help you find it. I went to the target and I was standing near the front of the ship in my apparitional form. What I did to guide you was to shine an apparitional torch into the gloom and wave it back and forth so that all of you would find the way."

I looked over to Saundra and mouthed the words, "No way!" She shook her head with a dazed look on her face.

Our class back then had been in a state of shock. There were soft murmurs of conversation between some of the class members, but it was remarkably quiet in the large room.

"And that was thirteen months ago," I finished my recollection. It was remarkably quiet in our meeting room at Marina Village too as I finished the story. "And to this day, that's been the only time that Dave has ever personally accompanied a class during a session. It probably never would have happened, except for the poor showing on our first try."

As the class chattered excitedly amongst each other, Patty spoke up, "That's not all. There's more to the story!"

I turned to look at Patty, the surprise evident on my face.

"Dave told me that when he was on the forward part of the deck waving the torch back and forth, he was looking for the first sign of the class. He said it was only moments later when the first student dropped into the target area not far from the wreck. Then in a cascade of apparitional forms the rest of the class dropped in one by one and headed for the target. He said it was one of the most exciting moments he's ever had in the classes," Patty finished.

A little less than a year later, I saw *Titanic* on cable at a friend's house for the first time. I recalled how eerily familiar the wreck looked lying there in the mud of the abyssal plain 15,000 ft. below the surface of the North Atlantic. It brought back the memory of that Saturday afternoon, the day I floated just below the railing on the starboard bow in the darkness and watched a light from my teacher pierce the gloom.

I remember that day as the single most impressive display of the power of remote viewing that I would ever witness.

The story must have impressed someone, because Patty had me reiterate it for the entire class during the class meeting, after the break. The funny part was when I told the class that Dave had chewed us out in no uncertain terms. He chuckled, admitting, "I was a bit more tightly wound in those days."

The class cracked up at that admission. That was the fun part.

The not so fun part was the afternoon target session. As hard as I tried, once again I just stayed in the tense, twilight world of Sanctuary, the minutes stretching into hours.

When you launch in ERV, the time flies by. But if something happens and you fail to capture the signal line, as I had, then watching grass grow is fast-paced in comparison.

There was now no longer any doubt in my mind that something was wrong. I was blind.

I had told myself earlier that it didn't matter. After all, I wasn't supposed to be psychic. So I wasn't really losing anything. But the string of failed ERV sessions exposed the lie. I wanted my sight back. I wanted it so bad it hurt. I was terrified that my newfound gift was gone forever. I was good at remote viewing. I wanted to get better. Why? I wasn't sure, but I wanted the chance to find out.

In the small group meeting I listened to the other members relate their experiences. Several had made the breakthrough to a successful session. I had spoken to the group previously, giving them some tips on how to get down far enough to enter ultra deep, the level of theta where ERV takes place. My advantage was the biofeedback training I had undergone. I knew what it felt like to be that far down. Once the other members of my group had an idea of what ultra deep felt like, they were able to use those clues to successfully transition to ERV.

Listening to them describe their success, I felt miserable and more than a little envious. It would have been far less painful had I never experienced the magic carpet ride. But having been there made it ten times worse.

When it was my turn, I had planned only on saying that I was still having some difficulty. As I started to speak, my emotions got the better of me and I had to stop. Working in altered states of consciousness can be an emotional experience, and combined with the trauma and sleep deprivation I was experiencing made me doubly vulnerable. I took a deep breath and tried again.

"I've got a real problem. I've used every trick I know, but I haven't been able to see anything. Why, I'm not sure. All I know is this; I've gone from the magic-carpet ride to blackness. I've gone psychically blind."

Even as I said it, the thought that I had lost my ability to remote view began to sink in, and I felt my eyes fill. I looked at the group, seeing the concern on their faces.

I continued, my voice slightly quivering with emotion, "This is really hard for me. I don't like to open up too much emotionally. I just want to say that you guys have a real opportunity here.

"For those of you who are still having trouble, don't quit. ERV is like nothing you've ever experienced before. It's nothing like CRV. I know; I've had some of the most outrageous trips, the so-called magic-carpet rides that Dave tells you not to expect right away. The Titanic story is just one example. I have others just as amazing. If I can do it, with the psychic ability of a sack of hammers, then there's no reason to believe you can't. But you've got to work at it. Anyone who says that ERV is easy doesn't understand. This is hard work. But I know you can do it. All it takes is the willpower and perseverance to succeed."

One of my classmates, J.R., spoke up as I finished, "When I first heard you speak earlier in the week, I didn't like you. I was having such a hard time with this and I was jealous of the fact that you were able to have such great trips with such apparent ease. But listening to you now, made me appreciate what you've told us. It made you more personable, more real. We all appreciate the effort it took to be so candid."

Patty also thanked me for my candor as the group broke up to take a short breather before the class meeting with Dave. As we did so, the four women in our group came over to me.

There was Tina, short, pert, with a bubbly personality. She was young and pretty, with a generous smile. Then there was Cynthia, as feisty as her hair was red. Buxom and energetic, with a raucous laugh, she was the clown princess of our group. Mimi, attractively tall and blond, had a serenity that would have done justice to a woman twice her age. And finally there was Ariane, tall and elegant with smoky dark eyes and hair a rich chestnut color. Beautiful both inside and out, her voice was a delightfully accented, throaty contralto.

In a wonderfully spontaneous show of support, these women, who were virtual strangers, put their arms around me, speaking words of encouragement. I was touched by their concern, and frankly at a loss for words. In the throes of this personal crisis, their attention couldn't have been timelier, or more welcome.

They clung to me, walking back to the meeting with me in tow. It was comical, watching us negotiate the doorway and hall, this mass of women with me in the center. They had me laughing by the time we got to our seats. "Jeez, you guys are stuck to me like barnacles!"

The way they stood by me made a huge impression. It was starting to dawn on me that the importance of remote viewing lay beyond just intelligence gathering. It's a path not just to knowledge, but also to experience the wonder of the interconnectedness of everything in this universe. The so called Butterfly Effect of Chaos Theory, where the fluttering of a butterfly's wings at one location can have an effect on the weather a continent away, is one way to look at it. Another is four women who selflessly took a complete stranger under their wing, because they felt his pain. They didn't have to.[22] But they did.

What would our world be like if everyone learned this? If everyone, regardless of gender, race, religion, or sexual orientation, could feel this interconnectedness, not as an abstraction, but as an everyday experience. It's possible; I know it because I've seen it in every class that Dave teaches. And every remote viewer lives with this connection every day.

It's an awesome experience the first time that you realize these connections between other living creatures. It changes everything about the way you look at life. Can hate and prejudice, greed and indifference and all the other negative human categorical imperatives survive this type of wisdom?

When we broke for dinner, one of my group mates stopped to talk to me as I was walking out. "John, you got a moment?"

I looked at Randy quizzically, "Sure, let's talk while we grab a bite to eat. I'm going with Heather and some of the others into Old Town for dinner." The two of us walked over to the parking lot where Heather and Diane were waiting for a couple of other classmates to show.

As we stood there, Randy turned to me, "John, I just wanted to say that I really appreciated your words. All of us did. That was powerful stuff. You said a lot of things that really made us sit up and take notice. Like J.R. said, your experiences and your honesty made a big difference. You have a great presence as a speaker. Have you given any thought to maybe teaching for Dave?"

I was surprised at Randy's admission. Teaching for Dave? I hadn't really given it any thought. "Well, the fact that I seem to have lost my sight makes me pretty useless right now. To be honest, I haven't really given much thought to what I was going to do with any of this stuff. It was just fun. I really enjoy the classes, meeting new people, and of course seeing Dave."

Randy's expression was noteworthy as he said, "Maybe you should."

We drove off to Old Town San Diego for a fine dinner, laced with conversation and laughter. I thought about what Randy had said. He was an ex-Navy submariner, not the type given to hyperbole. If he thought I would make a good teacher, perhaps I should give it further consideration. Still, I had to deal with my affliction first.

Since it was Thursday night, when we returned from dinner, the class would have an evening target session. After the session and feedback, we would have the class party, tomorrow being the last day of classes. These were fun affairs, kind of like a big slumber party for adults. Dave would show a movie, usually with a sci-fi theme. There was pizza and soda and chips to eat, or if we were lucky and Dave's best friend Mark showed up, he would bring his homemade chili. There was also lots of socializing. It was here that the friendships started at the beginning of the week solidified, with promises to meet and keep in touch, and to exchange practice targets.

Tedd and Dave's best friend Mark.

With the class sitting in a big circle, Dave began. "Your target tonight is one that I haven't used before. It has its roots in experiments that the Unit conducted back in the eighties. The target, which I'll get to in a moment, is one that was found using a technique called an open search outward.

"An open search outward is like a shotgun blast into the Matrix. The viewers are given coordinates but there is no specific target associated with them. The viewers simply go wherever the signal line takes them. If one of the viewers comes back with something interesting, then the coordinates are assigned to that target and multiple viewers are then sent against it. Viewers are sent to the target from time to time to add to the data. It's a useful and interesting technique. We used it as a way to see if there was anything interesting happening out there in the Matrix."

I had heard of the technique. While researching remote viewing before I took my first CRV class, I had read about an operational example. A member of the Star Gate Unit once ran remote viewer Capt. Paul H. Smith on an open search. The monitor was looking for something UFO related but Paul described an explosion aboard a ship.

Paul Smith

He described the explosion, death and injuries. The monitor wrote it up and sent it up the chain of command, but there was no response. Forty-eight hours later the reports came flooding in. In the Gulf of Sidra during the Iran-Iraq war, the frigate USS Stark had been hit by an Exocet missile fired from an Iranian fighter. Paul's description had nailed it.[23]

"Right now your tasking sheets and focus questions are being handed out. Let's take ten minutes to get ready to launch. Any questions?" Dave concluded. He answered several questions and then the class began getting their stations set up and familiarizing themselves with the tasking sheets.

I set about putting my sleeping bag on my inflatable and looking over the focus questions. This was the first time that Dave had done an open search outward in a class. My feelings were painfully ambivalent. I really wanted to have a successful session, but I was filled with apprehension at the thought of a repetition of the previous attempts. The thought of another failure during this first chance at an open search target was agonizing.

While I was straightening out my sleeping bag, I felt the touch of a hand on my shoulder. Turning around, I looked up into the dark, calm eyes of Ariane. She said nothing, only squeezing my shoulder and then she was gone.

She walked over to her sleeping bag that was next to Mimi's. As she crawled in, Mimi turned her head towards me, smiled and waved. I waved back, the facade of confidence as fragile as the first ice on a winter lake. But it felt good to know that the Barnacles were watching over me.

Sliding my eyeshield down with my earplugs in place, I let the cool-down tape take me to Sanctuary. I followed the voiced instructions explicitly. I felt my body slip deeper and deeper. My limbs had that familiar numbed heaviness, as if no longer connected to my body. Try as I might however, the space around me remained dark.

Even the mist of the Matrix, normally a swirl of violet, gray, and magenta, was barely noticeable.

I tried every trick I knew. I gave myself a break, lying there, passive, hoping something would happen. But not even CRV mode imagery floated into view. It was the same maddeningly empty blackness.

God, this was a nightmare where I got sent back to my first failed attempt at CRV the previous year. All I could do was ask myself, what the hell is going on? Why can't I see?

All too soon, the haunting violin strains of 'Nocturne', from "The Secret Garden" began to seep into my awareness. It was the warm-up tape and right after it was Jason's voice announcing the return to Sanctuary and the end of the session.

Return? Damn, I never left! I rolled over, taking off my eyeshield and earplugs, and looked around. The rest of the class was stirring; some of the students were already starting their session summaries.

Jason came back on the air saying that the party would start after group feedback.

It was just too much. The constant failures, the frustration, anger, and fear that I might not be able to do remote viewing again finally took its toll. I had really wanted to do this target, my first

Students recording their session summaries. The low light is typical in the classes during RV sessions.

open search outward, and the result just crushed me. I felt the hot tears rolling down my face.

I curled up in a ball in my sleeping bag, hoping that no one had noticed my embarrassment. Someone must have seen me alone in my workstation because a minute or two later Patty knelt next to me and asked quietly, "John, are you all right?"

It was all I could do to just croak out the words, "No, please, just give me some time alone."

She looked at me, concern evident on her face. She acknowledged my request and left me there with a softly murmured word of encouragement. I turned back to my pain, just lying there trying to pull myself back together.

Someone brushed past me, giving my arm a momentary squeeze, and was gone. It was Ariane again, not wanting to disturb me but just letting me know I wasn't alone.

While the others were in their small groups, I lay there racking my brain, wondering why this was happening. I finally pulled myself together into some semblance of order and joined the class party.

Once the food arrived, the party began. A video was put on and music blared from the speakers. Soon the room was filled with voices and laughter and just plain craziness.

Although I had no appetite, I was hungry, so I stood off to the side munching on a piece of pizza. The Barnacles; the women who had stood by me, Tina, Cynthia, Mimi, and Ariane, came over to ask what had happened. Mimi inquired, "John, what happened?"

"There isn't much to say. I failed again. I just can't see any more," I said miserably. The four women circled around me protectively.

Cynthia spoke up, as always cutting directly to the issue. "You need to talk to Dave and let him know

Two of the Barnacles, Mimi and Ariane.

what's going on." The other three women agreed.

I hated to admit it but she was right. I was out of ideas, "Yeah, you're right. Everything I've tried has failed. I don't know what's going on, and I don't know what more I can do at this point. I don't want to bother Dave with this. He's got the whole class to deal with."

Mimi sighed and shook her head, "John, that's what he's here for. You need to talk to him about what's going on. Do you really think he doesn't know what you're going through?"

Well, that was probably true. Patty would have said something to him for sure.

Tina and Ariane put their arms around me as Ariane whispered, "Talk to him."

"Okay, I'll talk to him," I relented. They were right, of course. There was only one person with the knowledge and experience to help me right now. That was Dave.

I walked over to where he was standing, one arm around Patty, watching the party with a detached amusement. As I walked up, he smiled in that open and honest way that I had come to know so well and drawled, "John, glad to see you're back with us."

"Hi John, I hope your feeling better." Patty added, the concern evident in her voice.

I smiled weakly, "Yeah, I'm feeling a little better, thanks." I turned to Dave, "I was wondering if you have a moment, I'd like to talk with you about what's been happening to me. I seem to have lost my vision. I've gotten nothing all week long. I've tried everything I can think of but no matter what I've tried, it hasn't worked. I can't even get CRV level imagery to show up. I was careful to follow the protocols and I made sure that I did all of the breathing exercises to get down far enough to do extended remote viewing. I'm positive I was down far enough, but nothing happened. It was the same maddening darkness. No Vortex. Nothing. I'm really afraid that my skills might be gone forever."

Dave shook his head, "No, you haven't lost your skills, John. At most it's temporary. What you have to do is to find out why. There's a reason why this is happening; why you aren't able to do ERV. The Matrix is sending you a message, and it's up to you to decipher what that message is."

I looked at him, the desperation I felt obvious in my eyes. Dave grinned and taking me lightly by the arm, said, "Trust me. Go have fun. You'll figure out what the Matrix is trying to tell you later. Your vision will return. Join your friends and put this aside for now."

When I hesitated, he repeated lightly, "It will return."

I turned back to my friends and the laughter, and put aside at least for the moment the turmoil I felt. I hoped he was right. I was sure about one thing, though. If the Matrix was trying to get my attention; it had succeeded. It had unerringly chosen the way that would get my attention in no uncertain terms.

This would not be the last time that the Matrix would take a teaching role. In the very near future, this incident paled in comparison to subsequent events. Dave's recommendations turned out to be sage advise. It would finally sink in over the next few months, the message that he had talked about. He was right; the Matrix had a lesson for me. It came none too soon, for the Masters class was fast approaching.

A Sorcerer's Apprentice

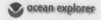 ocean explorer

◀ back

A view of the bow and railing of the *Titanic*.

Related Links

Titanic 2004 Exploration

Download high resolution image (348 Kb, jpeg)

Ocean Explorer Gallery

E-mail Updates | User Survey | Report Error On This Page | Contact Us
Revised July 12, 2004 by the Ocean Explorer Webmaster
National Oceanic and Atmospheric Administration | U.S. Department of Commerce
http://oceanexplorer.noaa.gov/explorations/04titanic/media/titanic_bow_railing.html

SESSION SUMMARY

MY IMPRESSIONS OF THE TARGET WERE
OF THICK SURROUNDING ATMOSPHERE — DARK —
CLOSE — OPPRESSIVE. AIR OF HARD TO BREATHE
AND GREAT PRESSURE. SMALL SPECKS IN
AIR BUT NOT LIKE AIR — THICK. VERY
COLD.

SAW AT FIRST WHAT LOOKED LIKE A
GRID BUT THEN BECAME WALL WITH BARBED
WIRE LIKE FENCE ONLY THICK. UNABLE TO
SEE ANYTHING ELSE EXCEPT SEARCHLIGHT BEAM
THAT SHOWN SUDDENLY. ROOMMATE NEXT TO
ME SNORED, DISRUPTING SESSION

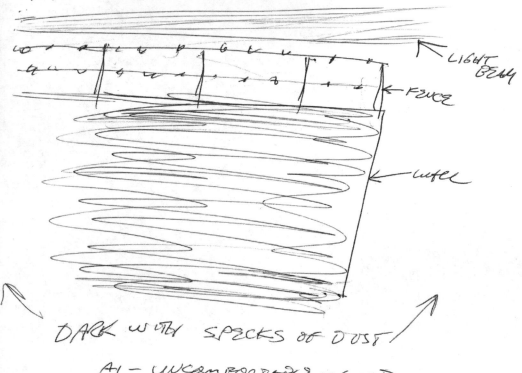

LIGHT
BEAM

FENCE

WALL

DARK WITH SPECKS OF DUST

AIR — UNCOMFORTABLE — COLD

CHAPTER NINE

Master Class

Change your thoughts and you change the world.
—Norman Vincent Peale

I felt like I was coming home when I walked through the familiar doors of the Bayside room at the Marina Village Complex in San Diego. I greeted Dave with a hug and a slap on the back, no longer hesitant about this show of emotion. It felt good exchanging greetings with Patty, Danielle, Rommel, Jason, and Stan.

Stan had been in the ERV class where I had lost my sight. Like Patty, he was a member of Tony Robbins' group and had a personal trainer practice in San Diego. He was here early, like myself, to help set up the room and equipment for the class. He and I were becoming fast friends.

The Masters. We were all excited about this class. It would be the first civilian Master class ever held by Dave. He had held one specialized class for a group of law enforcement officers previously, but this class would have elements that the previous one did not.

As we were setting up the screens for the PowerPoint projector, Dave smirked as I screwed up the ties that held them up, "Jeez John, you're tying everything up but the screens! Uh, need a little help there?"

I groaned, "Damn it, it's been three months since I last did this." I looked over at him and said in mock frustration, "I forgot how."

When everyone stopped laughing, Dave casually remarked, "By the way, Patty and I got married over Christmas."

He said it so nonchalantly that it took a moment before it registered, "What? Did you say you got married?"

I turned to Patty and asked incredulously, "Did he actually ask you to marry him?" Patty smiled and replied, "Yes, he did." I grinned and said slyly, "And you did?"

Patty blushed as the rest of us laughed. Dave, placing his arms around her with a kiss, said, "Yep, made her an honest Canadian."

While we were assembling the speaker stands, I remarked to Dave, "Boy, what a difference from that first class at UCLA. From boom box to computerized productions in two and a half years. Doesn't seem even that long."

"I know what you mean. Remember those losers I had working for me? Those were some tough times. I'm really glad that you and some of the others have stuck by me through it all. Patty and I would love to see you more often in our classes." Dave looked thoughtful for a moment then turned to me and said, "John, you should come along with us to Omega. It would be a blast and we could use your help as a group leader and assistant instructor. The Omega classes are usually big ones and we're always short of help. You'd like it out there in the country. Lots of interesting people to meet, good, healthy vegetarian food, and all you have to do is show up."

I knew that Dave was referring to the Omega Institute in New York. It is a holistic facility for mind-body training. They hold numerous classes and seminars there throughout the year.

Privately, I knew only one reason that I might not be able to go. I had not regained the full use of my ERV sight. I had tried several practice targets since then with mediocre results, certainly nothing like the results I had in the past. I trusted that the lessons I had learned in the previous three months would be enough to bring back my abilities.

In any case, it did sound like fun and I'd be working with Dave and Patty and the others. I had the time, so why not? "OK, you talked me into it. When's the next class?"

"If you have the time, we've got an ERV class here in the Marina complex in April and a CRV class at Omega in June. Then the following ERV Omega class is in September."

"Let's do it," I said after a moment's reflection. Right then I realized I did want to be a part of all this. I was surprised at how intense the feeling was, and how right it felt.

After we finished, the staff had coffee together. I looked at Dave drinking his usual five shot venti soy latte.

He saw me looking at him as he took a full sip of the potent brew. I shook my head with a smile, "How do you drink not just one of those a day but five or six and still be able to sleep at night?"

Patty smiled and echoed, "I don't know how he does it either."

Dave smacked his lips with relish, and replied, "Ah, coffee, the elixir of remote viewers. Ever since the Rangers, coffee doesn't affect me that much. We drank so much of the stuff that it takes these five shot lattes to get any lift."

Dave and Patty Morehouse

"Lift! Jeez Dave, if I drank one of those I could walk on the ceiling."Sharing the laughter with Dave and Patty and the others made me feel like I was a part of their family, not just a friend. I treasured that feeling.

More of the students arrived, talking and laughing, eager to greet Dave and the others. The thought that after the Master class I would be on the other side as a group leader and assistant instructor seemed like a dream. Me, the poster boy for the psychically challenged. It was just a short time ago that I was at my first CRV course, wondering if remote viewing was even possible for me. The thought that I was actually, well, used to be, good at this and would now be helping to teach other people was ironic. Of course, I still had to await the results of the first target session to see if my sight was back.

Wouldn't that be a kick in the head if my sight didn't return after all this, I reflected? Nothing to do but wait. I'd find out soon enough.

The arrival of many of the students for that pivotal Master class was good news. Three of the Barnacles were back, Mimi, Tina, and Ariane, as well as a number of other students that had become friends over the past year. Randy was back and so were Fortune, Heather and Diane.

There were over forty people signed up and it promised to be a memorable experience.

Once Patty had completed the administrative details, Dave took over the lecture.

"As Master level remote viewers, we now need to focus less on the mechanics of remote viewing, although you will be taught some advanced techniques. We need to go beyond that to what we as remote viewers can offer our planet. Your task now is to define reality for yourself, and to determine not only your own personal mythology, but also what our collective mythology will be."

Then, activating the PowerPoint program on the large screen, Dave called up his first presentation. "You remember the Five Assumptions from our discussion in ERV class. First, the physical world that is our everyday environment – this terrestrial plane – is not the only one. There are other worlds out there. Second, these other worlds interpenetrate not only our world, but also all of the others. In doing so they establish levels of hierarchy. Third, these various worlds and realms as well as dimensions have a constant dialogue or communication. Fourth, if the previous assumptions are true, then we are not alone in this existence.

"Finally, this existence that we inhabit as well as all other existences has a purpose and a meaning. There is a reason why."

Dave turned back to the class; "You as extended remote viewers have experienced the truth that we are omnipotent, omniscient, omnipresent beings that are co-Creators of this existence. Not through belief, but through direct experience.

"This aspect of ourselves has been called by many names." He displayed a diagram showing the various names: the collective unconscious, the Matrix, the holographic Universe, the Akashic Records.

"There is no shortage of beliefs or interpretations, nor is there a shortage of those who accept such beliefs as absolutes. The problem is that beliefs are one-way thieves of freedom, a desire born of anxiety to affect reality that only further distorts it. Embracing beliefs is easy – seeking truth is not. Beliefs service the eagerness of truth while knowledge nourishes the reverence of it."

Dave walked over to his director's chair and sat down, continuing the lecture. "Look at the havoc that differing systems of belief have wrought on our global community. Look at the turmoil in the Middle East; all because of different beliefs based on an interpretation of the truth, rather than the truth itself. Beliefs masking truth serve only to retard the scientific and spiritual development of our species. "Unconsciousness of consciousness has become a vehicle of retrogression, limiting us as a global society. What we can do as remote viewers to change the human condition is your task for this Master class. "First, I want you to identify a usable statement of the Human Condition. "Second, I want you to identify the top ten positive and negative human categorical imperatives. "Once this is completed it will be your task, both collectively as well as individually, to find ways to manifest those positive ideals as well as to suppress the negative ones in your daily lives," Dave finished.

That's a handful, I thought. It was going to be a busy day. There were other exercises to set up as well. Some were destined for completion days later. It was both exciting and thought provoking.

All the while there was the specter in the shadows. My previous failures haunted me. If I had learned nothing else over the last three months, it was to trust my feelings and listen to what Dave had told me. He had been right so far. The next day started early with morning meditation and Jason leading a yoga session. I threw myself into the exercises, determined to get the most out of it. I wanted to be ready for the calibration target to come. I was going to follow Dave's suggestions and protocols to the letter. I would leave nothing to chance.

Once the exercises were complete, we were given a break before returning for the lecture. I walked outside to get a breath of fresh air with Stan.

"So how do you think you'll do? Has your sight returned?" Stan asked.

He wasn't the first to ask; there were several members of the previous ERV class here that had asked as well. "To be honest, not really. I've tried several times since December with only mediocre results."

Knowing Stan's experience as a trainer, his reply was not unexpected, "Well, that's better than December." It was typical of him to point out the positive in any situation. I would find his patience and optimism sorely needed in the future.

"Yeah, but not by much. But I'm optimistic and I've been giving a lot of thought to what Dave has told me." As I spoke, Randy walked up and joined us.

I continued, "Hi Randy. I was just telling Stan I've decided to take Dave up on his offer to be a group leader for his next class at Omega. As a matter of fact, I've come to a number of decisions regarding my future and remote viewing. I've had a lot of things to think about since I lost my sight. I've discovered that remote viewing means much more to me than I had previously thought. So I'll be joining Dave more often in the classes."

I decided to confide in them another decision that I had made recently, "I've also decided that I'm going to write a book on my experiences in Dave's classes, as part of my personal mythology." Personal mythologies were, as Dave explained it, the conscious decision to effect change in one's life and to choose a future path.

Randy exclaimed, "Well, it's about time. I know Dave is glad to hear it. I told you that you should consider being an instructor. Dave has said it and most of the December ERV class said it as well. You're a natural."

I chuckled as I said, "Um, I'll give it a shot. I'll just have to shoot from the hip on this and hope I don't shoot myself in the foot!"

Both Stan and Randy laughed. Randy said, "Don't worry. We'll both be there to bail your sorry ass out."

On return to the class, Dave took the podium and started the briefing for our morning target session.

"Alright, everyone. Your first session will be a calibration target. Calibration targets are designed for comparison purposes and as a relative performance measure for remote viewers. They are usually targets with strong stage three or six gestalts, with plenty of measurable, verifiable attributes," Dave explained.

"This way it gives a remote viewer an idea of their relative accuracy rate. Then if a viewer is sent against a target where there is no feedback available, those results can be compared to the calibration results for a relative measure of accuracy. The majority of your targets this week will not have objective verifiable feedback due to their nature. The feedback will come in the form of the results that have been collected over the years on these targets. Your tasking sheets are on your work stations. Check the focus questions and lock those and the coordinates in your mind. Take ten minutes to get ready and we'll start the cool-down.

"Also, we are using a new cool-down CD that has pink noise on it instead of the ERV protocols. All of you are experienced ERV'ers so my narrative on the breathing techniques is no longer necessary. You'll hear the very beginning with the waves and the first portion of the narrative. Then the narrative will be muted as the pink noise is brought up. For those of you who don't know what pink noise is, it is simply a softer form of white noise that we will use to mask ambient sounds." Dave explained.

I looked over at Randy just before I slid the eye shield down. He gave me a quick V for victory sign. The cool-down started, and it was time. As I lay there, I remembered my sword training class when during the rank promotion exam I had to snuff out the flame of a candle with the blade of the sword.

The exam required you to kneel in front of a lit candle, raise the sword above your head, and bring the blade down just above the flame in a single stroke. Touch the candle and you failed. Stop too far above or use too tentative a stroke and the flame remained. You had to concentrate till the Universe shrank down to just the blade and the flame. Down to the Moment … of a single direct stroke when the flame would be snuffed out, the candle just below the blade, untouched.

Now was that moment.

As I drifted down to Sanctuary, I felt the familiar muscular twitches as my body relaxed. These were myoclonic spasms caused as my muscles released excess nervous energy as I drifted down to an altered state.

It was going to happen this time; I could feel it. I smiled as the Vortex began to form.

I was back.

I dropped into the target area in a swirl of the ethereal clouds. I experienced that sensation of falling in the pit of my stomach that signaled the onset of the most unusual effects in extended remote viewing.

Bi location. I could feel it happening, as the fog cleared away to blinding sunlight. Involuntarily, I raised my hand to shield my eyes and realized the futility of that gesture. The light passed right through my apparitional hand.

Feeling stupid, I waited a moment for my eyes to become adjusted to the light and thought it was a good thing no one saw that lapse.

I was standing at the base of a towering structure. I was dwarfed by the size of this block wall. It rose high above me and was composed of what appeared to be stone or concrete. The scale of this wall made me extremely uncomfortable, as if it was a wave composed of concrete poised to collapse and crush me.

Now I knew what an ant felt like next to a skyscraper. I was engrossed by the panorama around me, and didn't realize that I was slipping out of ultra deep. Cat's-paws of the Matrix fog suddenly replaced the scene.

Using the yogic breathing exercises, I felt myself floating away. It took a while to return to ultra deep but finally the scene rematerialized and I was standing in front of an impressive statue. Made of the same stone or concrete as the monolithic wall, it appeared to be a robed figure surrounded by blue sky. What surprised me was my visceral feeling that it was of Egyptian origin.

Then the fog closed in, and I decided to return to Sanctuary. No sense in pushing my luck and I was already more than satisfied with my session. My timing was perfect – the lights came up and the warm-up music began moments later.

I lay there, savoring the moment. Something on my pillow brushed against my ear. I looked down and there on the pillow was a red rose. I looked around the room. On everyone's pillow was a rose; a gift from Dave and Patty for each of the class. Simple and elegant, a Japanese poet or warlord would have approved.

I saw Randy looking over at me, a question framed on his face. I just stared at him for a moment before letting a smile creep across my face. I raised my thumb upwards slowly and watched Randy as his face broke into a wide grin.

After the break, we formed into small groups. Once again, I was fortunate to have Patty as my group leader. She must have been saving me for last because when it was my turn to speak about my session, she said, "For those of you who were not at the December ERV class, John had an event that gave the class a valuable learning experience. If he doesn't mind, I'd like him to share some of that experience with us as well as give us an update on what's happened since."

Everyone turned to look at me, and for a moment I felt like Steve Martin in the movie, *The Lonely Guy*. In a scene where he walks into a restaurant by himself, a spotlight suddenly shines down on him, emphasizing that he is without a date. The spotlight follows him as the maître d' takes him to a table right in the middle of the room and seats him. Everyone is looking at him and obviously talking about what a pitiful character he is.

I laughed when I saw the movie, but now I had a better appreciation for that moment. Now the spot was on me.

"Um, okay. For those who don't know, at the last ERV class I admitted the loss of my ability to remote view. Those of you who know me from previous classes know that I've had some really intense bi-locations, even though I don't think of myself as psychic. I've never had a psychic occurrence, prophetic dream, or seen a ghost. In my first CRV class with Dave, I was the only one in the entire class who failed on the first target. But with diligent practice and with the help of my previous training in advanced EEG biofeedback, I've had some of the most outrageous sessions in ERV with bi-locations that were mind bending in intensity."To be honest, I was having a hard time reconciling this ability with my belief system. I was brought up in the belief that ESP doesn't exist. My world was the world of science and the scientific method. Becoming a remote viewer was in direct conflict with those beliefs, and I just couldn't make the leap to acceptance of this ability. So I trivialized it. I became more concerned with results than with growth. Each session became an exercise in how good I was rather than how far I had matured. And it cost me."

My voice grew husky as I remembered the intensity of my emotions, "You have no idea of what it's like to start with nothing and then be handed the magic carpet ride, as Dave calls it, only to lose it because you were too immature to appreciate it."

As I said this, the emotions of that tumultuous time rose up inside me and I had to stop. Randy, who was sitting next to me, put his hand on my shoulder and gave me a reassuring squeeze.

I continued, "Take it from one who knows. Give this ability the respect it deserves. You emphatically do not want to go through what I did."

Then with a smile I announced, "And on a lighter note, I got my sight back on this target."

There was a smattering of applause and congratulations from my classmates. Randy shook my hand and said, "I knew you'd get it back."

"I don't know how well I did. For all I know I missed by the proverbial mile." I showed them my drawings of the target.

Patty spoke up, saying, "Let's go find out how you all did."

Our small group trooped out from the meeting room to the main floor where the rest of the class was assembling for the group discussion and target feedback. We arranged our chairs in a large circle.

Dave addressed the class, "Before we start, I'd like to take a moment and have John speak to the class about his experience from the last ERV class. He had a rather unique lesson which I think everyone could benefit from." My eyes grew wide as Jason came bounding over and handed me the microphone.

The request caught me off guard. It was one thing to talk about what happened to me to the people in my small group. I knew most of them from that last ERV class. Now I had over forty pairs of eyes all riveted on me. That damn spotlight seemed even brighter now.

I could feel the flush of embarrassment on my face as I struggled to collect my thoughts.

It may not have been my most shining moment, but I managed to repeat what I had said to my small group just moments before. When I finished, Dave thanked me and to my surprise, the class, in a spontaneous show of appreciation, also said thanks.

Then it was on to the feedback for the target. As Dave flashed the video feedback, I caught my breath as I recognized the target.

2083 – 8403.
TARGET: Hoover Dam in Southwest Nevada on Lake Mead.

Now the giant wall of stone or concrete made sense, and as I watched, the video showed two large statues with Egyptian headdresses at the base of the dam.

Not exactly like I had seen but close. Funny, I never saw the water on the other side and had thought that it might have been an ancient Inca or Egyptian ruin that I was looking at. That impression was probably because of the two large blockhouse structures at the base of the dam that held the turbines for power generation.

All in all, it had not been a bad session. I was relieved that my vision was back. It was as if my sight had never left. Perhaps it wasn't so much of a question of the Matrix allowing my sight back, but rather a realization on my part of the new reality that I was accepting.

During the week, Dave went on to teach us map dowsing and the use of the pendulum. I didn't have much luck with the pendulum. The rest of the class had mixed results, although one of the women answered ten multiple-choice questions correctly using only the pendulum to get the answers. It was an amazing feat.

The map dowsing exercise had us running our hand or a ruler held in our hand over a large blank piece of paper that had a reference mark on two of the edges. As we ran our hand or ruler over the sheet, we were to try and feel or see some intangible difference at a localized point on the page. When we did, we were supposed to make a mark there.

Taped to the wall was the master sheet where all of our marks were going to be plotted, by arranging our paper's reference marks on those of the master sheet. The master sheet was the same size as an actual geographic map of an event that we were trying to dowse.

I didn't like the ruler method, so I ran my hand just above my sheet of paper with my eyes closed. Since I was very visually oriented, I reasoned that when my hand moved over the location of the event, I might see or feel something.

I used the same breathing techniques used for a CRV session, to cool down for dowsing. After about ten minutes of waving my hand back and forth over the paper, I was surprised that I seemed to feel a spot on the paper that stood out.

It was more than just that the spot seemed to feel different in that one area. It just, well, felt right. I don't know why or how, but it did.

Making a mark on the paper, I opened my eyes to see how the rest of the class was doing. Actually, it was more like I wanted some confirmation that I was in the ballpark with my feeling.

That didn't mean I believed it, though. Here we go again, I thought, another assault on my fragile belief system. I took Dave at his word that these techniques worked, but given that the pendulum, at least for me, was a failure, I didn't have much confidence that my dowsing would yield any better results.

Looking around confirmed my skepticism. Everyone's marks were in different locations on the paper. I might not be a dowser or

Students in their ERV stations.

a whiz at the pendulum, but at least I can remote view. For that, I was a happy camper just the same.

Handing my dowsing sheet to Patty, I caught up with Mimi as she walked out the door. We were on lunch break.

"How do you think you did?" I asked, curious to see where she had placed her mark.

"I don't know; I never really felt or saw anything using either my hand or the ruler, so I just went with my gut feeling," Mimi replied cautiously.

"The ruler didn't work for me either, so I used my hand. It seemed like I felt a hot spot as my hand went over the paper, but I don't know. I was going more for my gut feeling too," I agreed. "Where did you put your mark?"

"I put mine in the middle, slightly high and to the right. How about you?"

"Umm, mine was near the center but down and to the right." Not where mine was, which confirmed what I had seen from several of the other students

Mimi shook her head and said, "I saw Barry, Dee, and J.R. and they all had different spots too. I don't know, I didn't get the same positive feeling I do when I remote view."

I agreed with her.

We met Stan, Randy, Ann Marie, Ramon and several other students and drove to a close by Souplantation for lunch. As we sat down to eat I asked everyone where they had placed their marks on the paper. Randy's was close to mine but everyone else's were in different places, not even close.

Randy, ever the comedian commented, "Well, we suck. So what. We sucked at the pendulum too. I suck. You suck. He, she, and it sucks. We all suck!"

Laughing with the rest I thought, yep, we sucked.

We were in for a shock. Dave strode up to the front of the room when class resumed. He was beaming and I could see that he was obviously pleased with the results.

I was seated next to Mimi and I leaned over and whispered, "Maybe we didn't suck after all." She nodded.

"Well, I'll have to say that the class did outstanding on this target, much better than the pendulum exercise. With a couple of exceptions, everyone nailed it. Let's bring out the reference sheet and you'll see how we plotted your results."

Jason and Patty brought out the reference sheet and taped it to one of the presentation screens. On it were numerous X's where each student had found something that they felt might have significance.

The class immediately buzzed with excitement. A clear pattern was evident. The X's started out in the upper left quadrant and went straight across the page, then suddenly curved down, around and started back diagonally up towards the right center edge of the sheet. The X's clustered around a small hand-sized part in the lower right quadrant of the sheet.

There were a couple of X's scattered around the sheet in apparent random fashion, but the majority were located along the clearly visible track.

Mimi and I exchanged incredulous looks, as did most of the class. How could we, working independently with only the encrypted coordinates as our guide, come up with such a coherent pattern? I just shook my head in disbelief.

"As you can see, the class locked on to something," Dave pointed out. He motioned to Jason and Patty, and they brought out a large geographic map of a portion of the northeast United States.

A track was plotted on it that duplicated the same path that the X's did on the white sheet of paper. Dave took his laser pointer and outlining the identical paths said, "OK, you can see the obvious resemblance of these two paths. They are virtually identical. When we plotted your results and placed them one on top of the other, they matched almost exactly." The geographic map shows the flight path of TWA flight 800 from the time it lifted off from La Guardia airport to the moment when it crashed into the Atlantic Ocean."

Everyone leaned forward to get a better look. It was impossible, but we had done it. My mark was located right in the debris field of the crash site. Mimi's had been on the flight path out from La Guardia.

Later, as we were leaving for the evening, I got a chance to speak with Patty. "Patty, that map dowsing session was just incredible! I wouldn't have believed it if I hadn't been there."

"I know. When the staff plotted the results and laid the maps on top of each other, it just about knocked us over. Dave said it was one of the best map dowsing sessions he'd ever seen," Patty replied. She had been just as impressed as I had been.

"This has been such an outstanding class so far. Everyone has learned a lot and had a great time to boot," I said enthusiastically.

Patty smiled, "Oh, we have more surprises in store."

I thought, what could they come up with that could beat this? I should have known better.

2083
8403

FOCUS QUESTIONS—EXTENDED REMOTE VIEWING

(SAN DIEGO) SESSION – 1

A. **GENERAL INFORMATION & INSTRUCTIONS:**

1. THIS TARGET IS TO BE VIEWED IN PAST AND PRESENT TIME (SIMULTANEOUSLY). **ASSUME NOTHING!** YOU HAVE NOT USED THIS TARGET BEFORE, HOWEVER, IT COULD VERY WELL BE LINKED TO ONE THAT YOU HAVE—OR PERHAPS NOT.

2. WORK THE SESSION MECHANICS AS YOU HAVE BEEN TAUGHT—AND THEN FLY! SEEK OUT ALL THAT YOU CAN FIND HERE. TEST EVERYTHING WITHIN YOUR VIEW OR GRASP. MOVE AS A CHILD WOULD MOVE IN A STRANGE NEW WORLD.

3. DURING FEEDBACK YOU WILL BE ASKED TO ADDRESS AT LEAST ONE DESCRIPTIVE AND THREE PHILOSOPHICAL QUESTIONS PERTAINING TO THIS SESSION.

4. YOU ARE RECEIVING THESE QUESTIONS NOW SO THAT YOU MAY CARRY THEM WITH YOU INTO THE MATRIX. IMMEDIATELY PRIOR TO YOUR DEVELOPMENT OF YOUR SUMMARY—REVIEW THEM CAREFULLY AND CONSTRUCT YOUR SUMMARY ACCORDINGLY.

5. DO NOT ALLOW YOUR CONSCIOUS MIND TO OVERLAY YOUR SESSION – LET GO OF THE OUTCOME, BE GRATEFUL FOR THE JOURNEY AND THE OPPORTUNITY OF IT. THAT IS ALL YOU CAN DO, OR YOU WILL IMMEDIATELY IMPAIR THE SESSION—TRUST THE MATRIX.

6. REMEMBER WHAT YOU HAVE LEARNED AND USE WHAT YOU ALREADY KNOW HOW TO DO—LET GO OF JUDGMENT—AND FLY.

B. **FOCUS QUESTIONS:**

1. WHAT DOES THIS TARGET SITE LOOK AND FEEL LIKE? (NOT TOO MANY DETAILS – DESCRIBE IT IN GENERAL TERMS). REMEMBER YOUR OBJECTIVE IS TO SEE BEYOND SURFACES.

2. WHAT IS HAPPENING HERE? AGAIN, LOOK BEYOND SURFACES AND WELL INTO THE MIND OF THE SITE OR WHATEVER MIGHT BE THERE—WHAT IS THE MEANING OF THIS PLACE—WHAT HAS, OR IS HAPPENING HERE?

3. THIS TARGET HAS A HISTORY—DOES IT HAVE A FUTURE?

4. WHAT DWELLS HERE? IF THERE IS POWER—DEFINE IT. DO YOU SENSE PRESSURE, LIGHT OR DARK, BALANCE… SOMETHING ELSE?

BLACK HOODED FIGURE SURROUNDED BY BLUE LIGHT

LARGE MONOLITHIC SLAB SIDED STRUCTURES WITH ELABORATE CARVINGS ON THE SURFACE.

MY IMPRESSIONS OF THE TARGET
TALL, HIGH, SLAB SIDED STREET?
REMINDED ME OF EGYPTIAN PYRAM
'R INCA RUINS. HEAVY AND MASS
'TH CARVINGS ON FLAT SURFACE

SECOND IMPRESSION OF TAR
WAS OF A TALL BLACK MO
FIGURE SILOUETTED BY BLU
LIGHT. HAD EGYPTIAN FEEL
IT.

Dave Morehouse leading a class in lecture.

Patty Morehouse leading a small group discussion.

CHAPTER TEN

Eater

We all live under the same sky... but we don't all have the same horizon.
—Konrad Adenauer

The following day there were more exercises. The class moved to a large empty meeting hall. There, taped to all four walls at chest height, were three-by-five cards that we had colored and designed days earlier. Each of us had created four of them. Randomly taped to the walls, colored side down, they totaled over two hundred cards.

This next exercise would have each of us trying to find the cards we had made, blindfolded. We would start with our back to the walls, and then move cautiously out to the center of the room. There, we would try and sense where our cards were, move to them, remove our blindfolds and check if it was our card. If not, the rules of the game said blindfold down and back out to the center of the room to try again. Dave and the staff were arranged around the room to help fend off potential collisions.

I didn't find any of my cards, but a number of the class did, some finding two or three. Through it all was Dave's calm voice offering encouragement and jokes to lighten the atmosphere. It was fascinating later to watch the video of the class during this exercise. At first, the class was exciting and fun. Then, after several people had found cards, the dynamic changed to one of competition, and the atmosphere became more tense.

After an hour, Dave called a break, and the class sat in the center of the room to rest and drink water.

As we relaxed, Dave caught our attention.

"The staff and I have made some interesting observations while you guys were poking around out there. We noticed in the beginning of the exercise that the class dynamic was light-hearted and excited. But as several of you found cards, that seemed to change. We noticed that the class seemed more self oriented and much more aggressively intent on finding their own cards."

He stopped for a moment, letting the import of his words sink in. It was true, too; I could feel the change in the room after about 40 minutes. I was just as guilty, remembering how I clapped when someone found their card, and thought, Okay great, now when do I find mine?

It was a sobering thought, and I wasn't the only one with a guilty look on his face.

"The real goal here isn't just to find your cards, although that's important. What's even more important is to find connections with the others in this class. You guys are out there in the middle of the room, sightless, vulnerable. The staff could see how awkward you were when one of you stumbled into another, afraid to open up and reach out for the other. That's when the real magic is supposed to happen.

"Think about it for a moment. See how difficult you are finding that connection in this protected environment. Is it any wonder that our world community is in turmoil, in an environment that has no protections?"

Everyone's eyes widened at that revelation.

Dave continued, his words penetrating. "You need to let go of the outcome. It doesn't matter if you find four cards or no cards. What matters is finding a spirit of community here with your fellow classmates. Once you as remote viewers can learn how to do this here, in this safe room, then you can go out in the world to show others.

"I want you to put your blindfolds back on and go once again in darkness into the unknown. This time put aside ego, and instead look for that sense of what this class is all about: all of us here in love and humility together."

We got up, and with a renewed sense of purpose, went back out onto the floor, sightless. The lightheartedness with which we had started the exercise returned. The awkwardness that plagued us earlier was gone, replaced by a new sense of comradeship. There was much more laughter and joking going on, Dave bantering with the students. It was an amazing transformation, with the added bonus of a number of people finding their cards, to tumultuous applause. I never did find any of my cards that morning, but I didn't care. I found something far more valuable in Dave's words, and the sense of togetherness the class shared that morning.

Just when it seemed I had gotten a handle on these adventures that I had experienced in Dave's class, my belief system suffered another assault. The Matrix pulled the rug out from under me again. That afternoon we were scheduled to do an open search outward target. I had missed my first chance at such a target in the December ERV class because of the loss of my remote viewing ability. Now I'd get a second chance. I was really excited, but I had no idea what was to follow. It would be a session that to this day elicits amazement and disbelief.

When we returned from lunch, the class assembled in the room for the pre-launch briefing by Dave. He took a seat in his director's chair and said, "Our next target session will be an open search outward. We have never used this particular target before in one of my classes because this is a special target. It was discovered by the creator of coordinate remote viewing, Ingo Swann.

"I was still in the Army at the time, assigned to coordinate the homecoming parade for the veterans of Operation Desert Storm in New York City. I had a chance to visit Ingo and I met him at his home in the Bowery.

"During the visit, he gave me the set of coordinates that you have in front of you. Ingo said these coordinates belonged to a target out in deep space. However, viewers sent against the target inevitably wound up describing a circle of spacecraft surrounding an object. There were lots of descriptions of the spacecraft and the beings that inhabited them, but no one had yet described the object they were orbiting. It seemed that the lure of all those extraterrestrials and spacecraft was irresistible to the viewers, drawing them away from the mystery as yet undiscovered.

"Your task is to penetrate the circle of spacecraft and find out what they are orbiting, why it's there, and why it's important."

Dave paused a moment to let the excited chatter die down before he continued, "Now, you've been slightly front-loaded because I've given you some information relating to the target. Remember to ignore the obvious. You are all experienced viewers and I'm confident you won't let your imaginations run wild.

"As a matter of fact, front-loading from an operational standpoint is routinely used to focus viewers on what's important and to reduce the time on extraneous portions of the target. So let's get our workstations set up and we'll launch in five minutes."

I was so thankful that my vision was back because this target session sounded like pure adventure. This was the reason I wanted to be a remote viewer, the promise of adventures unlike anything else on this planet.

On the way back from the water cooler, I stopped by and wished Heather and Diane good hunting and clear ether, the remote viewer's salutation. They returned the sentiment, and then it was into my sleeping bag and on with the eye shield and earplugs. Soon the relaxing sounds of the cool-down CD began, and before long I found myself in the quiet twilight world of Sanctuary.

As I waited for the Vortex to form, I went over my pre-launch checklist. I wanted to reaffirm the intent to disregard the spacecraft and observe the mystery at the heart of the target coordinates. Intent here was extremely important. Intent drives remote viewing sessions. My success in ignoring certain aspects of this mission would depend upon an ironclad intention.

The Vortex whirled into existence in front of me and I was off, the wormhole walls flashing past in a blur. Passing through the event horizon of the Membrane, once again I found myself surrounded by wisps of purple, black, and gray fog.

The stomach-turning sensation of falling washed over me, signifying the onset of yet another bi location.

The surreal fog surrounding me slowly faded away and I found myself floating in outer space, the heavens awash in stars. It wasn't like the sky that you see on a dark night, with lots of faint stars visible. This sky was extravagant with stars of different colors. It was like a panoply of jewels on a black satin jeweler's cloth. Glowing gas clouds of nearby nebulae fluoresced with multi-colored splendor. I was transfixed by the beauty before me and gave silent thanks for this wonderful vision. I was so caught up in the beauty that I almost forgot the reason I was here.

As I looked around, I realized I didn't know how far away I was from Earth. I didn't recognize any constellations. I had the feeling that I was nowhere near our solar system.

There was a strong glow from below my position. The heavens revolved around me as I oriented to view what was beneath me. What I saw took my breath away.

It was difficult to assess its true size because there was nothing to gauge it against, but my kinesthetic sense was that the object before me was approximately a kilometer or two in diameter. It was an oblate spheroid in shape, like a beach ball that someone was sitting on. The equatorial region was bulged outward and the poles flattened.

The object appeared to be spinning, with the predominant dimensionals of heavy weight and density. It was also glowing like a star. But unlike a star, its glow varied in the equatorial regions, from a bright pink to a cooler red. Occasionally there was a bright flash from deep inside the object.

Even more astounding, I could see bands of energy sliding across the surface like snakes. The flattened shape and convolutions of these bands of energy writhing across its surface reminded me of a giant brain.

I was thinking that it might be a neutron star but the surface was a plasma, not degenerate matter. Yet it was the size of a neutron star. There had to be something holding it together, hidden by the glowing gases of the plasma, otherwise centrifugal force would pull it apart. Opening my mind to the object, I intended to probe its structure when a sudden impression washed over me, rocking me with its implications.

This was not an it; this was a being! The impression was of intelligence. Alien most assuredly. There was computation, mentation going on. This thing was curious; it wanted to know. It sought knowledge.

I was struck by the incongruity of our two life forms so different in appearance, yet so similar in desire. Here was a totally alien creation, born of deep space under incomprehensible conditions, immensely old, another impression flooding in and yet it was no different from me. It, like me, was searching for its destiny. It was hungry for knowledge; curious about the universe around it.

Another impression formed in my mind that made this life form seem even more understandable. Loneliness. It had never met another of its kind in its journeys and craved other intelligences.

I realized now why the spacecraft were here. They were exchanging information. The spacecraft were beaming signals to this creature and responses were beamed back. This was a spectacular symposium on knowledge – a cosmic coffee klatch.

Suddenly the mists of the Matrix returned and the scene disappeared. In the distance, I could hear the music of the warm-up CD. It was time to return.

I wanted to stay.

I wasn't finished yet. I had so many questions to ask.

But there was only Jason's voice telling us to return to Sanctuary.

I was disappointed the session had ended, but also exhilarated with what I had seen. It was unbelievable.

The thought occurred to me that it was unbelievable. Did I believe what I just saw was real or a figment of my imagination? Or had I had a vivid dream? I was consumed with doubts. Then I remembered that the session had gone just like the practice session of the Hoover Dam. I carefully reviewed it in my mind. The dynamics were identical. It must have been real.

I sat up and raised my eye shield, and took a moment to remove my earplugs. Most of the class was up and writing summaries. I wondered what they had seen. Had they had the same fantastic trip that I had or would my adventure turn out to be nothing more than an entertaining fantasy?

I wrote my session summary and went out for a break. I was dying of curiosity and stood near Heather and Diane and several others to see if anyone mentioned a similar experience.

Everyone that I spoke to seemed reluctant to reveal what they had seen, perhaps for fear of ridicule. I didn't blame them. I felt the same way.

Yet when we broke into small groups and again for the full assembly meeting with Dave, I discovered I wasn't the only one who saw the life form.

Those who saw it offered much the same description that I had, albeit not in the same detail. There was no question that our descriptions were the same. Although I felt better when I realized that I was not alone in seeing this creature, I still wondered if what we saw could truly exist. Regardless of my doubts, I felt humbled by the experience.

On the last day of the course, after Dave and Patty wrapped up the administrative matters, the class gave gifts to the staff in appreciation of the work that they had done on our behalf.

Most of Dave's classes did this. I had started the tradition long ago when I had been in the CRV class at UCLA. At UCLA I had gotten a plaque saying thanks and listing the names of each of the students.

Today we gave Dave, Patty, and Jason engraved glass mugs. And we gave Danielle an engraved key chain with our thanks as well.

They were a bit self-conscious but appreciative, and each said a few words of thanks.

And then it was over. Within an hour, all of the students were gone except myself and several others who stayed to help pack up the equipment.

It was always the saddest time for me, seeing the people that I had spent the last week with leave. Some I would see again, others not. I had developed some strong friendships with several of them, and I looked forward to seeing them again.

The conflicts that had been the cause of my loss of viewing ability, I hoped, had been mostly resolved. But I knew deep in my heart that there was a small core of disbelief or lack of trust that was still hiding inside me. I could only hope that time would resolve these issues.

New adventures waited; the next time I walked through the doors of Dave's classroom it would be as a group leader and assistant instructor.

In the months following the Master class, I continued to wonder if that deep space creature could actually exist. I knew of no biology or physics that could support such a life form. Given that there could be no physical confirmation, I reluctantly put that session into the realm of the experiential, unable to be confirmed.

It was in my favorite bookstore in Torrance, that I made a startling discovery. It gave me pause when I considered the possibility of that creature from the open search outward actually existing.

Physics professor Dr. Gregory Benford of the University of California at Irvine is a well-known hard science fiction writer. His latest offering, *Eater,* had just been published in paperback. In it he describes a creature born of deep space, a creature that consists of magnetic forces surrounding a spinning accretion disk of plasma. Shaped like a flattened beach ball, the Eater is powered by a dense central object; a mini Kerr-type black hole. The Eater's intelligence is impressed into the magnetic fields swirling around the central black hole engine.

It sounded remarkably like the description of the creature that I saw thousands of light years away. Although the Eater of Dr. Benford's novel is a malevolent intelligence, unlike the creature I encountered, the physical description was too close to ignore. The flattened oblate spheroid, the writhing bands of magnetic energy, the intelligence superimposed on those magnetic fields, the dense central object, all were as I and the other members of the class had seen.[24]

I wondered what Dr. Benford would say if he knew that his creation might actually exist?

0301
0027   INGO SWANN'S TARGET

SESSION SUMMARY
SKETCH

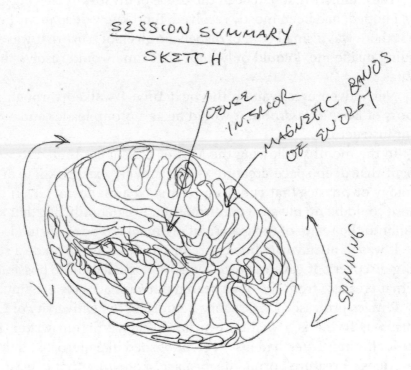

DENSE INTERIOR

MAGNETIC BANDS OF ENERGY

SPINNING

GLOWING HOT PINKISH YELLOW WITH SOME AREAS COOLER REDDISH.

DAVID MOREHOUSE PRODUCTIONS
THE MASTER CLASS

ΩNOTESΩ

MY IMPRESSIONS OF THE TARGET WERE OF A GIANT BRAIN. IT WASN'T MADE OF MATTER AND IT WAS HUGE. THERE WAS NOTHING TO SCALE IT AGAINST AS IT WAS FLOATING IN SPACE, SO THERE ARE NO CONCRETE DIMENSIONS. IT WAS OVOID IN SHAPE AND WAS COMPRISED OF PLASMA. PORTIONS WERE GLOWING A HOT YELLOWISH PINK AND OTHER PARTS WERE A DARKER COOLER RED. THE ENTIRE SURFACE WAS CONVOLUTED LIKE A HUMAN BRAIN, BUT THE CONVOLUTIONS WERE WRITHING ABOUT, TWISTING UNDER INTENSE FORCES. I COULD SEE THE MAGNETIC FORCE LINES AS THEY TWISTED AND TURNED. BUT IT WAS EMPHATICALLY NOT A STAR. THERE WAS COMPUTATION GOING ON, MENTATION, AN INTELLIGENCE, BUT ONE SO ALIEN AS TO BE BEYOND MY EXPLAINATION THERE WAS KNOWLEDGE, OPEN AND FREE, AND THE ONE THING THAT MADE ME FEEL OR KEPT ME FROM BEING TOTALLY OVERWHELMED WAS IT WAS SEARCHING TOO. THIS WAS NOT AN ARTIFICAL INTELLIGENCE OR MACHINE. IT WAS ALIVE, IT EVOLVED FROM ITS ENVIORNMENT OF SPACE.

27

Chapter Eleven

Remote Influencing

Humanity's happiness or unhappiness, as I construe, comes from its greatness; it is because there is an infinite in all of us, which with all our cunning we cannot bury under the finite.

–Thomas Carlyle

From out of the blue, not long after the Master class had finished, I got a phone call from my friend Saundra. I was surprised to hear from her, as I knew she was researching a book and had been very busy lately. We hadn't talked for several months.

"Hey girl, what's up? Haven't heard from you in a while."

"Well, I wanted to give you a call and invite you to our upcoming MUFON meeting next week," she replied.

I hesitated. I didn't want to hurt her feelings. She knew I wasn't a believer in E.T.s visiting Earth.

She must have felt my hesitation because she offered "We're having a special guest at the meeting that I thought you would like to meet. I invited Lyn Buchanan to speak about remote viewing and he accepted. After the talk he's coming over to my friend's house for a party and you're invited."

"Well, thanks for the invite; I'd love to," I quickly replied. I sensed her smile in response to my veiled hesitation. She knew me pretty well. After we exchanged pleasantries, she gave me the time and place and I hung up with a promise to be there.

Lyn Buchanan was one of the remote viewers assigned to Star Gate, the military remote-viewing program at Ft. Meade, Maryland. He was there at the same time as Dave and is mentioned in Dave's book.

I had a ton of questions for him, especially about another program that Dave alluded to in his book. The program was an outgrowth of the remote viewing program – an attempt to take remote viewing from a passive form to a more aggressive technique called remote influencing. According to Dave, Lyn was the one who had codified the protocols for remote influencing. I wondered if he would ever consider teaching the technique.

I met Saundra at the site just as the sun was setting in North Hollywood. She, as always, looked great. It was good to see her again.

"Come on with me. I want you to meet Lyn before the lecture starts because afterwards he'll be mobbed by people who'll want to ask him questions," Saundra whispered hurriedly. She pulled me up to the front of the meeting room.

Lyn Buchanan is over six feet tall, with graying hair and the pleasant, laid back demeanor of a Southern gentleman. It was his eyes, though, that spoke volumes. They were hooded, narrowed, like someone who has seen too many secrets, too many truths.

Saundra introduced us. "Hi Lyn, this is John Herlosky, one of Dave Morehouse's senior students. He's the one who took remote viewing classes with me."

"Hi John, it's nice to meet you. Saundra told me about you," Lyn said amiably.

I smiled, looked over at Saundra and said, "Okay, but I didn't do it no matter what she told you!"

Lyn and Saundra both laughed, Saundra saying, "Oh yes he did!"

Author and Lyn Buchanan

After a quick parry and riposte of "Did not," "Did so," I said, "You know we've actually met briefly once before at last year's IRVA conference." Seeing the look of puzzlement on his face, I raised my hand, "You wouldn't remember; we spoke only briefly before your presentation. I know you're going to be busy tonight and I've got a ton of questions for you. But I'll wait till the party Thursday to ask them."

Saundra opened the meeting with a short speech and introduced Lyn. After the applause had died down, he went on to talk about his experiences in the Ft. Meade military remote-viewing unit code-named Star Gate. He also talked about his experiences with UFO's.

I found that part of the lecture speculative, but I had to admit that, considering his background, it would be wrong to dismiss what he said out of hand. That was the one part of the UFO phenomenon that I did find interesting. There were so many witnesses, not crackpots either: credible people in good standing, who had seen something. I simply hadn't seen enough evidence to convince me that the objects observed were piloted vehicles from another world.

At the end of the lecture people wanting to ask questions mobbed him. Saundra walked over and shook her head, saying, "We won't get a chance to talk to Lyn tonight. There are so many people waiting to talk to him that it'll be late by the time he finishes."

"That's okay." Then, looking around to see if anyone was listening to our conversation, I said in a low voice "I'm also going to ask him if remote influencing really exists, and if he'll ever teach the protocols."

Jill asked, "Do you think he would?"

I shrugged, "I asked him the same thing at the IRVA conference and he said he wouldn't."

Saundra replied, "I thought that's what he might say. I asked him too, when I took his advanced class."

"It would be a shame to lose the technology. I know that Dave, and by the sound of it, Lyn as well, have a prejudice against it because of its possible unethical uses. But I would hate to see it disappear forever." I hoped against hope that Lyn might change his mind. I didn't want to use it against anyone, but I wanted it in my repertoire just in case.

Saundra echoed my thoughts when she sighed, "Well, all we can do is ask."

Thursday night brought a number of interesting people to the party. Since Saundra sponsored it, there were mostly people from the UFO community. The only remote viewers there were Lyn, Jill, Saundra, and a young woman who was a senior student of Lyn's.

It was a fun party with music and lots of good food. There were some fascinating conversations going on about all sorts of speculative topics; UFOs, Bigfoot, sprites, and E.T.s. But I was there to talk to Lyn, so as soon as he was comfortably ensconced on a sofa with a plate of food, I cornered him with Saundra and Jill.

"Lyn, what was it like to work with Dave at the Unit?" I asked.

Lyn took a moment and replied. "Dave was a good guy. He obviously was destined to go places. If he had stayed in the Army, he would have made General easy."

"How was he as a viewer?" This was something I had always wanted to ask someone from the Unit who had been there at the same time as Dave.

Lyn smiled and asked, "Have you ever seen him do a session?"

I told him briefly about our first ERV class target where he had accompanied the students.

"Yeah, that sounds like something he would do," Lyn remarked with another grin. "He was famous for that kind of stuff. He was an one of our best viewers, who had the unique ability to pick up conversations while they were happening, even if they were in another language."

I hoped one day that I could be that good. Jill and Saundra were impressed too.

I then broached the subject on all three of our minds.

"Lyn, Dave's book mentioned a technique called remote influencing. Does it really exist? I've heard people say that it does and I've heard people say that it doesn't."

Lyn's face changed, from lighthearted to dead serious. "Whatever you heard; whatever anyone has told you about remote influencing, the truth is that yes, it exists." Lyn looked as us and continued, "And I should know. I was the one who codified the protocols for it."

I saw Saundra and Jill looking at me expectantly. I figured Lyn would say no, as he had at the previous year's IRVA conference where I had first met him.

He had given a number of reasons. First, it could be just as hazardous for the viewer as it was for the subject.

Can you imagine being intimately connected with the mind of a madman? It is a two-way connection. If you use the protocols incorrectly, you could wind up with a piece of the subject's pathology stuck in your own mind.

Lyn Buchanan and Saundra

How would you feel if you had a sliver of Saddam's madness embedded in your psyche, and not be able to rid yourself of it for months or even years?

That thought had sent a shiver up my spine. Still, I could imagine useful purposes for the technique. It would be a shame to lose the knowledge. I had said as much.

But Lyn had just shaken his head. There were other reasons as well, which had to do with issues of trust and ethics. Until he had a resolution to those issues, he wouldn't teach it.

Thinking I had nothing to lose, I asked the million-dollar question.

"Lyn, will you ever teach remote influencing? When I asked you at the IRVA conference, you said that you wouldn't teach the protocols. I don't suppose you might change your mind?" I took a quick look around; he had a rapt audience. The entire room of twenty-one people was listening intently. His reply shocked all of us.

Lyn sat back in his chair and contemplated my question. "I've thought it over very carefully since then and I've decided to teach a limited class at my CRV conference this year in June."

This was a total reversal. I was curious about the change of heart.

"Lyn, why have you changed your mind? The last time I asked, you were totally against teaching it."

Lyn took a moment to ponder his reply; all he said was, "I have my reasons for doing so. And I won't say why."

Fair enough. I didn't want to look a gift horse in the mouth.

I quickly asked for the dates and venue. Fortunately they didn't conflict with my first teaching assignment for Dave at the Omega Institute. It was scheduled for June, but would be several days after Lyn's conference. It turned out that Saundra would not be able to attend because of a scheduling conflict. But both Jill and I were going to El Paso, Texas to Lyn's CRV conference. We were excited about the prospect of learning remote influencing.

Two weeks before the conference, I got an unexpected e-mail from Patty asking if I would like to help at a remote viewing class Dave was giving down in San Diego from April 29th through May 3rd. I wanted to. It would give me a chance to train as an instructor and group leader for Omega. The CRV conference in El Paso was the following day. It would be tight, but on reflection I realized that

I wanted to be in San Diego. I e-mailed Patty that I would be happy to attend. She told me not to worry about accommodations as I could stay at her home.

Once again I found myself at the Marina location where the Master class had been held. Once again I found myself waiting there, as Dave and Patty were late. I laughed to myself; some things never change. It wasn't long before I saw Dave's minivan pull into the parking lot. Along with him was his best friend Mark. With those two together, I knew I was in for a fun time. Mark is tall with an average build and sparkling blue eyes. He has a facile mind and an incredible sense of humor that compliments Dave's perfectly. I got out of my car, waved, and walked over to greet them.

"Hey Dave! Hi Mark!"

Dave's warm grin and friendly hug made me feel as if I was coming home, "John, happy you could make it. We can sure use you."

"Good to see you too. How have you been Mark?"

"Been busy with my video company. I decided to come out to help Dave keep this class from self-destructing. You know how helpless he is without me," he teased.

Dave shot back, grinning, "Yeah, right. They ran him out of town and he had nowhere left to go. So he shows up here like he's doing us a big favor!"

We started the arduous process of setting up the rooms. Patty and Jason would be coming along shortly, bringing coffee. Rommel and Ann Marie showed up only a few minutes after we started and pitched in. They were two nice people I had met in the Master class. Like me, they had offered to help. Ann Marie would assist Patty, and Rommel would help Jason with the audio-visual equipment. Stan showed up moments later and that completed the staff. It didn't take long before the classroom was set up.

Patty and Jason arrived as we finished up the last touches.

"Hi John, so nice to see you again," she greeted me.

"Hi Patty. It feels great to be back here." It did feel great. I was glad that I had accepted the invitation. I knew right then that my decision at the Master class to enter a new path for the future had been the right one. I wasn't sure what the future held for me; I still wasn't sure of my personal mythology, as Dave would call it. But I knew I was on the right road. And there was the camaraderie, and the amazing adventures I'd had so far. These were beginning and intermediate CRV classes. It would give me the perfect chance to review the mechanics of the protocols and tighten up my understanding of some of the more difficult questions that I might have to field. I'd be ready for the upcoming class at Omega, where I would have my own group.

Through the week-long seminar I watched Patty handle her group. I occasionally added comments to Patty's instructions and helped transfer the data from the students to the transparencies. It was good practice and I enjoyed working with her. At the end of each day we went out to eat or, when pressed for time, had a light meal at the house. In the evening after dinner, if Dave wasn't working on the next day's lecture, he and I sat down with a glass of wine and talked about some area of science or mathematics that was pertinent to the remote viewing lectures. The topics ranged from cosmology to aspects of quantum mechanics. Dave was intensely curious about any aspect of science that would help illustrate his lecture. Often he asked questions that I didn't have a ready answer to, requiring an "I'll get back to you." I had to break out my old *Introduction to Quantum Mechanics* book from my college undergraduate class, to show him the equations and what they implied about the world around us.[25] The more I showed him, the more he wanted to know. I had to go back into the book in the evenings after class to reacquaint myself with the math. That yellow-toned book became my constant companion from that day on. It gave me a measure of pride that some of the information and explanations I supplied to Dave would appear in the lecture the following day.

The day that Dave completed the Stage Three lecture for coordinate remote viewing, he assigned the class a practice target for the afternoon session. I asked him if I could work the target too.

"Sure, John. Actually, it's a good idea to have members of the staff do a target session during the class. It reinforces the idea that we all can do this and that the staff are viewers too." Dave asserted.

"I haven't done a target in coordinate remote viewing since the audit class at Saddleback," I offered. That was a year ago last spring.

"Well, this'll give you a chance to revisit the protocols. Take special note of any questions that come up during the small groups that you don't understand. That way I can fill you in and you'll be ready should a student ask the same question in the future. And you know they will," Dave said with a knowing smile.

I wouldn't realize it until months later, but the target that Dave chose would generate the most mind-shattering event that I had ever experienced in one of his classes.

When the students returned from lunch and had settled down in their seats, Dave addressed them. "Okay, class. The staff is handing out paper for this afternoon's target, so let's clear away everything off of your desks except your exemplars. You've just come back from a meal and you should be a little drowsy. That's good. It'll help you get into alpha rhythm that much faster. This is a Stage Three target. It is to be viewed in present time. Work on it through Stage Three. Try to keep working until you are told to stop." Then he turned and motioned to Rommel on the audio equipment and the cool-down started.

I was in alpha rhythm within a minute, but since I had to wait for the rest of the class I listened to the twenty-minute long narrative that would bring them into alpha too. By the time the CD ended, the lights were dimmed.

Jason strode back to the front of the room. He was to be the proctor for the session and would be reading off the coordinates.

"Okay, class, let's write the heading at the top of the page and declare any AVs or PIs. When you are finished, place your pens in the ready position to receive the coordinates," Jason announced.

AVs and PIs are remote viewing lexicon for Advanced Visuals and Personal Inclemencies. Sometimes as the viewers cool down they get visual data that is in advance of the coordinates. While in many cases it is correct data, the protocols require the viewer to declare and thus rid himself of the images, thereby clearing their mental stage for the coordinates. This way the advance images don't contaminate the session. Personal Inclemencies are anything of a physical or emotional quality that might hinder the viewer in any way. This includes being hungry or tired.

The class placed their pens on the paper and waited expectantly. I was solidly in alpha and my pen waited for Jason to announce the coordinates.

"Your coordinates are...two-seven-zero-seven. One-four-one-one," Jason intoned. At the sound of the last digit, you could hear the sound of pens shooting across the paper in response to the first kinesthetic contact with the target.

My ideogram felt like it was rising gently, but as if there were bumps or pebbles underneath. I decoded it as a land formation. I was quietly surprised. My previous ideograms had all had the same feeling to them – smooth. I had never felt texture before. Maybe I was finally maturing as a remote viewer.

Finished with Stage 1, I moved on to Stage 2 sensory impressions. Behind my closed eyes, images materialized and then just as quickly dissipated out of the ethereal fog of the Matrix. I wrote down the description of what I saw after several impressions, and got into the typical rhythm of a coordinate remote viewer. Detect and decode. View and write.

At first I seemed to be describing a landscape, but it wasn't long before I saw the distinctive ripple effect that my unconscious mind associated with water. There had to be water at the target. But the sensory impressions that implied a landscape began to change to those I usually assigned to a structure. I knew it was time to move to Stage 3 because the word descriptors that came to mind now died out and were replaced by images. I quickly sketched them on the middle of the page. I had the distinct impression the target was a ship. Not just a boat, something large and massive. My first thought was that it might have been the Titanic again or maybe the Queen Mary. But as the warm-up music intruded and Jason announced the end of the session, I had a sudden impulse that this was not a passenger ship.

It was a warship.

As the lights came up I started my session summary. When I finished I got up from my chair, stretched, and headed for the restroom. On the way I stopped by the staff table to talk with Jason.

"Hey, what was the target?" I asked him.

Grinning, Jason jibed back, "You're a viewer now. You gotta wait with the rest of the peons."

Leaning forward I whispered, "Okay, okay. But I think it was the Bismarck or maybe the Titanic."

Jason's jaw dropped. He quickly looked around to see if there was anyone nearby. Satisfied there were no other students near the table, he turned back to me and said quietly, "You're very close. Wait till you see the feedback and you'll see what I mean."

"OK, I won't twist your arm," I said, with a twinkle in my eyes. I was pleased that my session had hit the target. I went outside to join several students in conversation during the break.

After the small group sessions, the class gathered for Dave to go over the data we had generated. I had noted with excitement that my group members had done well and had duplicated much of my data. There was no question in my mind now. I would have been very surprised if the target wasn't a warship. The data screamed something massive so I thought my guess of the Bismarck might not be too far off. Patty, who already knew the choice of the target, was beaming. That was always a good sign, I thought.

"Well class, I'd have to say that you did an excellent job on this particular target," Dave announced, grinning boyishly. He pointed out that the data stream had convergence and congruence, two important considerations when conducting remote viewing sessions with a large number of viewers. Convergence meant that the data was focusing on a theme or object. Congruence meant that a large number of the class was seeing the same target, generating data that backed each other up.

With the suspense peaking, Dave turned to Jason and remarked, "Let's show them how well they did, Jason." When the video of the feedback flashed up on the screen, the class gasped. I had to smile. Jason had been right about my assertion.

2701
1411
TARGET: FAST BATTLESHIP USS NORTH CAROLINA WAR MEMORIAL.

I watched the video, which had been shot by Jason in Wilmington, North Carolina. The huge, squat bulk sat in the harbor, bristling with guns and turrets. She was one of the first of the new battleships that replaced the shattered hulks on Battleship Row in Pearl Harbor. The warship had been in the thick of the fighting in the fierce Pacific Theater battles. As a long time World War II history buff, I already knew quite a bit about her. I would find in the near future that I didn't know as much as I had thought.

The end of the week came as it had so often before, with feelings of sadness. I found now that I missed Dave and Patty when I was gone too long from them and the classes. Dave had remarked that he wished I could attend more often. I would see to it that I did.

The following day Jill and I flew into El Paso. I was a zombie at that point. I had been averaging five hours of sleep during the last week. After making some small talk with Jill, I realized that I couldn't keep my eyes open. While Jill turned to her book, I closed my eyes and promptly fell asleep. The flight passed quickly and after landing, we took a taxi to the hotel where the conference was to be held.

When we arrived at the hotel, Jill pulled out our itinerary and said, "Let's find our rooms and drop off our stuff. I want to clean up a little. Why don't we meet at the course registration room to check in? We'll meet there in, let's say, thirty minutes?"

"Yeah, that should be just fine," I agreed.

Thirty minutes later we met back at the registration room for the conference. Lyn was at the table.

"Hi Lyn. We made it," Jill greeted him.

"Hi Jill. Hi John. Glad you did," he amiably replied. There were about 30 people attending, and a dozen presenters, including Skip Atwater and Mel Riley.

The presentations were uniformly excellent and I learned a lot of new techniques and gained a greater understanding of the military training methods. Skip Atwater's presentation on those methods was particularly well received by those of us interested in the military program.

Lyn's course in remote influencing was the main reason most of us were here. It was a very technical presentation on how to influence the mind of a targeted person using CRV. It basically combined the Stage 4 matrix with elements of hypnosis and neuro-linguistic programming. At the end of the lecture, Lyn repeated the warnings he had laid out at the beginning of the class.

"This is a powerful technology that is not to be trifled with. I know all of you at this course will treat it with the respect that it commands. Otherwise I would have refused you entrance to the class. If you must use it, then use it in wisdom and compassion." He looked across the room full of rapt students and reminded us, "If you use this technology, remember to detox at the end of the session. I cannot emphasize this too strongly. Failure to do so can have the most disastrous of consequences."

As I walked to the next lecture, I wondered if I would ever have the need to use RI.

I was surprised by the presenter. He was one of Dave's former CRV students. David Edmonds had graduated from Dave's class and discovered his personal mythology. He became Corporate Intelligence Director for a company in Colorado called Cognisense.

Cognisense used remote viewing in corporate applications for such tasks as employee application screening, theft detection, hardware problem diagnostics, negotiation strategy and more. I was fascinated with his presentation and pleased he was living his personal mythology.

At the end of the lecture I went out into the lobby. I didn't have any plans and Jill was attending a lecture that I wasn't interested in so I had some time on my hands. I looked at my conference program to see if there was anything I might want to investigate. I noticed that one of the presenters had brought several computers for his presentation on associative remote viewing that could be used during the entire weekend. I had missed the presentation the previous day. After I read Dave's book, I had researched everything I could about remote viewing and come across the ARV technique. It was used primarily to find answers to forced-choice questions that would be difficult to target using standard remote viewing methodologies. A forced-choice question is simply one in which there are only two outcomes. Either one choice or the other is correct.

I wandered over to the room where the practice sessions on the computers were being held. I looked at the picture of the presenter and noticed him by a table with an unattended computer. I walked over and introduced myself. I didn't know it then but Marty Rosenblatt would inadvertently launch me into one of the greatest tragedies in American history.

Marty sat me down at the computer and showed me the MISTIE program for associative remote viewing. MISTIE stands for Minute Stock simulator for Training and Intuition Exploration. It didn't take me long to learn and I spent the next hour training with it. Afterwards I chatted with Marty and learned a bit of his background. He has an M.S. from UCLA in computational physics. That gave me pause. Computational physics is an esoteric branch of science that investigates some of the most difficult problems in applied mathematics and physics. It focuses on problems like simulating nuclear weapons effects. I was very impressed. Marty is intelligent and personable, unlike some scientists who are as stilted socially as they are smart. He had started and then sold several Internet companies and now ran his own, Physics Intuition Applications.

We hit it off immediately and decided to collaborate on some ARV projects coming up in the near future.

The best part of the whole weekend was the chance to sit down at dinner and later for drinks with two of the best known of the military remote viewers, Lyn Buchanan and Mel Riley.

I was excited to meet the man who played so prominent a role in Dave's book.

Mel Riley is short and slim with short blond hair and bright, humorous eyes that never seem far from a smile. He was as Dave had described him: good-natured with a self-effacing humor.

We had something in common. Before being recruited into the Star Gate program, Mel was a photo interpreter based in Germany. In World War II, my Dad was a photo interpreter for the Army assigned to the Italian Theater.

Mel Riley and Author

According to Dave, Mel's session drawings had a photographic quality to them. They had dimension and perspective. Lyn was the exact opposite. His drawings, like mine, were more rudimentary, with stick figures being prominent.

Jill and I were sitting by the pool at our hotel Saturday night after the conference had finished for the day. We were having drinks when Lyn and Mel appeared. We quickly offered them places at our table.

I decided to ask a question that had been on my mind since I first read Dave's book. I was curious to know what both of these men thought of *Psychic Warrior*. I broached the subject somewhat cautiously.

Lyn looked over at Mel for a moment, then turned to me, "Well, there is a lot of stuff in there that was personal to Dave that at the time he didn't share with most of the members of the Unit, Mel excepted. But the description of the everyday routine, if there was such a thing, is definitely accurate. As a matter of fact, I recommend the book to all of my students so they have a better understanding of the way we were mistreated."

I was about to ask him to expand on that when Mel spoke up. "Most people don't realize that. Here we were, given tasks that no other intelligence assets could manage. Not only did we succeed where others failed, but we did it repeatedly. Yet, except for a few brave individuals, the majority of the intelligence community shunned us as pariahs."

Lyn nodded, "They thought remote viewers were unholy or evil. They didn't believe in remote viewing and did everything they could to sabotage us."

Mel added, "Many of the generals in the CIA and DIA thought remote viewing was nonsense, despite proven results – results that no one else in the intelligence community could deny. The funny thing is that we got more support from the Presidents than we did from the people we dealt with on a daily basis."

I knew that from my research. Both Presidents Carter and Reagan were aware of and staunch supporters of the program. Admiral Stansfield Turner had briefed Carter on the remote viewers' success in locating a downed Russian spy plane in Africa. The aircraft could not be located by satellite imagery. The remote viewers had not only described the location of the crash site near a distinctive bend of a river, they had even drawn the tail of the aircraft sticking out of the jungle. Carter had been amazed that the drawing matched a picture of the crash site.[26]

"When something came up that defied the usual methods of intelligence collection, they were right there asking the Unit," chimed in Lyn. "Then, when they'd get it, half the time they didn't use it. And this after seeing success after success," Lyn finished, his voice filled with disgust.

Jill looked at the two men and asked quietly, "Do you think the government will ever use remote viewing again?"

Lyn shook his head; Mel took a moment to rub his chin in reflection, "Maybe, but it will take something big to overcome the prejudice against it. I'm inclined to doubt it, but stranger things have happened."

I would remember those words later.

CHAPTER TWELVE

Omega

What's important is that one strives to achieve a goal.

—Ronald Reagan

I watched out the small window with mixed emotions as our flight approached New York City. On the one hand, it felt great to be back in New York. It was the second time I had been in three months. Before this sojourn, it had been twenty years. Pretty strange, considering that I'm a native New Yorker, and my family still has a ranch there, upstate.

On the other hand I felt apprehension tinged with a mixture of anger, grief, and guilt.

The horror of 9/11 had happened 16 days ago.

Patty had called me a week earlier to confirm that I would be available for the Omega Institute to help teach an ERV class. She wanted me there because it would be a large class and she expected the pall of the recent tragedy to have an effect on the students.

It had had an effect on me, a very personal one because of a chance decision by a machine.

I arrived at La Guardia airport, worked my way through the heavy and pervasive security and took a taxi to the Amtrak train at Penn station for the 90-minute trip north along the Hudson River. The ride alongside the river would normally have brought back many pleasant memories from my younger days.

Instead, I found myself drawn inevitably back to thoughts of a library, and an experiment in remote viewing that had taken place there 96 hours before 9/11, run by my friend Marty, whose company sanctioned the project. The unexpected result shattered my old belief system forever.

The experiment had me at a computer, in this case, at the City of Torrance Central Library. There I logged on to Marty's web site and picked up a set of coordinates. These random numbers were assigned to an outcome. In this case, the outcome was whether a stock index had risen, stayed the same or fallen; a forced-choice experiment.

I would do a remote viewing session on these coordinates and record my observations. After that the computer would show me two pictures. I would choose the picture that most closely resembled my data.

These two pictures, chosen randomly from a picture file with thousands of entries, would be assigned to each of the two possible outcomes, those outcomes being either stocks up, or stocks level or down two days hence.

If the computer chose a picture of a mountain for stock up, and a picture of a waterfall for stock level or down, and I saw lots of rushing water falling in the RV session, then the computer would tell me that my choice for the market two days hence was market level or down.

Two days later I would receive my feedback based on the results of that trading day. If I were correct that the market was going to fall, then I would see the picture of the waterfall. If not, I'd get the other picture.

I thought back to the Friday before the tragedy. Since trading was suspended on weekends, my viewing session on Friday had been for the following Tuesday. It was a very strange session, stranger than any other ARV session I can remember.

The data, however, seemed to correspond to a picture choice of a faintly familiar cityscape as seen from across a river. I didn't recognize the distinctive World Trade Center in downtown Manhattan. Not knowing the significance of what I had seen, I simply wrote down the day that the computer said that the feedback for the session would be ready...Tuesday, September 11, 2001.

The following Tuesday morning, I was back in a library in Carson to access Marty's website and get my feedback for Friday's session. As the home page loaded, I glanced briefly at the news headlines to see if anything interesting had happened.

My eyes were drawn to a picture in the upper corner. I thought to myself, wow, the things they can do with computer-generated special effects. The picture was of a jetliner crashing into the side of a building. I didn't read the caption, as I had only a limited time on the computer. I typed in Marty's site and hit the Enter key.

As I waited for the page to load, I realized that the library had a television on the information counter. It was facing away from me and I could barely hear what was being said. That was a little odd as I had been coming to this library for over a month and they had never had a TV on the counter before. Before I could give it much attention, Marty's site came up and I ignored the TV as a minor distraction. I typed in the request and frowned when the picture flashed up on the screen. It wasn't the cityscape. It was the other picture, the one I hadn't chosen.

I rocked back in my seat. I was so sure it was the picture of the cityscape with the two large buildings dominating the skyline. This meant that the market had fallen, as the picture of the cityscape had been an up choice.

Damn. This would drop my overall average.

I printed out both pictures for my records, looking again at the other picture and shaking my head. I had been so sure I was right. I was really upset at missing this session. The old feelings locked up inside began to surface. The doubts and the disbelief had been waiting for something like this to happen.

Dejectedly I walked out of the library, completely forgetting about the TV, and drove home. I tried to put the result out of my head, but there on the seat next to me was my failure staring back at me. The pictures.

When I got home I went into my room and shut the door. I tossed the pictures on my desk and decided to lose myself in the boob tube. My heart froze at what I saw when I turned it on. It was the news of the attack on the World Trade Center. The picture on the search engine web site had not been computer generated. It had been real.

I watched in horror and disbelief as they played the tapes of the planes striking the towers. As I sat there stunned, I realized there was something eerily familiar about those buildings, the skyline, and the river that was close by. I couldn't put my finger on it, but I had seen them somewhere before.

It hit me as the news camera panned a shot of the twin towers from across the river. The feedback!

I jumped up from the bed and grabbed the printouts. The picture was what the news camera had just shown, except that my feedback had been a twilight shot of the Towers. As I read over the session I had done 96 hours ago, I felt a chill run up my spine. I had seen it all in the session – the two craters, the dust clouds, the dogs; all of it now made sense.

The round fuselage that I had first thought was a train, or maybe a plane, now took on a whole new significance.

I have to call Marty about this, I thought. Quickly dialing his number, I waited impatiently for him to answer. After several rings, while I feverishly hoped he would be home, there was a click and Marty answered.

"Marty, it's John. Quick, take a look at my session from Friday and at the target photos," I said in a rush.

"Just a minute John. It'll take me a minute to get into the site and pull it up." I could hear him typing on the other end of the line. "Have you seen what's happened in New York?" he asked quietly.

"Yeah, those bastards, those cold hearted bastards," As of that moment only the anger in my heart could speak. I knew there would be heavy casualties.

There was silence on the line for the moment. I knew Marty must have been looking at my session. I wondered what he would think.

I didn't have long to wait, "Wow, John! That's simply amazing. I'll have to remove that picture from the target pool. Its signal overwhelmed the correct choice. We'll never be able to use that picture again in an ARV trial."

As he typed in the background, commenting on the accuracy of the session, another thought came to my mind, this one more sinister, "Marty, when I did the session Friday, I didn't realize that the picture was of the World Trade Center." I paused for a moment as the full import of my train of thought hit me. "What if I had recognized it? I might have been able to do something!"

The thought that I might have been able to avert this tragedy were it not for my stunted architectural knowledge was agonizing.

Marty quickly spoke up, "John, you couldn't have known what was happening. That was a ten-minute session. Remember, what's the job of a remote viewer?" he asked, knowing that my response would yank me up short.

He had me there, which, of course, both of us knew. "A remote viewer detects and decodes; he doesn't analyze. But Marty—"

He cut me off. "John, there is no but. You know it and so do all remote viewers. It's one of the first things a viewer learns. Besides, whom would you have told? Who would even have believed you?"

I remained silent at the questions, and thanked him for his concern. Marty was a good guy, a good friend. After we said our good byes and hung up, I thought about his assertions. I hadn't said anything, but I knew whom I would have called. Whether or not it would have done any good, I don't know, but there had been at least a chance.

I watched the scenery drift by as I sat crouched at the window seat in the darkened train, guilt draped around my shoulders like a cloak. Now, there was no chance.

There was nothing I could do about the lost opportunity. It had slipped through my fingers like sand, and left me with only a hollow sense of guilt. The chance of a lifetime.

Gone.

I sat there quietly, alone in the darkness.

I left the train at the small town of Rhinebeck. I was met by one of RVTs many volunteers all around the country for the short trip to the Omega Institute.

The Omega Institute is a 100-acre wooded property dedicated to teaching numerous enhanced human performance disciplines, such as yoga, meditation, and massage. It also provides a venue for retreats.

I had been here in June for a week. There wasn't much difference then from the washed out greens and browns of Southern California's humid dry summers that I was so used to. But where Southern California was hot and humid, there was little rain to break the drought. Here in New York at least, you could look forward to the frequent thunderstorms to break the heat, not the puny, occasional brief showers of the Los Angeles basin. I hadn't heard thunder or seen lightning there in several years. Here the thunder boomed out like cannon shot and the lightning pierced the skies from horizon to horizon.

It was just as I remembered it from my youth, cool and humid, the skies leaden with gray and charcoal clouds, typical of late September. The promise of a late afternoon thunderstorm hung in the air. The grass and woods around me were the incredibly vibrant green that is the result of those rainstorms. The leaves were just starting to turn from the cool evenings.

In June, we had taught CRV methods to a class of over fifty people. It had been an interesting role reversal for me – on the other side of the table, answering questions rather than asking them. People were looking to me for answers, rather than me looking to Dave. I had a great time and was looking forward to being here for the ERV class. Many students from three months ago were back so I expected an even more enjoyable experience, as the ERV class was my favorite. My new friends Tedd, Cheryl, Franca, and Charles were scheduled to be here, as well as Robin, Carol and James.

I had moved into one of the small dorm-like cottages that everyone lived in. They were nothing extravagant, even Spartan, but with a certain homey comfort. I had met Dave briefly on arrival here, but both of us were tired from the journey. After a short greeting, we made plans to meet for breakfast in the morning.

Lying in bed in my little room, I listened to the patter of raindrops on the leaves of the trees. I thought how much at peace I felt here as I drifted off to sleep. I hadn't felt that way in a long time.

After breakfast with Dave and Patty and the rest of the staff, we assembled at the meeting hall to discuss the upcoming class and get our assignments. Dave had recognized the class's angst over the events of 9/11 and decided to replace the morning moving meditation with a walk in silence around the small lake on the Institute property.

It would give all of us a chance to collect our thoughts and to put things in perspective. Not alone, but in the company of friends. It would help all of us find closure.

Then Dave would address the class on the events of 9/11, and the importance of rejecting the path of vengeance and hatred.

We would be hard pressed because of the size of this class. We had to divide them into five groups. Patty, Lyn, Mark, Jason, and myself were the group leaders. This way we could go over their individual sessions and address any difficulties the students might have. With over fifty students between the five of us, time would always be an issue. We would have to keep a tight rein on the class.

As the students began showing up, I saw a tall, lanky, dark haired guy detach from a group of students and stride over to where I was standing.

"John, it's good to see you, my friend," Tedd said in greeting, giving me a robust handshake and a quick embrace.

"Hey you, how has everything been going since that last e-mail?" I replied. I had gotten to know Tedd pretty well in the CRV class a few months ago. We had gravitated towards each other, probably because we were both native New Yorkers and shared a spicy brand of humor.

Tedd leaned forward and whispered conspiratorially, "My girl-friend and I are getting married. Don't say anything to anyone because we haven't told anyone else."

"Damn, I didn't even know you had a steady," I exclaimed. "I thought you were playing the field."

Tedd was charmingly flustered, as if in admitting he had a steady detracted from his reputation. "Yeah, I've known her for a couple of years now and I just recently popped the question."

I remembered my conversation with Dave and Patty when they announced that they had gotten married and quipped, "And she said yes? Which did you do, drug her or get her pregnant?"

Tedd laughed, saying that his fiancée would be stopping by later in the week to meet Dave, Patty, and the rest of the staff.

Although I didn't have Tedd in my discussion group, I had Cheryl. She's a short, vivacious redhead with a gorgeous smile and a strong independent streak. She needed it; she managed musicians for a New York record label. The three of us had hung out the last time I was here. I knew she would keep the discussions lively.

With the class assembled, Dave entered and sat down in his director's chair.

I watched him; his movements were relaxed and he had that boyish grin on his face as he chatted amiably with several of the students sitting in the front of the class. I couldn't help but smile in response; he was in his element. The students focused on him, echoing his enthusiasm.

"Welcome! It is such a thrill for me and Patty and the rest of the staff to see so many adventurers on the path toward wisdom. We are so very honored to have you all here. We want you all to know that you are loved and cherished." A murmur of appreciation rippled through the room.

Dave continued, "I know all of you were shocked by the events of September 11th. We want you to know that we will endeavor to provide a safe and comfortable place of learning here at Omega.

"I want you to try and put aside the fear, anger, hatred and the other negative emotions of the human categorical imperatives. I know that may be difficult for some of you, especially those who may have lost loved ones in this tragedy. But you can't let those emotions overwhelm you. They will only force you to serve them.

"If we let the forces of Chaos rule us through our own destructive emotions, then we risk a Fourth Turning of unprecedented power. Already the voices in Washington are loud with vengeance and anger. A knee-jerk response that is full of hatred must inevitably result in a cycle of violence that will trigger more bloodshed, more slaughter."

Dave stopped for a moment, then continued in a low voice charged with emotion, "I don't mean that we should forget. I don't mean we should do nothing. I mean that we should think very carefully about how we should handle this situation."

"The cycle of violence spins today in Sri Lanka, the West Bank, in Mogadishu, and dozens of other places around the world. I spent half my life learning the art and science of taking human life. And I know that adding more mindless violence will only magnify the forces arrayed against us."

"This week we will move another step closer to wisdom, a step away from fear and anger. This is the reason all of you wonderful souls are sharing this week here with us.

"So let us dedicate this class to those who were lost, in the hope that reason prevails over those who will make the decisions," Dave finished quietly. "Let's take two minutes of silence in remembrance of the departed. After a quick break we'll start the lecture."

In an ERV class, the lecture portion takes only a day and a half. To my amusement, this class followed the pattern of the previous ERV classes that I had attended. Over the next day, the excitement and anxiety level began to build as the first target session approached. If they followed the pattern, most would be disappointed by their first foray into ERV.

"Alright, let's take a quick 15-minute break and then be ready to launch," Dave said.

The air was filled with the sounds of air mattresses being inflated by blow dryers as the students scrambled to prepare their workstations. The anticipation was palpable; the students animated. I felt their excitement. I remembered my first ERV class. I barely slept the night before, with Saundra, Jill, John, and I talking into the wee hours about what might lie ahead. I walked past Cheryl and Franca, a tall, willowy brunette from the previous CRV class at Omega, wishing them a good trip. As the cool-down CD started, I felt a little envious. As an instructor, I wouldn't be doing the viewing. I would be one of the class monitors assigned to make sure that the room stayed quiet. In other words...

Snore patrol.

I walked quietly around the room, checking on the viewers. As I did so I reminisced about my own experiences during my first ERV class, the excitement, the doubt.

There were times when those doubts would surface, usually just before a target session, or just after a session that didn't go as well as I hoped.

I knew now that remote viewing was for real, or at least I thought I did. What I still doubted was my own ability. There were times, like the Mars session, when my ability seemed certain. But then there were others that made me wonder. I knew I was being too hard on myself back then. At that time I had fewer than 40 sessions under my belt. How many times had I heard Dave admonish his students about the vicious cycle between ego and self-doubt? You did your best. That was enough.

Still, I had always been driven to succeed. Dave's words on ego versus self-doubt were one of the most difficult lessons that I had to learn. And I wasn't quite sure that I had really accepted those words yet, 9/11 notwithstanding.

A few of the viewers stirred and got up, taking their masks off. I glanced at my chronometer and suddenly realized how much time had gone by. Dave walked into the room moments later and signaled to Jason, who was monitoring the room with me at the sound console.

Jason nodded and slowly muted the pink noise while bringing up the warm-up music. "Alright viewers, let's end the session, and when you are ready and only when you are ready, return to Sanctuary. Complete your session summaries and you are free to go to lunch. Be back at 2:30 pm for small groups."

The students began to write their summaries. I looked around the room at their faces. That would tell me immediately who did well and who didn't. As with most classes on their first targets, the reactions seemed mixed.

I happened to catch Cheryl's eye and walked over to her work station.

"Hey, how did it go?"

Cheryl's normally pretty face screwed up in frustration, "I didn't see anything, anything at all."

"Let me see what you've written," I said quietly. After reading her notes I replied, "Cheryl, you've got a lot of accurate data here. I don't want to give away the target, but from what I see here, you did well on your first try."

"But I didn't get any visuals. I really wanted visuals," she said plaintively.

"Come on, let's go grab some lunch and we can talk," I replied. I saw Tedd at the door. "There's Tedd. Let's see how he did."

"So how was your trip?" I asked Tedd, as we walked the short distance from the room to the cafeteria.

"Not bad, I think. I got some stuff written down, but I'm not sure if it's good or not. I had a solid vortex though. That alone was worth it," Tedd said excitedly.

"I know. I remember my first time on the magic carpet ride," I replied, recalling the trip to the Titanic. As we walked to the cafeteria, Franca joined us. At Omega, the meals were major social events. Everyone could people-watch while they talked about the day's events.

Meals are strictly vegetarian at Omega and served buffet style – all you can eat. The fare was eclectic but the quality and quantity were excellent. Dave and I loved it. Patty however, was less enamored. Her staple fare consisted primarily of peanut butter sandwiches.

When we were seated, it didn't take long to notice that the remote viewers seemed to be the center of attention. Once our excited conversations, filled with the esoteric descriptions of remote viewing sessions began to drift through the room, I noticed the effect. It was like the commercial for a well-known stock brokerage firm that had the adage, "When so-and-so speaks, everyone listens." It was comical watching the people from the other classes as they strained to hear our conversations over the general din, marveling at the arcane language.

I turned to Cheryl. "You asked me how to get more visuals, right?" Cheryl nodded. "Okay, first of all, remember that ERV is a very personal experience. Everyone sees differently. Some people are visual, like Dave and I. Others are aural or kinesthetic. It's good that viewers do see differently because if we all saw the same way we might miss information."

"I know, but..."

I interrupted her with a smile, "I know, I know. That having been said, remember that remote viewing is intent driven. The viewer's intention drives the session. If you want more visuals, then you need to have the intention of having more visuals."

Cheryl cocked her head and asked quizzically, "How do you do that?"

"Before you launch, you tell your unconscious that you are going to have more visuals. The best time is when you're in Sanctuary waiting for the Vortex to form. This is the time that whatever you want to happen should be presented to your unconscious."

Cheryl looked dubious, "So all I have to do is basically really want visuals and then program myself to have them?"

I grinned at her, taking a grape from her plate and popping it in my mouth, "Hey, I'm a man. When has a man ever lied to you?" At that, Franca and Tedd laughed.

Cheryl groaned, rolling her eyes at me. "I'm doomed never to have visuals."

"Nah, you'll do just fine. Just do like I said. After all, I'm a native New Yorker like you. Trust me," I assured her.

After lunch, we returned to the hall for small groups. When everyone in my group had arrived, I had each member give a short synopsis of their session. While they were talking, I glanced at their drawings, tracing the relevant ones to a transparency. I also wrote down sensory verbal data that corroborated the target.

After everyone had a chance to speak, I said, "For your first time at this I'd say, compared to other classes that I've seen, you come in maybe average or a little below. Most of you had a decent amount of sensory verbal data but I would have liked to see more drawings."

To forestall the pleas that I knew were coming, I held my hand up as several of my group raised theirs. "I already know what you're going to ask. How can I get more visuals? Get some paper to take notes and I'll give you my recipe for ERV success." There was a scramble as everyone went through their notes looking for blank paper. Then the noise subsided and all eyes were on me.

Outwardly I was calm, but inside my stomach churned. It was a little unnerving having all those pairs of eyes on me, with a grand total of one class as a group leader under my belt. I could sense their desire. It wasn't hard to understand as I remembered how I waited for five months after my first class before I got to take ERV.

I had worked target after target so that I would be ready; used biofeedback techniques to hone my skills in meditation to facilitate the drop to a deep hypnagogic state. I wanted that magic carpet ride that Dave described in his book.

I was lucky. All my preparations had paid off with not one, but several bi-locations. I had some good observations on how to duplicate the strong visuals. But I also knew that ERV was a very personal experience; what worked for me might not for someone else.

I saw the trust in their eyes and suddenly the weight of responsibility hit home. I didn't want to let them down and I didn't want to let Dave down. It was a measure of the trust he had in me that I was here.

My mouth was suddenly very dry. I took a moment to clear my throat, "Umm, I wasn't going to give you this originally. I was just going to tell you what I told Cheryl at lunch. What I told her is true, but it still lets you flounder around out there.

"I have found that what I'm going to tell you works. But there's a caveat. It worked for me because I've had training you haven't. There's no guarantee that it will work for you. Do you still want me to tell you?" I asked quietly.

There wasn't even a moment of hesitation. They all said yes.

"OK. First is what I call the Ninefold Path."

Keythe spoke up, "Like the Buddhist Eightfold Path?"

I grinned, "Yeah, if it worked for Buddha, I figure it'll work for me." That brought a giggle. "The nine points are these. First, follow the methodology as taught. Listen carefully to everything Dave says. He's distilled months of training down to this class. You can't afford to miss anything he says. Also, be on time for class.

"Second, forget what other techniques you may have learned for now. I know some of you have had training in other disciplines. Wait till you're comfortable with the methodology of ERV before you try and experiment with it. Once ERV becomes second nature, then you can play with it to better fit your personality." Of course Dave had said all of this during his lecture, but I knew some of them needed the reinforcement.

"Third, you need to be tired. I can't emphasize this enough," I said seriously.

"If I get too tired I'll fall asleep," complained one of my group members.

I waved my hand at her, not in dismissal, but in affirmation, "Maybe, but I guarantee that if you get lots of sleep you're going to come in here wide-eyed and spend the next 90 minutes on your back, bored out of your mind. You'll never get deep enough in theta.

"You've got to go down deep – right on the edge of sleep. It's hard work. That's why ERV isn't for everyone; not everyone has the drive to work at it. They want the magic carpet ride, but they just

Author with Cheryl and Keythe.

want to lie back and let the show begin. It doesn't work that way.

"If you're in alpha or high theta you can get data. But if you do, it will be in CRV form with none of the CRV protocols in place. That's a setting for disaster."

I waited a moment to let that sink in.

"So what can we do?" Cheryl asked quietly.

She was so attractive when she was like that, so intent and serious. "Listen to what the group leaders and Dave and Patty say. The breathing techniques are designed to get you deep enough. Learn them.

"Next, be mindful of food and liquid intake prior to a session. It can really be frustrating when you gotta go to the can, man." I drawled with a grin.

"When you're in Sanctuary waiting for the Vortex, don't just lie there. It's the perfect time to reinforce your desire for visuals."

Once the students finished writing, I continued. "Any time you think that you're not deep enough or the information just doesn't want to come, then you need to use those deep breathing techniques that Dave taught you. Once again, those techniques are the window to a successful ERV session. Use them, they work."

I couldn't have asked for better timing when Keythe asked, "How do you know if you're getting deep enough?"

"There are two things that you should look for as you get close to the zone of ultra-deep. First, you'll notice sudden short sharp muscle spasms as you relax deeper and deeper. Don't be worried; that's what you want. They're called myoclonic spasms and are the result of excess muscular tension bleeding off because of the lowering of excitation thresholds in the muscles.

"Second, will be a profound sense of falling, as if the floor has dropped out from underneath you. It's usually of very short duration but it can be uncomfortable and disorienting. But when it stops you should be right where you want to be."

I cautioned them again, "Remember, this was my experience; it may not be yours. But it worked for me and others have reported similar experiences.

"Finally, if all else fails ... remember the mission. Refocus on what you're trying to accomplish." Smiling, I reminded them, "And above all else, have fun."

Cheryl spoke up, "You mentioned the Five Intentions. What are those?"

"The Five Intentions are the way to get what you want from ERV. Once again, ERV is intent driven, so if you want to have, for instance more visuals..." I said looking at Cheryl meaningfully, "then you want to have the intention of having more visuals. Reinforce those intentions and if you work at it, it will happen.

"The Five Intentions are; the intent to have more visuals, the intent to move in the target area, the intent to remember everything, the intent to return to consciousness if I fall asleep, and finally the intent to succeed at ERV.

"The Five Intentions should be constantly reinforced prior to a target session as well as during a cool-down. I also recommend that each night before you fall asleep you reinforce them again." I shrugged my shoulders, saying, "How badly you want success; how hard you are willing to work for it, is the real key.

"When I learned ERV, I worked my ass off to succeed. I did lots of CRV targets before the class. I took EEG biofeedback from a clinical psychologist to make sure I could access ultra-deep, and practiced the cool-down so I would have the greatest chance of success. You need to dedicate yourself to success too."

Keythe spoke up again, asking, "But none of us has had that type of training; what can we do?"

"Just do what Dave has told you and remember what we've talked about. Trust me. I'm not a natural psychic, but I can do this. So can you." And with that, I cut them loose to take a break. After the break, we'd be back for the large discussion group and feedback for the target.

Later that day Dave called me over.

"John, Patty says that Charles is having a hard time. Can you check up on him? He was in your group last time and your experiences might give him an insight."

It sounds silly but my chest was about to burst with pride when he said that. A big grin spread across my face; I couldn't help it.

"No problem. I'll grab him for dinner tonight. It'll give us a chance to talk. I'll take care of it, don't worry."

Dave smiled back, saying simply, "I know you will."

Charles had been in my Omega CRV class three months earlier. He was a good student and had done well. We had become friends during the week as one of my group. Here was my chance to see if I really could make a difference. On the way to the cafeteria, I saw Charles walking slowly, by himself, to the entrance. It wasn't like him. Although not as gregarious as some of the others, he had a quick sense of humor and fit in well. I increased my pace and sidled up alongside him, "Hey Charles, how was your session?"

Charles looked up, startled by the interruption.

"Oh, hi John. Ah, it didn't go so well. Actually it didn't go at all," he said, his head dropping dejectedly.

"Well, if anyone can say this ... it's me. I know where you've been; I know what it's like. Kinda sucks, doesn't it." He knew I knew. And suddenly, I realized why that crafty old Ranger asked me of all people to talk to him. Dave's wisdom hit me like a brick, deflating my ego a little, too.

But it picked up when Charles said quietly, "I'm thinking of heading for home. This just isn't for me."

Dave had been right in more ways than one.

"Then you would be making a big mistake, Charles. Believe me when I tell you that you can do this; that you *will* do this. Dave sent me over to talk to you because you know my history with him. If I can do this, you can too. And I'm going to show you how," I said earnestly.

Charles looked at me.

I replied with a sigh, "I'm not BSing, Charles. Give me a chance. Then, if it doesn't work for you, at least you gave it your all. Besides, you don't want to miss all this wonderful food and company, do you?" I said with a laugh. I knew, like Patty, he wasn't crazy about the all-vegetarian fare.

"OK, what the hell. I'll give it a shot," he replied, a small grin appearing.

Several others joined us in the cafeteria when they found out that we would be discussing hints for ERV. Suddenly, there were half a dozen people at our table. I gave them a pep talk and reiterated what I had told my group earlier. I knew they could all do it. I think they just needed to hear it from me. They all knew I failed the first time I did CRV and ERV.

Now I saw what Dave had already seen, that the students could hear it from him but would think, "He's a master of this stuff, has done it for years. I haven't had years. I can't do this." Now they heard it from one of their own: a student like them not that long ago. Someone who wasn't a natural.

After dinner, I decided to go for a walk and explore the campus. The lush woods reminded me of our family's ranch in upstate New York. The ranch was 275 acres of forest with a spring-fed pond the size of a football field. My parents had originally bought it as a summer and weekend retreat but relocated there full time to get away from suburban life. I had grown up in a natural wonderland. The ranch had been a tree farm at one point but we had let it return to wilderness. It looked much like the Institute grounds with the exception of the bungalows and meeting buildings.

When I had been here in mid-June, the deer flies were in season and it had been impossible to go exploring in the woods. They had swarmed all over me at each attempt, forcing me away. Now, they were gone for the rest of the year and the woods were mine. I still had to keep a lookout for ticks but with caution they would be no problem. The sun was low on the horizon and the interior of the woods appeared forebodingly dark. The coming darkness had subdued the creatures of the forest and the normal sounds of birds and insects was now muted. Dressed in greens that matched the surrounding foliage, I slipped through the forest unseen.

It was great to be back in the woods. I had learned how to stalk and track when I was a teenager back at the ranch. My father taught me to respect nature. He was an accomplished woodsman and hunter. It was he who taught me how to shoot, a skill that served me well when I entered the police academy.

I reveled in the rocks and trees, immersed in the quiet dignity of nature. This was my cathedral, the jays and crows in the canopy overhead, my angels. Unknowingly, I was about to meet the nuns.

Like a cat I climbed silently up to the top of an outcropping of boulders and came upon three whitetail deer – adult does. They were only fifteen yards away, oblivious to my sudden arrival. I crouched there, savoring the magic moment. As I watched, they slowly moved off into the trees. The last doe languidly turned her head and stared directly at me. I froze, holding my breath, hoping to blend into the surroundings. The animal stared at me for a moment; then, with a flick of her tail, she was gone.

I stood there, smiling at what had just transpired. After living in the city for so long, it was like going back over twenty years to the last time I had been at the ranch. It was a wonderful way to end the day.

Later that evening, I was lying awake in my room, again listening to the rain patter on the branches and leaves of the trees surrounding our bungalow. I thought about what had transpired today, and how it had affected not just the students, but also its effect on me.

I hoped I had made a difference. I was worried, though. Maybe my tips wouldn't help them to the breakthrough that they wanted so badly.

I didn't want to let them or Dave down. I had told them that if they followed Dave's teaching and my tips, they'd have a better chance at a successful ERV session.

But what if they didn't? I could picture the nightmare; everyone does great except for my group and the others who sat with me at lunch and listened to me shoot my mouth off. Oh boy, party time, I thought. I'd find out tomorrow. Just before I drifted off to sleep, the memory of the encounter with the deer materialized. It was just what I needed; I fell asleep unburdened.

I stopped off to see Patty the next morning after breakfast and the meditation hike.

"Hi Patty, how's your group doing?" I wanted to find out if my people were the only ones having trouble.

Patty looked up at me from her computer over the top of her glasses, "They're doing okay overall. Some are still struggling though. Dave is going to go over a few things this morning before the next target. That should help them."

"What's the next target?" I asked. Patty leaned forward and whispered in my ear.

"Chernobyl."

They were getting one hell of a target. Literally.

During the short lecture portion of the morning session, Dave answered questions from the students. After several questions it became clear that the class was apprehensive.

"OK, you guys are getting too caught up over this," Dave said pleasantly.

"There's not that much to this. Cool down and relax. All of you can do this. Just relax and have fun. Don't get too jammed up because your Vortex isn't bright or doesn't spin fast. It doesn't matter. Go with what you get."

A question came up, "If I land at the target and don't see anything, should I go back to Sanctuary and try again?"

Dave gently scolded the student, chuckling to soften the impact. "Why would you want to go back to Sanctuary and restart the whole sequence?" Spreading his arms to emphasize the point, he exclaimed, "You're already at the target! If you don't see anything, what should you do? You should be doing the yogic breathing exercises to get back into deep theta, then move."

With no more questions, Dave gave them ten minutes to get ready for the target session. I looked over at my students. Cheryl happened to look up and I smiled back at her, giving her a thumbs up sign. She returned the smile, but I could see the apprehension in her face.

As Jason started the cool-down, I reminisced about what Dave had done for my first class in ERV. I thought about how he had joined our class at the target after our abortive first attempt. I looked over at Cheryl lying in her sleeping bag quietly, remembering what she had said about her desire to see more visuals. Maybe I could take a more active role in helping her, not just stand by and hope that my advice would do the trick. If I was going to do it, I realized, I'd have to hurry. The cool-down would be coming to a close shortly. Biting my lip and hoping that I wasn't making a monumental mistake, I made my decision.

I would join her at the target, just as Dave had joined ours.

Quickly stretching out on the floor and pushing my jacket underneath me as a makeshift mattress, I started the ERV protocols. This would be dicey; I'd have to time my arrival carefully so that I wouldn't startle her at the target. If I couldn't reach the target before she did, I would have to abort. I couldn't risk coming up on her unannounced and causing her to experience a slingshot return as I had when John had snored, ruining my session during my first ERV class in Carmel.

My breathing went into Trojan Warrior II mode. I didn't have time to use the full ERV breathing techniques because the cool-down tape was almost finished. I felt myself swiftly drop lower and lower into the arena of ultra-deep, the brain state where extended remote viewing takes place. Several times my body jerked uncontrollably as myoclonic spasms wracked my muscles, their excess energy draining from me like water through a hose. I quickly entered Sanctuary and changed the rhythm of my breathing to bring on the Vortex as fast as possible. This was where the Matrix could make me or break me. If the Vortex didn't form right away, it would be too late. It would be only moments before the tape ended and Cheryl would be on her way to the target.

The swirl of Matrix mists gave way to the sudden arrival of the Vortex, the wormhole spiraling open in front of me. Immediately I was off, the walls of the spinning signal line flashing past. I felt the stomach wrenching sensation of falling and then passing through the Membrane. I was at the target site. There was no sign of Cheryl.

I was concentrating only on Cheryl, hoping my intent to be visible only to her would keep any of the other students from seeing me. It wouldn't do me any good if I succeeded with her but then startled someone else, ruining their session.

Where is she, I wondered? The longer I stayed the greater the risk that someone else would see me. I couldn't stay any longer.

Then I saw her apparitional form closing on me. I smiled inwardly as I waved, willing her to see me. I saw the surprised look on her face as she recognized me. Immediately, to keep her from losing her concentration on the target, I invoked Sanctuary, executing an emergency return.

Just as in the Titanic and Mars missions, I snapped back to Sanctuary, feeling the vertigo and nausea take hold. I lay there while the symptoms passed. Thinking how Cheryl had appeared to me in the Matrix, I wondered how I had appeared to her. To me, she had been invisible except where my vision was focused, which was on her face. There, I could see a transparent outline of her visage. She might well have seen me in a different manner though; ERV was that personal. Then another thought intruded. What if this was just a figment of my imagination? With a frown, I thought, what a colossal ego to have thought I could have pulled this off. Pulling the eye shield off my face and taking out my earplugs, I glanced over at Cheryl's quiet form. She wasn't moving.

I shrugged my shoulders. Good, I thought to myself. It was a boneheaded idea anyway. At least I didn't seem to have disturbed her.

Ninety minutes passed and we brought the class back. Nervously I scanned Cheryl's face, looking for any sign of success or failure. She, like everyone else, seemed to be caught up in her summary, which was a good sign that my plan hadn't had any effect. Since the class was free to go to lunch once they were finished, I'd get a chance to talk to her on the way out. I waited impatiently while she completed her summary, wondering if my idea had backfired.

She got up from her mattress and looked around. Seeing me, she made a beeline to where I was standing.

As she approached, a radiant smile bathed her face. She stopped in front of me and said, "You went to the target with me, didn't you."

Keeping my face carefully neutral, I said nothing.

She stamped her foot impatiently and asked again, "Tell me! You went to the target with me, didn't you? Seeing me smile, she grinned and accused, "You did, didn't you." This time she said it as a statement, not a question. I paused a moment then slowly nodded.

"I knew it! I saw you there waving, then you were gone. That was so cool." she exclaimed. She reached up and hugged me, whispering, "Thank you."

I returned her hug and replied, "Trust me, it was my pleasure."

Outside, I looked for the members of my group, wondering how they had fared.

They seemed to be pleased with their results. I couldn't wait for the small group sessions after lunch. There I would see how well they had done.

What we found was one of the single best sessions to date in an ERV class. The class as a whole was outstanding, but as we went through their notes with mounting excitement, we found that individually, the students had done wonderfully as well. Some even called the target by name. Even the few students who were having difficulties made breakthroughs. Dave and Patty and the rest of the staff were ecstatic.

On the last day of class, I stopped off at the Meditation Hall as the evening twilight draped the campus. The transition from daylight to darkness was my favorite time of the day, when the Sun gave way to the ascendancy of the Moon. I loved watching the colors drain from my surroundings and the sounds change from the bustle of day to the more subdued rustle of the evening.

The Hall was set up as a Buddhist-style meditation room. It was a single building surrounded by waterfalls and pools with Asian fish and frogs. It's my favorite place in the Institute. The interior is beautiful redwood unadorned with furniture. I took my shoes off and entered the hall. It was empty, thankfully. Sitting down in the semi-lotus posture, I took several breaths to calm my mind. I thought about my experiences with this class. Although it didn't have the same level of excitement for me as the previous ones, it held something far more precious.

On reflection, I realized how much I enjoyed being with Dave, Patty, and the others, and teaching this wonderful art and science. I always felt like I was coming home when I walked through the door. The stress and tribulations of the outside world faded away.

I wondered where all this was going to lead me. I seemed no closer to my personal mythology, except for my decision to write about my experiences. The journal I had kept since my first CRV class had grown into the beginnings of a book.

I didn't know if I could finish it or if I would have enough adventures to fill it.

But I had nowhere else to go. I'd take the road less traveled by, and see if Robert Frost was right. Would it make all the difference?

CHAPTER THIRTEEN

A Thousand Hours

The man who has no imagination, has no wings.

—Muhammad Ali

I was on the I-5 freeway in early December, driving south on the familiar route to the Marina Village complex in San Diego where I had first taken the Master class.

I was excited about the prospect of helping Dave and Patty teach the final course for that year. The reason I was excited was because this class, which was the ERV course, would give me a total of 1000 hours of classroom time spent with Dave. On reflection, it was hard to believe that I had been with him that long.

It had been one hell of a ride. It didn't seem possible that I could top what I had already experienced. After a thousand hours, you'd think I would've known better. Those hours would barely be enough to prepare me for what was to happen next.

Blissfully unaware of the shattering events to come, I was enjoying the early morning ride. The freeway was nearly empty of traffic in San Diego County at this time of the morning. The sun was up on what appeared to be another fabulous Southern California day.

Students at Marina Village. In the front row are Mimi, Stan, Ariane, and Tina.

As I pulled into the lot at Marina Village, I noticed that Dave's van and equipment trailer weren't there. I got out of the car to see if the room we had reserved was open.

This was a class of 40 people and Dave would be short of group leaders.

As I walked back to the lot, there was a rustle of gravel and Dave's van pulled in.

I waved to them as they exited the van and received a shout of recognition from Dave and Jason. Dave's best friend Mark pulled up a moment later in his truck and we exchanged greetings. The rest of the staff arrived as we were off-loading the van and equipment trailer. I had to marvel; Dave had new presentation materials and equipment to increase the effectiveness of his lecture. He also had all new manuals and handouts as well as new multimedia teaching equipment.

During the first day of lectures I sat in a chair at the back of the class, listening. I had heard this lecture so many times that, after the first couple of exposures, I tended to tune it out. If Dave added new material it would get my attention and I'd follow along. Usually though, I would be working on my book, taking notes, or helping by checking over his use of physics and math in the lecture.

At one point, he was saying, "The world is filled with the Legions of the Status Quo locked in a useless struggle with the future. You, as extended remote viewers, now have the tools to transcend the future. If you spend precious time wondering why you find yourself at odds with your life, you resolve nothing. You don't need to waste that energy. Your life is perfect."

At that, my ears perked up. This sounded different. I looked at the students. Their eyes were locked on Dave. I thought to myself as he paused after that statement, "My life is perfect? Last time I looked, my life was so far from perfect you'd need a telescope to see it!"

Dave must have been reading all of our minds because I could see the look on the student's faces that said they, too, weren't living perfect lives.

Dave looked around the room. His voice, strong with conviction, continued, "Yes, I know you're thinking that your life is nowhere close to being perfect. That's because the events that occurred in your life were not perfect. The events that occur in it may not be. But, your life is perfect, has always been perfect, will always be perfect.

"I've had some really terrible things happen in my life. I was forced to resign from the Army that I had served for so long. I can't be buried in a military cemetery. I lost my marriage, my pension, just about everything that was important to me. But those are only events. My life is perfect. Who I am today, what I am today is because of those events that tested me. I wouldn't change any one of them for anything. They're part of me. They're what made me the man I am today."

I sat there, shocked at the realization. It hit me like a physical force. Quickly glancing around me, I could see the entire room had been moved by his words.

Dave pointed to the class, "Ah, you see what I'm talking about. Uncle Dave hasn't gone senile just yet!"

There was a round of laughter and applause. But Dave wasn't finished. "Don't get caught up in the events of your life. If you give energy to the future, to the illusion of what may be, then that energy may go to manifest the very future that you fear.

"The only solution is to be centered in the moment of your life." Dave quickly pulled up one of the presentation slides from the computer, "Remember the Delta function we discussed earlier?" Using his laser pointer, he outlined the far right of the graph of the Delta function.

"If you are concentrating your energies out here in the ocean of probabilities of the future, then you have nothing left for the very time that you can effect a change in your life. And as the graph shows, it is only in the now, the moment, where your actions can influence what will be."

Moving the laser with a flourish to bring home the point, Dave turned to the class. "You have a choice. Live your life like the legions of the status quo, forever locked in the unconsciousness of consciousness, or live a life full of promise and possibilities."

Spreading his hands for emphasis, Dave finished, "The past is dead and gone; the future a sea of probabilities. Only in the moment, in the space between what was and what will be, can you affect meaningful change. The choice has always been yours."

"Let's take a ten-minute break and then we'll start the first target session."

I couldn't move, transfixed by Dave's words. They had gone right to the heart of the uncertainty that I had about my future. I had been stressing out lately over where I was going after this class. My sabbatical would be over and I would have to go back to a real job soon. I hadn't even started looking. With the loss in personal capital from the breakup with my fiancée and the financing of the unsuccessful Trojan Warrior II project, to say my finances were challenged would be a monumental understatement.

After hearing Dave's lecture though, I suddenly felt that everything would work out. I *had* been living too much into the future. My mind lately had been full of fear and apprehension for what could be, not for what was. I could live, as Dave had said, in the moment. I could take steps to make sure that whatever future occurred, it would be one that I could live with. It was an epiphany; one that couldn't have been more timely. I wanted to tell him but he was surrounded by students demanding his attention. Evidently, epiphanies were not in short supply. It would turn out that, with the demands of the class, I didn't have the chance to relate my newfound wisdom until days later.

I was staying with Stan, my friend from the ERV class where I temporarily lost my ability. He lived just outside San Diego not far from the class venue.

Stan is a big guy with a booming voice, a good-natured manner and upbeat outlook on life.

Two days later, just before the class lunch period was over, I saw Dave talking to Patty at the door to the classroom. As I walked over, Patty gave him a kiss and walked across the parking lot towards her car. Dave turned to me, stretched, then asked warmly, "John, how are things with the class?"

Remembering the epiphany of the other day, I remarked, "You know, with this class, I'll have a thousand hours of instruction or participation with you. I've heard that lecture so many times I can quote it from memory."

Feeling somewhat awkward, I continued, "I have to admit though, that your comments about having a perfect life really hit home."

Dave looked up at me quizzically, "What do you mean?"

"Well, the lecture; it was different this time for some reason. A difference in the wording or a change in the way you normally try and bring home the points. I'm not exactly sure. But it hit home when you talked about having a perfect life despite what's happened in it. It made a huge impression on me, and I'm sure it had the same effect on the class."

Dave looked thoughtful for a moment, running his hand through his hair. "Thanks John. Come to think of it, there were a lot of similar compliments from a number of the class. It's funny but that lecture is pretty much the same as it's always been."

"Well, maybe, but then maybe that's the first time it registered with me."

Dave replied, eyes sparkling, "I can't believe you actually counted the hours."

"Yeah, hard to believe it's been that long since my first CRV class at UCLA," I remembered, shaking my head in wonder. "God, its been such an amazing time and I've met such wonderful people. I'm still awed by the incredible events that I've witnessed. At the mention of UCLA, Dave asked, "How're Jill and Saundra doing?"

I laughed. "Still pursuing the Holy UFO. Actually Saundra had a falling out with her MUFON group and is continuing her research on her own. Jill is working on getting her script sold, so they're both pretty busy. But I get e-mails from them on occasion. They both said to say hi."

"Well, say hi to them for me too." Then something must have tickled Dave's childlike sense of humor because suddenly he picked up his and Patty's paper plates from their lunch. He turned one upside down and stuck it on top of the other one, then, holding it above his head, he exclaimed with a feigned expression of fear on his face, "Oh no! Look, a UFO is trying to abduct me!"

Dave ran around in ragged circles holding the paper plates above his head like a flying saucer.

I couldn't help but laugh so hard my sides hurt.

Patty walked up as he went careening by. Her jaw dropped on seeing her husband, former Ranger company commander, military trained remote viewer, Doctor of Education, running around like a lunatic holding those paper plates over his head. She shook her head, smiling at her husband's antics.

Still giggling insanely, I yelled to Dave, "Wait! Let me get my camera. We'll get proof positive for Jill and Saundra of the existence of UFO's."

Camera in hand, I motioned to Dave to hide behind a bush so that only his hand and arm holding the plate were visible. By now, the students were starting to return from lunch and were watching the two of us run around like madmen. One of the students asked Patty what we were doing.

Patty laughed, saying, "I have no idea."

Susan asked, "Is he like this often?"

And Patty replied chuckling, "Sadly, yes, he is."

After taking several pictures of Dave behind the bush, one with his head peaking around the side, I said to Dave conspiratorially, "I'm going to e-mail those two and tell them I'm sending them pictures that were taken over Area 51. Then I'll give them these in a manila envelope, saying that they were sent to me anonymously."

Dave, still laughing so hard he was having difficulty speaking, gasped, "Oh man, those two are going to kill you!"

Back in lecture, I had asked Dave if I could do this next target session with the class and he replied in the affirmative. As long as there were proctors available, the staff that was unoccupied could join the class and do the target.

I pulled out my inflatable and hooked up the air pump. As the mattress filled with air, Jason stopped by and asked, "Are you doing the target?"

I looked up at him, replying that, yes, I was going to join the class.

Jason launched one of his effervescent smiles and gave me a thumbs up. It was echoed by several of the students who were setting up their ERV workstations nearby. Their enthusiasm was infectious; it made me feel good that I'd be joining them today.

"Lock and load!" I shot my favorite aphorism back at Jason, grinning.

On that note, the cool-down CD started and the lights dimmed. I climbed onto the mattress and snuggled under the covers. Soon, the familiar breathing exercises had me safely wrapped in the quiet, twilight world of Sanctuary. There, I continued the ritual, feeling myself drop deeper and deeper. The sounds of the cool-down drifted away as I turned ever inward.

It didn't take long for the Vortex to spin open and I was off, the walls of purple and gray flashing past. Moments later I was through the Membrane and with the stomach-churning sensation of falling, I landed at the target.

As always on arrival, the mists of the Matrix spun around me, and it took a few moments of breathing techniques before it began to clear away. In a flash of recognition, I knew where I was. At least I thought I did.

Then my training asserted itself and I ignored the feelings of recognition and decided to explore further. A remote viewer must take nothing for granted. Besides, with over 100 targets to choose from, the chance that Dave had chosen the target that I thought he had was small.

I was in a tight passageway made of steel. At the end there was a steel hatch instead of a door. Passing through it, I came upon a ladder leading up to another hatch. The hatches were closed, but that offered no resistance to my form. I continued upwards until I floated out into the open. Now, there was no way that I could contain the feeling of having been here before.

Because, I had been.

I looked out over the huge squat shape sitting in the harbor. The light and dark gray camouflage in the distinctive dazzle pattern; the long barrels of the main armament; the distinctive crane for handling the scout floatplane, it was all so familiar. I had been there once before during the CRV class that I had assisted just before leaving for El Paso. With 1000 hours of classes I guess it was inevitable that I would do a target that I had done in a previous class. I couldn't help but smile. It was a fluke, to be sure, that Dave had chosen a target that I had been to once before, but I wasn't complaining. It was one of my favorite targets.

I floated above the fast battleship U.S.S. North Carolina, a war memorial in Wilmington, North Carolina.

There was no point in staying any longer. I knew the ship inside and out. Still, it was good to visit an old friend. I returned to Sanctuary, taking several minutes to relax. Once I had completed my summary, I joined Stan and several of the class for lunch.

On our return, we followed the usual routine by breaking into small groups to discuss the results. It didn't surprise me that my students duplicated much of the data I had, leading me to believe that the target was indeed the WW II battleship. Technically, it would be confirmed only with the feedback. If this target was the Carolina, it had always brought good results in Dave's classes. The Carolina's signal line was unusually sharp and well defined. I had always thought it was because the ship had won 15 battle stars for participating in most of the major battles in the Pacific during World War II.

Once we finished the discussion group, we broke for ten minutes then returned for the feedback and discussion with Dave. After seeing the combined results, it was obvious that the class as a whole had duplicated my group's success. The combined data also confirmed what I had suspected about the target identity. After displaying a number of transparencies with data from the session on the overhead projector, Dave turned to the class. "As you can see from the wealth of data, this is a significant target with a strong gestalt. Before I have Jason display the feedback, I want you to know that you did extremely well as a class on this target."

Motioning towards the back of the room where we were sitting, Dave continued, "The staff has seen this target used before with other classes and it has always generated excellent results. This class kept up that tradition.

Jason, let's show them the feedback."

I had seen it several times. Jason had shot it with a digital video camera while Dave was in North Carolina teaching a class. The same squat shape I had seen appeared on the video screen, the fast battleship U.S.S. North Carolina. He had walked all over the ship recording the exterior as well as the various spaces below decks. I nodded with recognition at seeing the crew spaces, the rows and rows of huge 16-inch shells stored in the turret barbette, and the aircraft crane on the stern of the ship. The crane was the one feature that seemed for some reason to stand out. Most of the students who were given this target seemed to focus on it.

The members of the class began to talk excitedly amongst themselves as the features of the ship were shown. Hushed exclamations of "I saw that!" or "Look, I drew that!" floated through the room, as the students examined each other's work.

I glanced over at Patty. There was a look of pleasure on her face. She caught my look and we both smiled, sharing the satisfaction of the results of the class.

When the video was finished, Dave took questions on the target. Patricia asked, "Dave, I smelled paint or turpentine. Would that have been there?"

Nodding, Dave replied, "Yes, the ship is being renovated after years of neglect. The funds were finally appropriated and work is continuing today to bring the ship back to its original World War II condition. So, if you detected the sights of welding or the sounds of heavy machinery, that's the reason."

That was good news. It was a great feeling to know that this piece of history would be preserved.

With an ironic twist to that thought, Dave cautioned, "I see a number of you nodding at the news that the ship is being restored. Not everyone, however, agreed with that decision. There was a lot of resistance to the decision to restore the ship. And you would be surprised who were the ones who were the most vocal."

Dave's next words caught me completely off guard.

"Many of the original ship's crew lobbied hard, not for restoration, but to have the North Carolina towed out to sea and scuttled."

An involuntary, "No!" escaped my lips. I was doubly shocked at the revelation. Immediately I asked, "Dave, why would they want the ship sunk? I would have thought that they would be the ship's biggest promoters."

A look that spoke volumes appeared on Dave's face. I had seen that look before on soldiers and sailors and airmen that I had known. It was a look that bespoke the senselessness and horror of war that has no glory, only survivors and the dead.

"Remember in our first class we spoke of inanimate objects having a memory, an imbued spirit of what took place around them?

Does anyone here believe that a place like Dachau wouldn't have a memory, an essence, or a spirit of the things that took place there?"

Answering the rhetorical question, he said, "Of course it would. That's why when we speak of levels of viewing ability, this is the level where you are seeing into the spirit of a place or object. That is the third level of viewing.

"The veterans felt that the ship was tired and should be sent to her final resting place. They felt it was not in the best interests of the ship to have it restored. However they were outvoted and the funds were finally raised."

I muttered under my breath that I was glad they didn't get their wish.

After the class was finished for the day, while Stan and I were driving back to his house, I remarked, "Wow, you know I still can't believe they wanted to sink such a great ship. It seems inconceivable that veterans who served aboard her would want to sink her after everything that happened. They lived and died aboard that ship."

"Yeah, it does seem a little strange that they would elect to sink her rather than restore her. But I can see a certain logic in what Dave said their reasons were," Stan replied in his deep voice. I couldn't share that conviction. It seemed incomprehensible that these men would even consider that alternative. Once we got back to his place and ate, we settled in for the night. Stan at his computer, and me channel surfing the cable TV. Since there was no extra bedroom, I had my air mattress on the floor of the study.

Around midnight my eyes were getting heavy. I looked over at Stan at his computer. He had drifted off to sleep at his desk; one arm hung down at his side and his head was lolled forward. It had been a long day. I decided to turn off the TV and hit the sack. Switching off the light left me in semi-darkness. I was so tired the light on Stan's desk wouldn't bother me. It took only moments before the tendrils of sleep enveloped me.

I don't know how long I was asleep. All I remember is suddenly being someplace else, wide-awake. The feeling was surreal, as if I was in two places at once. I had only felt like that once before. It had been in the Master class where we had conducted a beaconing target.

During the original remote viewing experiments conducted at Stanford Research Institute, Hal Puthoff and Russell Targ had used a beaconing target. A beacon is a person in an remote viewing experiment who is given a target location chosen from a target pool by a third party. The third party chooses a sealed envelope from a group of envelopes at random, each containing a photograph and description of a landmark within 50 miles of the experimenters location. The third party is then no longer involved with the experiment. The target pool, made up of the 10 to 20 photographs of random landmarks around the city, are chosen by someone also not involved in the experiment. This keeps the target locations in the pool removed from the experimenters insuring that no one has any idea where the beacon will be at the time of the experiment.

At the appointed time, the beacon opens the envelope and goes to the landmark described within and stays there for the duration of the experiment, usually an hour. He then returns the target to a room and places it on a table containing the contents of all of the now opened envelopes in the target pool. A third party judge is brought in and looks at the target locations on the table and tries to match one of the targets to the description that the subject doing the remote viewing gave to him. In most of the cases, the judge chose the correct photo or chose the correct photo on the second try.[27]

During the Master class, Dave went one better. He had not one beacon but two. Not only that, the beacons were chosen a world apart; one in Stockholm, Sweden, the other in Sidney, Australia. The remote viewers in our class had to simultaneously view each of the beacon's locations and describe locations halfway around the world. Dave had done this to illustrate that humans are omniscient, omnipotent, omnipresent, wondrous beings.

The PEAR research group had gone even farther. They did the same beaconing protocol as the SRI groups had used. The beacon had the pool of ten to twenty targets, that were sealed and unknown to him, delivered by a third independent party. At the appointed time he would choose at random one of the targets and open it. He would then drive to the location of the target and concentrate on the aesthetics of the location. Then, after being there for a period of time to allow a session by the remote viewers, the beacon would open all the envelopes and take them to the independent judge. The judge would then once again try to match the session to the correct location.

In this case, the remote viewers in the PEAR experiment did the viewing before the targets were even given to the beacon. They had to leap ahead in time and view the target that would be chosen randomly, describe the correct target that had not yet been chosen, and hand over their sessions to the judge. The judge would not get the target pool until hours after the viewing session. The viewers, judge, and beacon were held incommunicado during the length of the experiment to ensure no one leaked information.

It had made no difference. The remote viewers still described the correct target with the same accuracy as the regular viewing experiment. Even more eerie experiments were tried to fool the remote viewers. In one instance, the beacon decided spontaneously to shelve the target pool and instead chose a location that only he was familiar with. He added the location to the pool targets and gave them to the judge. Once again, it made no difference. The viewers still described the target well enough that the judge chose the correct target. The experimenters even tried having the beacon not even choose a target. He simply gave the target pool to the judge. The judge could not match the viewer's session to any of the pool targets. That's because they found that the remote viewers had described the location where the beacon was when he was supposed to choose a target.[28]

When I did the double beacon in Dave's class, it was a very strange experience. We don't really have words to adequately describe the sensation of being in two places at the same time. Yet here I was trying to come to grips with not only being in two places at once, but also being in myself in two places at once.

One of me was outside, a passive observer watching someone. That other someone was myself as well, the person I was watching, the active participant.

I realized that the active participant me was dressed in combat fatigues and equipment. I watched my doppelganger look through a night-vision thermal imager, even as I looked through that very same imager. It was as if I was a silent partner to myself, an alter ego with no control over this other self.

We were on the side of some outcroppings of rock overlooking a flat sandy plain. In the distance below us there was a two-lane road that was slightly elevated by a dirt and rock berm. I had been looking through the viewer at the road. The road led off into the distance to the right, and to the left my view was cut off by the rock outcropping. It was still dark but there were no sign of city lights on the horizon. The vista of stars across the sky was breathtaking.

At any other time I would have been thrilled at the sight. Now the only thing that rang through my mind as I looked around wondering was, "What's going on? Where am I? Is this a dream?" Yet that other part of me I watched knew exactly why we were there. The voice crackling through the earpiece He/I wore made that evident a moment later.

"Charlie six one, six five." Six five was one of my men at an observation post located on the lower portion of the south end of the rock outcropping. How I knew, I didn't know. But I knew.

"Six five, six one." He/I replied, whispering into the mike jutting down from the helmet.

"We've got movement from the south. Single APC. Possible recon," came the clipped reply. I knew something was going to go down; we weren't expecting any incursions tonight. I shook my head. How did I know that?

"Roger, stand by." I watched myself turn to the right, kneeling on the rock with my right knee to help stabilize the heavy thermal imaging device.

It was so strange being in two places at once. The memory of the Master class when we had the dual beacon target – two people simultaneously viewed who were half a world apart – tugged at my mind. It was the only handhold I had in this netherworld.

There was no question that this other person was me. I knew it was me. My outside observer could see the other me clearly. It was me, and yet it wasn't me. I was looking through this me's eyes, but I was separate from that me, another passive observer watching through my own eyes. It was very disorienting. Even as I wrote these words two and a half years later, it made me dizzy just thinking about it.

Looking through the thermal imager, it was easy to see that the oncoming enemy armored personnel carrier was not expecting any of our forces this far south. They had their blackout lights on and were lit up in the night-sight.

"Charlie five one, six one, weapons free. When you have a clear shot, take him," I felt myself say. My doppelganger said it with a certain fierce anticipation. I knew it was to be our first live combat. This was unreal. I waited in vain for the nightmare to end.

It didn't. And it was going to get worse.

Much worse.

Charlie five one was the main battle tank assigned to this recon unit. It was located behind me to my left. Charlie five two was an armored personnel carrier that had been converted to an anti-aircraft vehicle. It mounted a 20mm Gatling gun capable of firing over 1500 rounds a minute against ground targets and 4000 rounds a minute against aircraft.

That's a staggering 66 rounds a second of high explosive and armor-piercing shells the size of a large man's thumb; nearly a solid stream of death that could carve a plane or light armored vehicle to pieces in the blink of an eye.

The Gatling gun was the closest weapon the military had to a death ray. It was located just below me. Both vehicles were sited to provide the maximum amount of coverage of the road and the adjacent area.

"On the way!" crackled in the earpiece and simultaneously there was a sharp BOOM as the tank's main gun roared. I watched the tracer lance out at over a mile a second.

Because of the range, the tank commander had decided to use a sabot round instead of a high-explosive round normally used against such a lightly armored vehicle. These are depleted uranium penetrators that would slice through the thinly armored sides of the enemy vehicle like a hot knife through butter.

Only it missed.

Somehow the enemy had either sensed our presence, or was lucky, but they had pulled off the road just as the tank fired and were headed directly towards our position. The sabot round had struck just in front of the vehicle and had skipped off into the desert.

I heard my other self swear under his breath as the radio announced, "They're under our arc!" in an excited voice.

The enemy APC had executed the primary tactic against an ambush, close with the enemy. They had managed to get under the tank's ability to bring the main gun to bear.

I heard myself say over the com-link, "Clear the Gatling. I've got control." The night vision device my double had was a thermal imager. It was also slaved to the Gatling's gun director. My other self quickly flipped open the safety cover and flicked off the safety. He then switched views from the observation view to the fire control sight.

I watched through his eyes as he placed the gun sight reticle over the rapidly approaching vehicle and squeezed the trigger on the side of the sight housing.

There was a sound like canvas being torn or a long drawn-out burp that lasted about three seconds. And in that three seconds the enemy armored vehicle found death.

The concentrated stream of high explosive and armor piercing rounds literally tore the vehicle apart, carving great tears and rents in the lightly armored sides. It slewed to the left and nearly overturned, the hulk coming to rest at an angle. As I watched, streamers of smoke burst from the holes and I could see fire begin to brew up inside. There were sharp reports punctuating the night as ammunition inside the vehicle began to cook off.

I thought that no one could have survived such an onslaught. It had been totally overwhelming. But I was wrong, a moment later a hatch opened and a single soldier attempted to crawl out of the burning wreck.

Part of me wanted to scream. Part of me smiled viciously as I watched myself place the sight on the soldier. Part of me cried, "Oh my God!" while the other me sneered, "Adios." Then we pulled the trigger.

As a former police officer, I have witnessed death in many forms. I had seen it all, from the young female immigrant that met a violent end at the hands of an axe-murderer, to the lonely, quiet passing of a transient from exposure.

Death and cops go together like ham and eggs. It's just a part of the job, although some never really get used to it. I recalled myself as a young rookie officer rolling on my first homicide. It was in a housing project in the middle of winter at two o'clock in the morning. There were two inches of snow on the ground and the temperature was below freezing.

As we drove up on the scene, there were several squads that had arrived before us. A number of officers were standing around what appeared to be a body in the middle of the road. Our headlights illuminated the body, which had long blond hair.

I felt my throat tightening as we parked and got out of the squad car, silently imploring, please God, don't let my first homicide be a woman or a child. It was apparent as we approached the crime scene though, that the victim was a white male in his twenties. He had three bullet wounds to the chest that we found out later were made by a .357 magnum.

The body had melted into the thin veneer of ice on the road. The tragedy prompted the usual defense mechanism for the veteran officers who had seen scenes like this far too many times. They made jokes about it. As a rookie, I was shocked, but later began to see the justification. If you're laughing, then you're not crying. Comments like, "Well, we won't have to draw a line around the body, because his outline will obviously outlive him," and "I've got my pedestrian violation for the week," served to help survive that kind of outrage.

I was no stranger to death. But of the myriad ways I have seen the demise of a human being, I have never witnessed what I saw when my doppelganger pulled the trigger.

The burst of cannon rounds literally disintegrated the soldier. In the view from the thermal imager, which added a muted false color component, his body suddenly disappeared in a blossom of crimson.

I gagged at the sight, then blinked in confusion. Disoriented, it took me a moment to realize I was no longer in the desert. No rocks, no sand, no death. I was back in the house, the familiar walls around me again. The transition happened so quickly that it was as if I had never been there. But it had happened; it must have happened.

I was sitting up and I noticed Stan was no longer asleep. He was looking at me strangely. At first, the sudden transition left me so nonplussed that my mouth just hung open. Stan asked in a concerned voice, "What's wrong? What happened?"

I blinked a couple of times to pull myself together, my face pale. "You're not going to believe it," I said in a shocked voice. I related to Stan what I had just experienced. He sat there in rapt attention, a stunned expression on his broad face.

"I tell you, Stan, that was no dream. Everything was as real as this room, the night sounds, the cool breeze, even the sounds of the insects." There was a hint of desperation in my voice. I was still affected by the experience and my voice shook.

"There were no inconsistencies like you have in a dream. You know what I mean, in a dream there's always something out of logical order, something that doesn't fit. But this ... there wasn't anything out of place! It was as real as the two of us sitting here."

"Except you're not a soldier," Stan replied.

"Yeah, never have been in the military either. Closest thing was working with some of the SEAL's from SEAL Teams One and Three during the Trojan Warrior II program," I reflected, distractedly rubbing my knee. For some reason it was bothering me, as if I had been kneeling too long on something hard.

Something hard? The realization hit me with a shock.

"Oh crap!" I exclaimed, pulling off the blanket and rolling up the leg of my sweatpants.

Startled, Stan asked in alarm, "What's wrong?"

Looking down at my knee, I could see that the skin was reddened. That wasn't all. There were indentations in the skin, as if I had been kneeling against something hard. Like a rock.

I looked up at Stan, my face ashen, "I was kneeling on the rocks on this knee. Look at the skin."

"Jesus!" Stan exclaimed, staring wide eyed at my knee. The two of us stared at each other in silence.

"I think I just had my first Vision," I said to Stan in a shaking voice. "Only, I don't believe in Visions. Damn, this shouldn't have happened to me. I don't have things like this happen. And I never wanted this to happen, either!" I said frantically.

"Wow, you need to talk to Dave tomorrow. He should hear this," Stan stated flatly.

I nodded reluctantly, still shocked over the event, "Yeah, I definitely need to talk to him about this. This is going to be a problem."

When I had read Dave's book I found the sections about remote viewing utterly fascinating. However, the more eclectic parts where Dave described his Visions were just too far outside my comfort zone. Not that I didn't believe him, but his experiences were his, not mine. I had no frame of reference for his experiences, and frankly hadn't wanted any. I wasn't a natural psychic like Mel or Lyn. And I hadn't been shot in the head like Dave.

So I preferred to simply put aside those sections of the book. That was easier for me to deal with. Remote viewing itself was barely within my comfort zone. Only because it had been developed by the second largest think tank in the US, by two renowned laser physicists, was I able to deal with it. I had done remote viewing; I knew it worked. But, visions? Visions were something else altogether.

Visions were out in the area where the signpost up ahead said you are now entering the Twilight Zone. Where ancient mariners' maps had the legend, "Here there be Monsters!"

I looked at Stan, my eyes imploring, "I don't have Visions. I don't believe in Visions."

"Well, it sure sounds like one to me," Stan said, shaking his head emphatically. I didn't know, and wasn't sure I wanted to. It would have to wait till morning. The two of us turned in. I lay there in the darkness wondering what had happened to me. That had not, repeat not, been fun. The chilling possibility occurred to me that if it had happened once, what would keep it from happening again? The darkness around me seemed foreboding, sinister.

I would find out that my night was going to get much, much longer.

Chapter Fourteen

The Vision

The most beautiful experience we can have is the mysterious. It is the fundamental emotion that stands at the cradle of true art and true science. Whoever does not know it and can no longer wonder, no longer marvel, is as good as dead, and his eyes are dimmed.

—Albert Einstein, *The World As I See It* (1949)

I drifted into awareness slowly, like the opposite of falling asleep at the wheel of a car on a long trip. I was surrounded by the twilight world of the Matrix. The mists of purple, magenta, gray, and black, swirled around me, back-lit by an occasional flash of light, like heat lightning on a summer evening.

It took me a moment to collect my wits. I wondered: was I dreaming? What was going on? There was nothing else to see. It wasn't Sanctuary, as my customary protective circle of light was missing. I seemed to be standing alone in the emptiness of the Matrix.

Not again, I thought. This, once again, wasn't a dream. I was lucid, and too aware of my surroundings. It was more like an ERV session.

Except, I wasn't doing a session. I was supposed to be asleep after a very long day.

I looked around, wondering, what now?

"It's all about choices. It is your greatest gift. You have the privilege of choice, I don't."

The voice echoed around me. It was female, but not feminine. There was a hard strength in that voice; a voice of power and contained violence.

"What do you want?" I called out. I couldn't believe this, twice in one night. I shook my head in disbelief.

"David was right. I don't want to be a memorial," the voice became softer, sadder. "But unlike you, I had no choice. From the moment of my birth, I have had … no choice. I was born in a time of great conflict and great evil. I was born a warrior."

"Who are you?" I asked, but I thought I already knew who, or what, it was.

"I am the totality of all who served aboard me; all the hopes and fears, the dreams and nightmares, the camaraderie and shared experiences of those who built me and served on board. I am all of the very best that those young men represent."

The voice became harder, quivering with emotion. "But I am an abomination. I am a creature of War. I was born to kill, to destroy. I know nothing else. I cannot be converted to something not of War."

The voice was thick with emotion, almost sobbing. "You can't possibly understand what it's like to know that you are an abomination, that your only purpose in life was to take life, to destroy life. I am everything that those young men who served aboard me hated about those they faced on the battlefield. They were willing to sacrifice everything to end that evil. Some of them died aboard me."

I was speechless. I knew now that this wasn't a dream. But why would she (and I couldn't think of the voice in any other terms), come to me? There wasn't anything I could do to help.

My hand went to my forehead. This was too much, too soon.

The voice continued, now quieter, "I wanted nothing more than to end my days as so many of us did, at the scrapyard or the bottom of the ocean that had been my only home. I was no longer needed and no longer wanted to live as a symbol of war. No one wants to live as an abomination. I only want to move on to the next plane of existence, to start anew. But I can't. I am trapped here so long as this ship exists. I cannot walk away. I have no choice."

I didn't know what to say. I started to ask why she was talking to *me*, when the Voice interrupted. "I am not alone here," the Voice murmured softly. "The members of the crew who have passed on are here with me. Rather than abandon me to my fate, they made the choice to join me, so that I would not be here alone. We are all trapped here. So now you see why the surviving members of the crew want me taken out to sea. To go home."

I was shocked at the sublime tragedy of her situation. The ship was being lovingly restored to a place of honor, yet all she wished for was dissolution. And her shipmates who had passed on, courageously and knowing full well the consequences, made the decision to deny themselves their destiny and return to this purgatory so that she would not be alone. There they would remain, trapped, until the memorial was razed.

The Voice returned, "You have the gift of making a choice. Remember that." Echoing, the voice faded and was gone.

I opened my mouth to tell her to wait but it was too late. The familiar surroundings of Stan's study had instantaneously returned around me, replacing the fog of the Matrix. I could hear the sounds of water running. Stan was probably in the shower.

Glancing across the room, I could see light coming through the picture window. The clock on the desk confirmed it moments later as the alarm went off. I was shocked to discover that it was time to get ready for class. It had seemed like I had just put my head down on the pillow.

I tried to imagine being trapped forever in an iron tomb, the crewmen voluntarily abandoning their destinies to be trapped there too.

I heard Stan walk out of the bathroom. I quickly got up and brushed past him. As I entered the bathroom, I heard him call out to me, "John, are you okay?"

I managed to croak out an affirmative. "I'll tell you when I'm finished taking a shower."

As the warm water coursed down my body, I replayed the experience of moments before. The irony and sublime tragedy had deeply affected me. Later, I would discover that those raw emotions weren't entirely my own. Some of them were echoes of the anguish expressed by the Voice.

After the waves of sensation had subsided, I left the shower and walked out of the bathroom. I found Stan waiting for me.

"Are you okay?" he asked again, the concern evident on his face.

"No, not really. It happened again. Another Vision," I sat down, utterly drained.

"Jesus, what happened this time?"

I looked up at him, my eyes red and swollen. Stan stood there listening intently until I finished. He shook his head in disbelief.

Every rational part of me wanted to disbelieve, too. "It sounded like the spirit of the North Carolina, I think," I said cautiously.

"Maybe the North Carolina is your guardian angel," Stan said brightly, trying a bit of humor to calm me down.

A forty-five-thousand-ton guardian angel?

"There's no sense in trying to figure out what happened right now. We should head for class. At least there you can talk to Dave," Stan offered sagely.

He was right. There were no answers right now. Once again I had found myself in a situation that I had no experience with. There were no safety belts or parachutes here. My greatest resource was the man I had shared the adventures of the past three years with: my teacher, my friend.

When we arrived, I looked for Dave, but everyone was so busy getting ready for the class that I knew I'd have to wait for a break. It was typical for his classes. The mornings were busy with getting the room set up, the handouts ready and the music selection confirmed.

Dave and Patty were already busy at their computer consoles, printing out hard copies of the previous targets and editing new handouts for the class. I decided to help Jason and Rommel with the computerized multimedia equipment. What I had to talk to Dave about could wait.

Not that I really had a choice. Patty had just handed me a stack of handouts. I immersed myself in the daily chores; it helped take my mind off the previous night's trauma.

I was able to corner Dave though, while the class was doing a session later that morning. "Dave, have you got a moment?"

I had caught him at the door. "Sure John. Just let me go to the bathroom. It's the first chance I've had all morning." He stared at me for a moment, and then asked, "What's up?"

He was looking at my hands; I looked down, surprised that I was wringing them. Embarrassed, I shoved them in my pockets. "Um, something happened last night. Something that goes way beyond anything I've ever experienced."

I tried to make light of what I was feelings. "And considering what I've experienced in your classes, that's saying something. I need to talk to you about it, if you have the time."

Dave pursed his lips, "I'll tell you what. Things are going to be hectic until lunch. You and I can break away then and grab a bite to eat. That way you'll have my undivided attention. Well, almost undivided. A sandwich is sounding pretty good right about now. You may have to share my attention," he teased lightheartedly.

"Thanks Dave, I really appreciate it," I said with obvious relief.

"No problem." He abruptly turned and was gone through the door.

I immediately felt better. Dave had been there, had gone through this sort of thing. His experiences would put what happened to me in perspective. And right now, perspective was something I desperately needed.

The morning went quickly. Once the students were released for lunch, Dave and I drove to a nearby deli. Once we had ordered and picked up our food, we sat down at an outdoor table and started to eat.

Dave said casually, "Okay, so why don't you tell me what happened last night."

I finished swallowing and, taking a deep breath to calm my thoughts, began to recount the previous night's incidents. As I talked, Dave sat staring into the distance, calmly chewing his food. He didn't say anything; he just let me talk. He didn't look at me.

For some reason, that made it easier to talk, the words spilling from my lips. Surprisingly, I managed to get through the account of the slaughter of the enemy soldier without choking up.

"Dave, I didn't have to. But I did. That other me squeezed the trigger and burned that guy." I shuddered with the memory. "I've seen death in so many ways when I was a cop. But I've never seen anyone shredded like that. It was obscene. That's the only word I can use to describe it. And that person who pulled that trigger was me. I know it as sure as we're sitting here.

"That's the scary part. It was so real. You know how dreams are. And I swear, last night wasn't a dream. The whole experience was like the one you described in your book. The only thing is, I don't have visions. You know my history. I've never had an experience like that in my life. I believed your experiences. But that type of thing was for someone like you, not me. I've never been shot in the head." I stopped, partly out of breath, and partly because I wanted to see what Dave would say.

For several moments, he didn't respond. He sat there eating quietly. Then he wiped his lips with a napkin and turned to me. "That wasn't you, John. At least not the John we both know. The other one was maybe from some other time, some other place.

You had a choice. That's why you're here with me now, instead of some battlefield. I think I've gotten to know you pretty well over the past few years. And I can tell you; you wouldn't have pulled the trigger. Not in this time, this place."

I thought for a moment about that. Would I have pulled the trigger in this time? I would think about it for the rest of the class.

"Dave, what was the voice? Was it like Stan said, an angel in the guise of the ship? Or was it some spirit or trickster?"

"It wasn't the ship itself, rather the essence of all those who served aboard. Also, that first sequence was probably generated by your unconscious. For reasons only it knows, it was using this as a way to get your attention. It's like when you temporarily lost your remote viewing ability; it was your subconscious trying to tell you something. The Matrix was sending you a message. You'll have to figure out what it all means."

"Well, it definitely got my attention, that's for sure," I said with feeling.

We finished eating and got back in the van for the short trip to the classroom. As we parked I remarked to Dave, "Quite a watershed, this class. 1000 hours, a vision, and finally getting what you've been saying for the past three years."

"Yeah, makes you wonder what's next, doesn't it."

Evidently I wasn't the only one who had been 'blessed' with a vision. Several members of the class had similar experiences, although none quite so dramatic. Dave brought it up when the class was assembled.

"It seems several in the class have experienced epiphanies or other strange happenings over the past week. John had a particularly powerful one last night. If your classmates are willing to talk about their experiences, those of you who are interested should see them during the breaks. You might benefit from it."

During one of the breaks I was sitting in the classroom doing some typing. Ariane came over and sat next to me.

"Hi John. I'd like to hear about your experience last night. But only if you want to."

I thought, the last thing I want is to look like a fool, but I couldn't say no to her.

She sat there, quietly listening to me recount the experience. I had hoped not to look foolish but the memory was still strong and I found myself having to pause to keep control. Ariane said nothing. She reached out to squeeze my arm in sympathy. I let the emotion of the moment pass, and then finished my account.

"Ariane, it was so real. Just like we're sitting here, everything vibrant. Nothing was out of place or out of sync like a dream. During the first part of the Vision, I could feel the wind against my cheeks and hear the sounds of insects. The smell of sand and rock, and then, when the guns went off, the reek of gunpowder. I saw that soldier disintegrate in the gunsite. It was so real it turned my stomach."

Then I confessed, "You know, to tell the truth, I've been thinking about the Vision, and about how a part of me wants to dismiss it as a dream. I mean, this kind of stuff isn't me. At least wasn't me."

Ariane looked at me intently, "Don't say that. You received a wonderful gift; don't destroy it over your own prejudices," she implored.

I shook my head, "I know. I should feel privileged. But last night wasn't fun. It was terrifying watching me blast that soldier. It makes me wonder who I really am."

Ariane took my hand and said softly, "That isn't you. I've come to know you. You're kind and compassionate. Accept what happened in the spirit in which it was given, like Dave said, and learn what it is that the Matrix is trying to tell you."

I looked into those calm dark eyes and felt the tension slip away. "Thanks Ariane, again. You seem to have a knack for being there when I need you. Don't worry. I'll take yours and Dave's advice. Every time I start to think this was just a dream, I keep coming back to the one sure thing that makes me know it wasn't."

Ariane cocked her head to one side, the question unsaid.

I looked at her. "I have never used the word abomination ... ever. It's not a word that I would ever choose to use in a sentence. To have chosen that particular word, besides everything else that happened, tells me it couldn't have been a dream."

She nodded, "I don't think it was a dream either."

CHAPTER FIFTEEN

Schrödinger's Cat

Where did we get that Equation from? Nowhere. It is not possible to derive it from anything you know. It came out of the mind of Schrödinger.
                                         –Physicist Richard Feynman

I spent the rest of the day talking to a number of the class who were curious about what had happened. It wasn't easy. I got emotional relating the more dramatic parts of the Vision. The intensity didn't fade, as it would have with a dream. Years later, when writing the account of what happened that night, I had to stop for a moment. The emotions from that experience came flooding back, surprising me with their intensity.

The remainder of the week I was apprehensive over what might transpire while I was sleeping, but the nights proved to be uneventful. I woke up feeling refreshed. The rest of the class passed without incident. No visions, no trauma-drama. I was glad; I wasn't sure I could handle any more.

The end of the week was a familiar echo of other classes. Saying good-by to all my friends was as sad and poignant as always. When we had loaded up all of the equipment in the van and trailer, and after my classmates had left, Dave turned to me, "Hey, why don't you come over to the house. Patty, Ariane, and the rest of the women are going to make dinner for us."

"Sounds good to me. I'm starved!" I replied enthusiastically. We formed a convoy for the trip back to the house.

Dave and Patty's house sits on a hill in a nice subdivision near the small town of Carlsbad. It is a beautiful home with a view of the ocean in the distance from the second floor.

While Patty and the others bustled about getting dinner ready, Dave and I sat in the living room with glasses of red wine. Once we were comfortable, Dave turned to me and asked, "Tell me more about Quantum Mechanics and how it relates to my lecture."

Whenever I came to one of his classes to help, once we had the time, the two of us would sit down and discuss questions of math or science that he had. If I didn't know the answer, I would research it for a later time.

"Okay, you remember what we talked about last time, Schrödinger's wave equation and the uncertainty principle. It turns out that there are several interpretations of exactly what the equations are telling us about reality. Remember, scientists still argue over what the equations are telling us. So keep in mind I'm only an undergrad on all this."

Dave smiled and nodded. I took a deep breath and started, "These different interpretations arise from a fundamental schism in science. On one hand you have the realists, who believe in a concrete physical reality separate from the observer who perceives it; and on the other, you have the idealists, who believe that reality is an illusion of sense data such that you can't remove the observer from the nature of reality. The realists look at the world though classical physical theories of Newton and Einstein. The idealists look with the eyes of Schrödinger and Heisenberg's quantum theory.

$$\frac{\partial \psi}{\partial t} = -\frac{+2\pi i}{h} E\psi$$

Schrödinger's wave equation. Notice the plus and minus signs that show this equation as a symmetry.

"The first interpretation that probably most scientists ascribe to is called the Copenhagen Interpretation. It's called that because of physicist Niels Bohr and a number of others who worked on it, mainly in Copenhagen in the 1920's. It says that an unobserved system evolves deterministically according to the Schrödinger wave equation. When the moment of observation occurs, the system evolves in a random fashion instantaneously to an outcome that has a probability given by Born statistics. The 'collapse of the wave function' was the description given for the process. It was Bohr's way of saying that the equations of quantum mechanics were not a realistic picture of the world. The indefinite world of quantum mechanics was fine for the subatomic realm but the world around us had a classical realism."

"I remember from the last time you were here with the Yellow Book," Dave remarked.

"Well, it turns out that there are some problems with this understanding. First, the collapse happens instantaneously over an extended distance in apparent violation of relativity."

"Non-locality," Dave chimed in.

"Yes. Second, the observer is given special status; he causes the collapse by the act of observation, even though he has no idea what the actual mechanism of the collapse is. Most scientists are uncomfortable with that explanation. It seemed too arbitrary. Schrödinger's equation essentially describes a symmetry between energy and momentum, and space and time. Schrödinger himself said in a lecture that his equation describes different histories of a particle and all of these histories really happen, not just a single history as Bohr would have physicists believe.[29]

"In 1957, a graduate student working on his thesis under physicist Dr. John Wheeler came up with something better than the Bohr explanation. Hugh Everett III looked at the equations as Schrödinger had. His explanation of quantum theory did away with many of the problems of the Copenhagen interpretation, but the implications of his work were astounding."

"What was his theory called?" Dave asked.

I took a quick swallow of wine to moisten my mouth. "He called it 'The Relative State Formulation of Quantum Mechanics' or the 'Theory of the Universal Wavefunction.' Everett said that when two systems interacted they became correlated."[30]

"Like quantum entanglement?"

"Yes, exactly. When these systems become entangled, the products of that interaction become a superposition of relative states. Each of these states is a separate system evolving distinctly and in isolation from the others. And each of these elements that evolve must be considered in their own right, relative to the others. There is no special single outcome. Just as Schrödinger said."

Dave took a moment to digest what I had said. I knew he was familiar with the old idea of the collapse of the wave function. Now we were leaving that concept behind and replacing it with an idea that was almost heresy. I saw the light dance in his eyes as he looked at me over his wineglass, the implications dawning.

"You're saying that there isn't just one outcome to a measurement. You're saying that all of the outcomes from a measurement are real."

I nodded.

"But how is that possible, unless ...." He looked confused for a moment. I didn't blame him. It was the same way in my college course. Quantum mechanics is counter-intuitive; things happen in the quantum world that defy everyday understanding or logic.

"Multiple universes!" he said with a grin. "That's it, isn't it? It has to be." Then the full ramifications hit. "But are these real universes?"

"Yes, according to his view, although parallel and multiple universes appear in our classical theories even without Everett's formulation. Remember what Everett said. You have to look at each product in relation to the others. There is no special state. Like Relativity, which has no special frame of reference either, all frames are equally valid in relation to each other. It's the same with the products of the superposition. Everett said each is just as real as the others. So there is a universe where you never became a remote viewer; where you became a General; where you were born a girl instead of a boy. Every time an observation of an irreversible process occurs, the observer splits according to the wave function into all possible outcomes, each with its own universe and lifeline."

"But which one is really me?" he asked. I didn't answer. I didn't have to.

"They're all me, right?" I nodded. "Yes, remember, they are relative to each other. There is no sense in choosing any one universe over the other in his formulation."

"Where are these other Everett universes?"

I waved my arm across the room, "They're all right here."

Dave looked puzzled, "How is that possible?"

"It's possible because these different universes are exclusive. When an observation is made, the observer splits into as many observers as necessary to cover all the bases, so to speak. In addition, the wave equation is linear and the operators in the calculation are commutative. Therefore, no communication is possible between these worlds."This formulation does have some difficult technical issues. Specifically, Everett's formulation is Lorentz invariant, meaning all signals must obey special relativity. No signals faster than light. That precludes non-locality, which John S. Bell showed was intrinsic to quantum theory. The Universe is and must be connected on a very fundamental level. Particles with entangled states can instantaneously affect each other light years apart in apparent violation of special relativity."[31]

"Can entanglement be used for communication," Dave asked?

"No. Entanglement exchanges correlations between particles. Mathematician John von Neumann proved that this exchange of correlations could not be used to send messages faster than light."

I took another sip of wine then continued, "Einstein is known for saying "God does not play dice," because he was greatly disturbed by the probabilistic nature of quantum mechanics. He always thought it was an incomplete theory. But his greatest objection to QM was non-locality. It was this objection, the "spooky action at a distance", that led John Bell to his result that non-locality is the truth of our Universe.[32]

"So that brings us to decoherence which combines the best of Everett's theory with non-locality. All of the possible observers covering every observation de-cohere to a single observer with a consistent history. And because this is happening at every moment we actually exist in a fuzzy state of many very close histories that we see as a single existence. The other possibilities fade from existence in less than a millionth of a millionth of a millionth of a millionth of a second. The existence that we experience must be consistent with the past. That precludes the possibility of reality suddenly changing to a completely different reality with no relation to the past."

"Now what does this have to do with remote viewing?"

"Hey you two! Dinner's ready. Quit your blabbing and get something to eat," Randy yelled from the kitchen. We grinned at each other. When we discussed this arcane stuff we tended to tune out the rest of the world.

We went into the kitchen. Grabbing plates and utensils, we helped ourselves. The variety of food was excellent, with mouth-watering choices. The kitchen was alive with laughter and conversation; the warmth of our emotions filled the room. Once Dave and I had loaded our plates, we went back into the living room to continue our discussion.

"Hey, where are you two going?" Patty called out to her husband.

"John and I are discussing concepts in Quantum Mechanics," Dave replied with a smile.

Immediately Randy interjected, "Hey, you two can tinker with the quantum later! Your food will get cold and it is so good you won't want that to happen. The women worked really hard on this crap so get eating and forget the blabbing!"Dave shot back, "We're going to eat the crap! We just want some stimulating conversation to go with it."

Patty slowly shook her head in resignation, "We worked so hard and they're calling it crap."

Dave finished the colloquy grinning at his wife, "Yeah, but its really good crap."

I was laughing so hard I spilled some of my wine.

Back in the living room I continued where we'd left off.

"Remote viewing is probably quantum in nature. We know from experiments conducted with Ingo Swann that remote viewing also appears to violate special relativity. Remember his viewing of Jupiter's rings before they were discovered six months later? Swann was on target within minutes. Jupiter is half a billion miles away. Light takes three-quarters of an hour to get there from here."[33]

Dave pondered that for a moment before he replied, "So you think quantum entanglement may be at the heart of remote viewing?"

I sat back in my chair, "Yes, I believe so. More and more, the latest experiments and observations are finding that quantum effects are not confined to the subatomic world but are actually being found at increasing levels of complexity. They may in fact operate in our everyday life. They have already confirmed quantum transitions during electron transport in plants during photosynthesis.

"I ascribe to two quantum physical theories we have of consciousness which has been put forward by famed physicist Dr. Roger Penrose and anesthesiologist and consciousness researcher Dr. Stuart Hameroff called "Orchestrated Objective Reduction" or Orch-OR, and the Theory of Holonomic Brain Function by Dr. Karl Pribram and Dr. David Bohm.[34]

"Penrose and Hameroff believe consciousness derives from fine scale quantum processes located in the microtubules within brain cells. It's very controversial but I like Penrose's math," I said smiling. "Of course, we don't know for certain if remote viewing is quantum in nature. We know remote viewing is not affected by distance or shielding, like electromagnetic energy. Also, remote viewing is not constrained by time. All of these issues point toward a quantum connection. I also believe that holography and interference is evolved. Some physicists, notably Gerard t'Hooft, believe the multiverse is actually a four-dimensional space-time, holographed onto a two-dimensional membrane.[35] Kind of like the depiction of the Matrix in the popular movie of the same name. Our existence, which appears to inhabit three dimensions, would actually be an illusion brought about by interference effects. Remember that a hologram can be broken apart but that won't destroy the information on it. Each separate piece of the hologram contains the total amount of information of the whole. Perhaps consciousness can access this master hologram and decode the information contained within. Pribram and Bolm's Theory of Holonomic Brain Function is similar to Orch-OR in that it has to do with quantum transitions in the brain. However, instead of these transitions happening in the microtubules, they happen at the synapses where the ion clouds of neurotransmitters holds sway. The ion clouds of all the synapses in the brain form a superposition until it collapses into a decision.[36]

I believe that both theories are correct and it is these interactions that form holograms in the brain. This hologram interaction with the Universal Wave Function is what gives us psi effects. It would mean that Ingo Swann's depiction of the Matrix is correct. The Matrix is a hologram of the totality of the Universe, which interacts with the holograms in the brain by those two theories. It would explain why psi is such a weak phenomenon and why it appears to act faster than light. It's weak because we only have an interaction of interference effects not a direct connection with the Universal Wave Function. And it only appears to be faster than light because of the interaction. The data is always there in the hologram, there is no FTL signal. Once you remove the apparent FTL signal transmission, you now are within the restrictions of Relativity and are Lorentz invariant. "One last observation," I added. "Remember the Delta function in your lecture? How only the moment matters. The seas of possibilities extend not only into the future but also into the past. The Universe has no definite past or future. Quantum mechanics states that the past and the future are indefinite, linked by the superpositions in the Universal Wave Function interference effects. Fits pretty well to your lecture, doesn't it?" I finished.

Dave sat there contemplating our conversation, then he turned to look at his wife in the kitchen. He turned back to me and said, "Come on. You only have a little bit more time with us before you have to leave. Let's spend it with our friends." I agreed and we returned to the warmth of the kitchen and our friends.

After dinner, we all sat in the living room and talked, enjoying the time we had left together. As I sat there, the conversation with Dave about quantum mechanics and parallel universes ran through my mind. Parallel universes. What if the first part of my Vision had been in an alternate reality? Could remote viewing penetrate the dimensionalities of the configuration space where that alternate self was located? If it could, then that would explain how I had seen an alternate self in a reality separate from my own and why it had appeared so real. Then it wouldn't have been a dream after all, as I had said. If that was true, then Dave's assertion that I would not have pulled the trigger in this time, in this reality might be true. Nevertheless, I had to wonder, was I really the same person as the person in my Vision? Did I have the same hate, anger, and indifference to death as my doppelganger?

I thought about Dave and Ariane's assertion. I thought about my own doubts. Would I have squeezed the trigger?

It came to me at that moment. I had my answer. It lay in a twenty-five year-old memory from my days as a rookie police officer.

I was working a solo squad on the night shift. I had only two years on the job at the time. Since I wasn't assigned to a particular car, I did what we call war-horsing, bouncing from assignment to assignment. It allowed me to get more involved with our district. It also seemed more exciting, with a new part of the district to explore every night. That night I got all the excitement I ever wanted. Like the saying goes, "Be careful what you wish for..."

I was taking a tour of one of the many strip malls in our district. This one was adjacent to a polo field that was owned by the equestrian center.

As I drove through the parking lot, I noticed a woman in one of the shops with her hands raised in the air. I had slowed the squad car to see what was going on when two men in green hooded army jackets burst from the doorway to the shop. One pointed to my marked squad car and they both fled in the direction of the polo field.

I grabbed the microphone for my radio and yelled, "Squad 44 has a robbery in progress at the strip mall in the 4400 block of Good Hope Road!"

As the dispatcher acknowledged and called for assistance, I jammed on the accelerator to follow the robbers. Once they got to the field I would have to follow on foot. A four-foot earthen berm separated the mall from the field. It was far too steep for my squad-car to negotiate.

The two figures crested the berm just as I squealed to a halt in front. As I leapt from the car, I pulled my "handie-talkie" from its case and shouted into the mike, "I'm in foot pursuit through the polo field next to the mall. Two male suspects in army field jackets. They're headed for the projects at the south end of the field." I knew if they got there, I'd never find them in the maze of buildings.

Had it not been for two fortunate occurrences, they would have made it. A foot pursuit carrying twenty pounds of equipment and body armor is a short one. Unless you get to the perpetrators in the first fifty yards, they'll be gone like last year's lovers. These two were in jeans and go-fast shoes…sneakers.

But I had the advantage of driving that first fifty yards. Second, being not too long out of the Academy and running regularly, I was still in good shape. There was no veteran's donut-filled tire around my middle.

That advantage translated to my rapidly closing the gap between us. One of them took a quick glance behind and got a shock seeing me right behind and gaining fast. He yelled something to his partner and they split up, running on diverging courses toward the projects. One of them threw down what appeared to be the victim's purse.

Well, as Clint Eastwood did in the movie *Magnum Force* in a similar situation I thought, follow the money. I continued closing on the suspect that had thrown down the purse.

I drew my service revolver and, catching up, screamed "Freeze, police!"

Nine times out of ten that just makes them run faster, but that first fifty yards had burned this guy out. He stopped abruptly and whirled around. As he did so he thrust his hand into his jacket pocket.

My heart froze. I thought, Oh my God, I'm going to have to shoot him. Time seemed to slow down as I watched him start to pull something silver out of his pocket. The pulse roared in my ears as I screamed again to freeze or die.

At that time, I was a member of the intramural police shooting team and regularly shot on the range. At the range of twenty-one feet, I could put all six rounds in the space of a fist on target in the blink of an eye. This suspect was a lot closer.

I placed the illuminated sights of my Smith and Wesson Model 19 Combat Magnum over his chest and pulled the hammer back. The cock of the hammer in the cold air sounded like the crack of thunder in my ears.

In the space of a heartbeat I saw him continue to yank something silver out of his pocket. If I was going to beat him to the draw, it would have to be now.

The .38 caliber, 158 grain lead semi-wadcutters traveling 850 feet a second, would tear through the sternum and muscle of the suspect's chest wall. A fraction of a second later, slightly flattened and tumbling from striking bone, they would penetrate the pericardium, the sack containing the heart. The slugs would rip through the organ and lodge under the shoulder blade and spine. With a shocked expression on his face, he would slump to the ground with only seconds of life remaining before the loss of blood pressure and the lack of oxygen to his brain would kill him.

At least it would have happened that way had I pulled the trigger. To this day, I don't know why, but I didn't.

I watched him pull the silver object out and toss it to the ground. I looked uncomprehendingly at first, and then rage rose in my throat.

It was a can of beer. A lousy can of cheap beer. And for the first time I took a close look at the face staring wide-eyed at me from under the hood; the face of a teenager.

He couldn't have been more than thirteen years old.

I stepped up, raising the gun over my head to strike him, screaming, "You fool! You almost got shot! Why didn't you freeze like I told you?" I was so angry; I wanted to smash that young, foolish, ignorant face.

He quivered in fear and in a small boy's voice managed, "I didn't want to get caught with beer on me. My mom would kill me."

I brought the gun back down, barely in control, "You almost did die, you stupid ass!" I stood there, shaking in anger and fear. I seemed to tower over him even though he was actually only a few inches shorter than I was. I couldn't say anything more. Breathing heavily, as much from the near disaster as from the pursuit, I handcuffed the kid. My hands were shaking so badly that it took me several moments to get the cuffs on.

As I was struggling with that, I noticed headlights approaching from the entrance to the field. My backups had arrived.

Back at the station, I talked with the detective who interviewed the teenager. We both shook our heads. "Could you see the headlines in the paper tomorrow if I'd shot him?" I remarked to the detective.

"Oh yeah. Only too well. Cop shoots … no, executes unarmed teenager in deserted polo field. At night. It would have caused a riot. You would have been justified, but it wouldn't have mattered. It would have been just another case of police brutality to that community. The press would've had a field day and everyone would've wanted your blood.

"It's a funny thing though. He's not a bad kid. He's just hanging around the wrong crowd. The victim said he wasn't the one who robbed her. The other suspect did it and according to her, he jams the purse in our friend here's hand and yells run. So like a young dumb teenager, that's what he does. He doesn't have a juvie record and has got good grades in school according to his mom, who is on the way to pick him up. And from the sound of it, she's not too pleased," the detective finished, rubbing his chin in reflection. He looked at me and after glancing quickly around, turned back to me and asked in a low voice, "I'm curious. Why didn't you shoot him? Ninety-nine percent of the department would have fired in that instance and they would have been justified too. But you didn't. Why?"

I took a moment to put my thoughts together, "I almost did. When he whipped around and jammed his hand into his pocket I thought he was going for a gun. I was concentrating on his hands when he turned around so I didn't realize how young he was. I had cocked the hammer back so my service revolver was on single action. Just three pounds of pressure on the trigger and it would have fired. When I saw the flash of silver coming out I thought for sure this was it." Just thinking about the incident brought back the adrenaline rush and a quiver in my voice.

"I was wearing body armor but I wasn't about to let him have the first shot. I had no desire to play Russian roulette with the possibility of a shot striking someplace where the armor didn't cover," I stated flatly.

"OK, so why didn't you shoot?" the detective reiterated.

"I don't know." I shrugged my shoulders when I saw the look on the detective's face. I didn't know why. I should have fired. But I didn't.

The detective looked at me for a moment and then observed, "The only one luckier than you tonight is that young son-of-a-bitch! I wonder if he has any idea how close he came to stinking up the inside of a coffin?"

I would see that same teenager six months later, riding his bike with some friends in an alley. He was laughing and joking, playing with his buddies; young and without a care in the world. It had been so close. I don't think to this day that he had any real idea of how close he came to dying on that dark cold night, on a deserted polo field. And it proved the assertion that both Ariane and Dave had told me.

I wouldn't and didn't pull the trigger.

The memory also resolved another question that had been on my mind since Marty and I had discussed the 9-11 ARV session. I had put this question to Marty: Does a remote viewing session constitute a quantum mechanical observation? If so, then does what a remote viewer see in the future have to take place? By his observation, has he caused the superposition of possible outcomes to de-cohere or coalesce to a reality? If the answer was yes, then that reality must happen. My conviction had been that it was an observation. Marty had not agreed. Now I could see, after all of the recent work for Dave, that my ARV session that had seen the demise of the Twin Towers had not caused the superposition of possible outcomes to decohere to the monstrous event called 9/11, because all outcomes occur. I was simply in the universe where 9/11 occurred. That it happened in this reality was just a throw of the dice.

It also answered the question about Dave and Ariane's assertion and my doubts.

I looked down at my chronometer. It was time for me to leave. I had a two-hour drive back through traffic to L.A. and I had stayed as long as I could. I said good-by to everyone, secure in the knowledge that I'd see them again.

I saved saying good-by to Ariane for last. Embracing her, I said with feeling, "Thanks Ariane for everything. I'm so glad you were here this week. It made a huge difference for me." I thought about the fact that once again, she had been there for me. I hoped that one day I would be able to repay her thoughtfulness.

She gave me a quick kiss and replied shyly, "Have a safe trip home. We'll see each other again I'm sure."

Dave walked me out to the car. As he did so he turned to me and said quietly, "John, if there's anything I can ever do for you, just ask. You know I would do anything to help, if I can. You mean a lot to Patty and me." The simple but engagingly sincere offer and admission caught me off guard. Surprised but grateful I replied, "Thanks Dave, I appreciate the offer." I looked at that open and honest face I had come to know so well over the past three years. I thought to myself that this had been an amazing week, an amazing three years. As I opened the door to my car I turned and looked back at him, silhouetted in the moonlight. "One hell of a ride!" He nodded, a crooked smile creeping across his features, "One hell of a ride."

He had been right all along.

CHAPTER SIXTEEN

Explorer's Class

Never doubt that a small group of thoughtful committed citizens can
change the world. Indeed, it is the only thing that ever has.

—Margaret Mead

"All passengers please fasten your seat belts. We are starting our descent into San Francisco International. The
temperature is 63 degrees with an overcast sky. And we
thank you on behalf of the crew for flying Jet Blue."

It was the spring of 2003 and I was flying into San Francisco to
meet Dave and Patty. A month earlier I had gotten an invitation
from them to attend the first Explorer's class. This was the class he
had worked for so long to present. Only Master level remote viewers were invited, which means that they had at least 150 hours of
classes under their belts and a minimum of thirty practice targets
completed. There were over forty master level viewers who were to
attend, most with far more experience than the required minimum.

The Explorer's class was not for instruction; it was the first operational class. The targets were chosen from the edge of knowledge, and as such, there would be little real feedback available. We
would be going "where no man has gone before."

We were all excited about what this represented. It was the culmination of years of hard work and sacrifice. The event was sponsored by the VFW and was being held at the War Memorial in
beautiful downtown San Francisco. It seemed a fitting location for
the first Explorer's class.

As the plane descended, I thought about the previous four
years. It was still difficult to believe everything that had happened.
I had experienced the most incredible adventures of my life. I
had been changed; my life had been changed. The statement that

graced the back cover of *Psychic Warrior* had turned out to be true. It had warned, "Your life will never be the same!" And it wasn't. I had traveled past the event horizon of my experiences with Dave Morehouse and stepped through the looking glass into a new life in a brave new universe. I never would have believed the things I had seen; the things I had done over the past four years. Still somewhat skeptical, but with an open mind, I had gone to his remote viewing class and never looked back.

I wondered what might have been had I not seen his book in that bookstore so long ago. Of course, I thought wryly, there was a universe where I had never met Dave. I was glad some other me was in that position. Sorry guy.

After I had deplaned, I stopped outside the terminal and looked for Jason, Patty's son from a previous marriage. Patty had said that he was going to meet me out in front, and a few minutes later RVTs stalwart minivan pulled up.

"Hi Jay!" I greeted him as I opened the van door. Everyone called him Jay.

"Hi John! Glad you could make it. Did you have to wait long?" Jason asked. He was young and laid back. Handsome and tall with Patty's dark good looks, he reminded me of the other Jason in the RVT organization.

"Nope. You got here just after I did. You timed it better than a taxi."

"Cool! Any other luggage?"

I shook my head. I like to travel light.

"Alright. We're staying at the Hilton but we're going to be crowded. Joey and Jeff are in the room with us."

I didn't mind. This was the first time I had been to San Francisco so any accommodations were fine by me. With Jeff, Joey and the two of us it promised to be a fun time. Jeff was Patty's cousin and Joey was a good friend from one of Dave's classes. As we drove to the hotel, Jason pointed out the scenery. The Golden Gate Bridge was spectacular, and the bay was beautiful. The Hilton was located downtown, and as we approached I thought the downtown skyline was impressive.

The following morning the four of us met Dave and Patty in the lobby for the trip to the VFW where the class was to be held. Once we had our coffee, we boarded Dave's minivan.

As we were driving I asked Dave a question, curious about what my role as a member of the staff would be.

"John, you're not staff this week. You're a member of the class. So are Joey and Jeff. Staff duties are being handled by Mary and Marv," he replied smiling, looking at my reaction in the rear view mirror.

This was new. That meant I would get to do all the targets. A slow smile crept across my face as I looked back at him.

Sweet.

The drive to the War Memorial was short. The building has an older façade and several floors. It's located near the impressive Opera House in the Arts district. After the usual routine of offloading equipment and setting up the room, I noted wryly that my exalted status as class member didn't exempt me from this RVT staff ritual. No matter, it actually was a form of praise from Dave for those fortunate to be accepted as volunteers, as he had a soldier's predilection for order. We used the time not only to put the classroom together, but also to talk and catch up on everything that each of us had been doing since the last time we had been together. Like soldiers, we accepted the hardships and celebrated the triumphs, and sometimes the tragedies that occurred in RVTs universe.

Soon my classmates began to arrive. I was expecting my buddy Tedd, but I wasn't sure who else would be attending. Imagine my surprise when more and more of my former classmates began to show. J.R. and Gabriele from the class where I lost my ability; Fortune from my first ERV class; Rommel and Annmarie from RVTs staff; Dave, Barry, Alane, Carol, Fran, and Talia from the Masters class; Theron, Maryann, Maria, and Merv from Omega.

It was old home week!

I spent the next half-hour rekindling friendships. I had a feeling this would be a great week. San Francisco, the first Explorer's class, friends from past classes and new friends to be made, and the promise of adventure. What more could I ask?

Finally it was time to begin and after some administrative details and announcements by Patty, Dave came to the front of the room. This was a special moment, not just for the commemoration of the first Explorer's class; but also for another celebration. All of us had been with Dave through the entire series of classes. We had all made sacrifices in time and money over the years to be here today. Each of us had worked hard in class and in outside training, long hours of practice, and review. I thought back to the spring of 1999 when I took my first CRV class at UCLA, not long after Dave first started teaching in 1998. I had been with him ever since and done and seen things that were right out of a science fiction novel, only they were real. Now all of that training and dedication were going to be put to the test. None of us knew what a historic class this would be. Events were soon to go far beyond what even Dave had planned.

"Welcome to all of you. Welcome to my dream. From the moment I first started teaching remote viewing, I have worked to realize this class. This was my dream, a class composed of the best remote viewers that have gone through all of my training, together for the purpose of going beyond knowledge, to explore human destiny. I am so proud of all of you stalwart friends who have made the sacrifices necessary to be here today. This week we will go to the edge of knowledge and look beyond, using the skills that you have learned and practiced. This will be unlike any class that we have shared previously, as there will be no teaching of techniques. This will be a totally operational class. The target sessions will be run just as they were when I was at Ft. Meade. Some of our targets may come from outside sources with real world applications, so strive to do your best."

Everyone in the class was rapt with attention.

"To change the way we see things takes compassion and dedication, and this you all have; and once again we are here as a family from across the globe to make a difference.

Collectively we came to transform spirit, ours as well as the rest of the world. We came to learn a new manner of seeing. But we see with a restructuring of perception, not merely to stand in the comfort of the habit of our lives, our beliefs, but rather to challenge our own perspective. It is when we reach beyond the edge of knowledge that the same becomes altogether different."

The smile faded as he continued. "The world has gone to war as we begin this class, during our watch; entering us into the Fourth Turning of Global Societal Evolution. Or at the very least, introducing us to it. Each of us has grieved in our own way, then rallied and joined together to hope for peace. Peace for the children, for all humanity, and all life on this physical plane. This transformation of grief to hope in the face of human fury is psycho-spiritual transformation.

"The recognition that we are more than the physical, that there is a very real place beyond this physical existence, and that we are the source and that source is indeed us. It is the recognition that we have never, never... " Dave's voice shook with emphasis as he repeated the words, "been disconnected from the source and that the wisdom of all things is within each of us! It is knowing that we have all lived before; that we will all live again, and that we have always known each other on some extraordinary plane in the Matrix. Transformation is knowing that we are responsible for ourselves, but more importantly, that we are responsible for the collective whole of humanity.

"What we see in this life, in this world will be seen through these reconstituted eyes, the eyes of the Remote Viewer. Our eyes will be full of a new vision of the world, a vision of love and compassion, of promise and possibility."

Dave paused a moment to let what he said sink in. Then he concluded in a soft confident tone, "You are my heroes; you are my dream, you are the great clarity the world now needs. The world is no longer able to give meaning to what it sees, though it sees perfectly well what is there. The world needs you to give it clarity; that's why you are all here: We few, gathered together to accept this duty to all of humanity, for all of humanity. Thank you all for accepting that responsibility. Thank you all for being here."

We took our first break and I thought about what Dave said about responsibilities and remote viewing and where I fit into all of this. I had spent the last four years with him and had struggled to put all of what I had experienced into perspective. Four years trying to find answers. What was my personal mythology? Where was I going from here? How was remote viewing going to be a part of my life from now on? All I knew was that having come down this path, as Dave's book had warned, I could no longer turn back to what I was. To deny everything I had done and witnessed would be impossible. I wouldn't even if it was possible. I could not walk away from these non-physical eyes any more than a sighted person would willingly choose blindness.

The hand on my shoulder startled me and I quickly turned my head.

"Hey John! You looked like you were in a trance, my friend."

It was my friend Tedd. "Hey buddy, just sweeping out some cobwebs," I countered.

"Well come on. Let's take a break and shoot the poop outside." We walked outside. I spotted David, Cheryl's friend from Omega, over by the water fountain so we joined him.

"Hi David, glad you made it. Is Cheryl coming?" I asked.

"No, she won't be here. She's still working on getting ready for the Master class and practicing ERV. She felt she wasn't quite ready yet," David replied.

That was too bad. Cheryl is a neat lady. She and David were close friends. The three of us chatted for a few minutes then it was time for the class to continue.

At the end of the morning lecture series we broke for lunch. Tedd and I joined David and some of our classmates and looked for a nearby restaurant. As we walked through the downtown streets I struck up a conversation with two of the other people with us. The first was a tall, statuesque woman with blond hair named Jana. She was congenial with a strong independent streak. In many ways she reminded me of Saundra, although Jana had no experience with UFO's. She and I had liked each other from the very first meeting and by the end of the week had become good friends.

The other classmate was from halfway across the world. Taz was from Tasmania of all places. His real name was Guy but everyone called him Taz. His determination to be here was admirable; on a minimal budget he had managed to make it all the way across the Pacific Ocean to the Explorer's class. He was of medium height with shoulder length curly brown hair. He had a killer accent and a great sense of humor. We hit it off, not knowing that we had a shared destiny in the events to come this week.

We managed to find a Chinese restaurant that could table us together and once seated Jana asked me how I had gotten involved with Dave.

"Like most of the class I read his book. But unlike most I was a skeptic. I didn't buy into the possibility of psychic ability. I had never had a prophetic dream or a premonition, seen a ghost or anything. As a matter of fact, I was known as Remote Viewing Technology's poster boy for the psychically challenged," I related. When she and the others had stopped laughing, I continued. "True story. In both my CRV and ERV classes I failed on my first attempt. In fact, I was the only one who got nothing in my CRV class during the first target session. Everyone else did just fine."

"But you obviously continued with it. What kept you interested?" she asked.

"Two reasons, really. One, I was intrigued with the notion that you could learn to be psychic; that psychic ability is innate in all of us. Two, Dave has always maintained that he was not a natural psychic, yet he's acknowledged by his peers as an excellent remote viewer, extremely talented. I've seen what he can do first hand." I related the story of my first ERV class where Dave had accompanied us to a target. Everyone was captivated.

"As a matter of fact, because I did keep at it I found that I'm actually good at remote viewing. I've had some amazing adventures with Dave in his classes. So much so that I'm writing an account of those adventures that I hope to have published," I explained.

"Well, that's great. I can't wait to read it." Jana replied.

"Yeah, I'm hoping that this class will provide some fodder for the book, but there's another reason I'm writing it. I'm using the book as a means of finding my personal mythology," I continued. "I've been with Dave since the spring of 1999, a year from when he first started teaching. That was four years ago and I'm still trying to figure out where I fit in with all this. Hopefully all these experiences will show me the way." Little did I know that my wish would be granted in a most spectacular way.

We returned to the War Memorial, and settled into the classroom. Scheduled next was our first target session. "Patty is handing out your tasking sheets. As you can see, they're fairly straightforward," Dave said grinning.

Boy, he wasn't kidding. Usually there were a number of focus questions listed for the target, but our tasking sheets were virtually empty.

We were given:

TARGET TASKING SHEET:
TARGET IS TO BE VIEWED IN PAST TIME

FOCUS QUESTIONS:
DESCRIBE WHAT YOU SEE AND FEEL

"How's that for no front loading!" Dave added. "OK, let's set up your workstations and we'll launch in ten minutes."

I walked to the place on the floor where I had set down my inflatable and other equipment and began the task of setting up. As my air pump began to hum it was joined by more than a dozen other pumps as my classmates inflated their workstations. It was music to my ears.

I looked around at my fellow classmates. I enjoyed being with people who weren't caught up in the unconsciousness of their own lives. I thought of how much I was tired of dealing with people who couldn't see beyond themselves: the Me Generation of video games and Teflon responsibilities. I looked over at Dave and Patty behind their computer consoles as they set up the cool-down music. I thought how much I missed being with them when I was gone; how much I felt fulfilled when I was remote viewing, when I was in their classes, either helping or viewing. I glanced over at Taz a few spaces over, catching a smile and a thumbs-up. I grinned, mouthing the words "lock and load" and returning the gesture. I realized that this was what I wanted. This was where I wanted to be.

The lights began to dim as the music began, and I snuggled down on my mattress. Once again it was time to enter the Matrix. The place where I had found my truth, as so many others had. It had been in front of me all along. But like the Ch'an student who tries so hard and goes through a personal crisis during his training only to find enlightenment was always within himself, I too had needed the same journey through Oz. All of the adventures, all of the personal crises, the doubts, the uncertainty, and yes, even pain, were necessary for enlightenment to follow. It seemed only appropriate that enlightenment should happen during this time, this class; the culmination of my training. It also seemed ironic that I, a martial artist of thirty years experience, trained in the fist and the sword in an arcane martial tradition that dated back over 15 centuries to the beginnings of the Shaolin Temple and the Knights of Korean Justice, had missed the truth until now. Then again, even Dorothy had to make the journey to Oz.

I began the ritual for ERV. The breathing exercises brought me quickly to Sanctuary. The swirl of the Matrix surrounded me as I stood in the center of the soft blue light. I took a moment to savor the experience and then it was time to go. The Vortex brought me to the event horizon of the Membrane and I arrived at the target.

Before I had the chance to figure out where I had landed, there was a tremendous flash of light. Then nothingness. It had been like an explosion but strangely without sound. No remnants of what had exploded, at least on first inspection. Only darkness. Then something materialized before me; something I least expected on this, the first target in the Explorer's class.

It appeared to be a wall. A wall made of some sort of building blocks inserted side-by-side rather than end-to-end. I thought this was very strange. What did this have to do with the target? What was the target? I remembered the Titanic session from Carmel. Maybe the wall wasn't a wall. Perhaps I was seeing something else.

I knew I was spending too much time in analysis. Already the mists stirred around me. I had slipped out of the zone of ultra-deep. I concentrated on my breathing once more and shortly thereafter the fog cleared away. The wall was gone, but replacing it was something even more incongruous, even more unexpected.

It was a man and a woman holding hands. I didn't recognize them; they appeared to be a generic couple. To my consternation, they faded out and were replaced by the mists again. I lay there thinking, what the hell am I looking at? I knew I was analyzing again but now I had a reason. I wasn't sure I was on target. I might have missed the signal line. It had happened before. My results on a few targets had no correlations. It didn't matter if I was in CRV or ERV mode. Sometimes viewers just didn't catch the signal line for the designated target. That was one of the reasons for the three laws of remote viewing, one of which was never to trust the results of a single remote viewer. Remote viewing had been designed as a group effort, a process, not an event.

I was about to return to Sanctuary and try again to contact the signal line when in the background I heard music, as if it was coming from down a long corridor. My time was up. I returned to Sanctuary and ended the session, reluctantly. Disappointment was again my companion. I found it hard to believe that anything I'd seen had any relevance to the target. I couldn't get a clue to what I should have been concentrating on from the focus questions because there were none. I wrote down what little I saw and got up from my workstation. I would have to wait until after lunch for the feedback. Jana, Taz and I headed for the door.

On our return, Dave gave us the feedback for our target, "On this target session you were sent into the Universe to find and experience a collapsing star, a supernova."

There was a wave of surprise at this disclosure. I was completely taken aback by the news. The big flash of light I had seen fit the target but what about the wall of building blocks and the couple? Those didn't seem to fit. I was disappointed in my performance. I considered my results substandard. It was not an auspicious beginning. I was so caught up in myself that I almost missed what Dave was saying. It was the uncharacteristically quiet voice that grabbed my attention.

"The concept of this target was simply the death of a star and the gestalt surrounding this event. Since this is the first time I have ever sent a class into such an event, I really have nothing to give you as far as feedback is concerned except the notes you brought back on your own. There is no telling what might come from such an experience. Perhaps nothing, perhaps an overwhelming abundance of imagery and sensory data. In the death of that star, what is released is the sum total of all that it was, all of the knowledge contained in its life of millions of years, now cast adrift into the quantum foam of the Matrix field."I feel the death of a star was a direct reference to my soul, to my pursuit of knowledge and my path to wisdom. I found this death to be an intellectual phenomenon rather than simply an act of physics played out in a violent fury."

And with that, Dave left us with a question to ponder, "Why would the death of a star be any different from the passing of a human being?"

Something he said nagged the edge of my mind. Something about the sum total of the star being cast adrift caught my attention. It was the key to my session. I knew the truth was there if I could figure out why my mind locked onto his words. Try as I might though, the solution eluded me like a thought you just can't resolve and gets further away the harder you try to force it. I would have to let my mind make the connection in its own time.

The following day Dave came to the front of the room for an announcement, "Today's target will be a very special one. As you know, I told you that there could be an operational target this week. A client has approached us with a request for information on such a target. This will be an operational tasking with possible consequences based on your results."

The buzz was immediate. Everyone began to whisper excitedly. Dave continued after giving the class a moment to calm down. "I know that you'll do your best. Your results will be compiled by the staff and forwarded to the client. If the client is sufficiently impressed there may be a second tasking session. To facilitate getting you on target, there will be an element of front-loading.

All of you are experienced viewers so this should not pose a problem for you. In operational settings like this it is not unusual for viewers to be front-loaded. This is to focus you on the target and keep you from wasting time on extraneous elements of the target or its surroundings. Get your stations ready and we'll launch in 10 minutes."

This was it, the moment we had all been waiting for. The chance to put everything we had learned into actual practice on a live target; not a training session, but an operational tasking that might have important consequences based on our results. Taz was fitting out his workstation nearby; he looked over at me and smiling said. "Good luck, mate!"

As we completed our preparations, Dave returned to the front of the classroom. As he did so the lights dimmed and the music began. "Okay, as I said, you'll be slightly front-loaded. This shouldn't present any problem for you; you're all experienced remote viewers. Just don't let your imagination get away from you. "With a grin he assured us, "And it's not Osama or Saddam so clear your minds. Access the target and describe. The target is to be viewed in present time. Good luck and good viewing."

The lights were down and the tape sounds washed over the room. My breathing slowed and I turned ever inward away from the outside world. Deeper and deeper I sank into semi-consciousness, looking for the ERV viewing realm on the edge of dreams. The sounds of the tape faded away and my body lost sensation. Once again I entered Sanctuary where the colors of the Matrix spun around me. As I waited for the Vortex to form, I reviewed my mission, reinforcing my desire to see the person that was my target. I felt a calm exuberance more than excitement. I savored the moment until the tempest of the Vortex swirled open and I was off on my first operational mission.

As I passed through the Membrane, I felt the familiar but still unsettling sense of falling and then I was at the target. The mists of the Matrix surrounded me momentarily before they cleared away to reveal a man. I didn't recognize him as anyone important or someone I was familiar with. He was a white male of Mediterranean appearance in his late thirties or early forties. It was difficult to be sure as he had dark hair and was unshaven and unkempt in appearance. He appeared to be wearing rags. My impression was this was someone that had some sort of problem with his heart. He was alive but he also appeared sick.

Thinking I might get an idea who he was by seeing my geographical location, I expanded my awareness and drifted out of the building I was in. It was a modern multi-story building that felt to me to be a residence. It appeared to be made of stone and was relatively new. I must have slipped out of the zone as I pondered this revelation, as the scene darkened to the twilight vista of the Matrix. I was familiar with this phenomenon by now and I simply returned to the yogic breathing exercises. It wasn't long before the mists faded away, this time revealing a spherical edifice that I took to be some sort of statue. It had a distinctive flared base and was black in color. I was about to change my location to get a better view of this unusual object when I heard music drifting into my awareness. A disembodied voice said to return to Sanctuary and complete my session summary.

Disengaging from the target, I returned to Sanctuary and after a few minutes to collect my thoughts and refresh my memory of what I had seen, slipped my eye-mask up. I blinked owlishly in the light and, once acclimatized, I rolled over and wrote a narrative with drawings of what I had seen.

After the break, Dave called up the known feedback for our target as Patty handed out the hard copies. I was shocked when the computer presentation came up on the screen: It was the last thing I expected.

OPERATIONAL TASKING # 1 EXPLORER'S CLASS 2003
TARGET COORDINATES: 2003 1627
TARGET SUBJECT: COMMANDER MICHAEL SCOTT SPEICHER, USN
FIRST PILOT SHOT DOWN DURING THE FIRST GULF WAR.
FIRST LISTED AS KIA, NOW LISTED MISSING IN ACTION.

I didn't know that we still had a missing man in Iraq. I hadn't seen anything recently about him. The picture on the screen of a man in a Navy uniform was similar to the image I had seen, but my viewing had shown an unkempt man, one with possible heart problems. But the man I saw looked similar to the man depicted on the screen.

"Commander Speicher is the only man in US history ever listed as killed in action and then through subsequent investigation had that classification changed to missing in action. I was approached by the members of this VFW post and asked if we would do a session on Commander Speicher. The results will then be forwarded to the Speicher family attorneys. All of your sessions will be copied and be returned to you. The copies will be given to the VFW," Dave informed us. "If they feel the information is worthwhile, they will ask for a second, more in-depth session as well as a map dowsing to see if we can pinpoint a location to suggest looking for him."

That evening at dinner with Dave and Patty, and my roommates Jay, Joey, and Jeff, I thought about the day's events. It didn't seem fair that the US government had left this man behind all these years. I said as much to Dave.

"You won't get an argument from either me or any veteran's groups, John. But consider this, the US government refused to accept any responsibility for the effects of Agent Orange until the early 1990s. Our government deploys depleted uranium ammunition, the only country left in the world that does, even though there is evidence that there are serious environmental and health issues in its use. Think about it, even the Russians no longer use DU rounds. The US government has closed veteran's hospitals and reduced veteran's benefits. We still have MIA issues that haven't been resolved since the Vietnam War. Why should this be any different?"I thought how I might feel if it had been one of my SEAL friends from Trojan Warrior II. What if it was Keith, Shawn, Tom or Jeff who had been left behind? How would any soldier feel if they knew that they might be abandoned for the sake of expediency? It was an unsettling thought.

The following morning I found I had a new respect for the War Memorial as we walked through the doors.

When the class had assembled, Dave strode to the front of the room, "Good morning, everyone. It seems you have justified my confidence in all of you. I have received another request for more information on Michael Scott Speicher. Evidently they were sufficiently impressed with yesterday's session to have you do another, more in-depth, session to expand on what you learned.

So that is what we shall do. You'll do another target session on Michael Speicher using the same coordinates that you used yesterday. When you have completed the remote viewing session, I would like you to do a map dowsing to try and pin down his location."

Dave paused for a moment then he said quietly but with barely concealed sentiment, "I am so proud of all of you. You have made my dream a reality." He returned to the work at hand. "Okay viewers, let's get ready and we'll launch in ten minutes."

I walked by Jana on the way back from the restroom. She was busily setting up her mattress, getting ready for the upcoming session. "Hey Jana, ready for this session?" I asked.

She looked up at me, "Hi John. This should be exciting. I had no idea we would be doing any operational work. I was expecting more of the same of our first target. This was totally unexpected."

"Me too. This is very exciting, but I hope something good comes of it. Wouldn't it be wonderful if our efforts helped to bring Speicher home?" I knew his family would be hoping the same.

"Yes, that, of course is the most important aspect. Here's to a successful mission for all of us."

I hoped she was right. I returned to my mattress, noting that Taz was already ensconced on his mattress, his eye-shield down. I smiled, wishing him silently a productive session. The lights lowered and the cool-down tape began its programmed task to lower us to the realm of ultra-deep, the theta state on the edge of dreams. My breathing slowed to follow the rhythm of the sounds of ocean surf. I felt the long slide down as I entered Sanctuary and waited for the maelstrom of the Vortex. When I had turned inward far enough, the wormhole spun into existence and I was off. Dropping through the event horizon of the Membrane, the all too familiar feeling of falling swept over me. The sensation was like being on a roller coaster that has dropped out from underneath you. It turned my stomach, but fortunately it was short-lived and as the feeling subsided I found myself at the target.

I was looking at a building. I recognized it immediately as the same one I had seen on the first session. I tried to take in as much detailed information as I could, but I had to be careful for two reasons. First was the fact I had to rely on a passive memory of what I was looking at. Any attempt to use more aggressive techniques to remember what I was seeing could change my brain state, pulling me out of the viewing zone. I would have to spend precious time to re-establish target contact that could have been better spent viewing. Second, I was fighting the time dilation effect that I experienced during an ERV session that made it seem like I had only minutes at the target.

From my point of view, standing in apparitional form about 100 meters from the target, the building appeared to be a low, flat structure of modern architecture. It was two stories high and appeared to be made of an adobe or sandstone type material, tan in color. The entrance had three large arched doorways that appeared to open on a large courtyard. Peering through the arches, I could see the second floor landings. My kinesthetic sense was that this building was a residence, but had an aura of government associated with it. The building did not appear to be a prison. I mentally rocked back on my heels, wondering if I could have missed the target.

It could happen, had happened to remote viewers. If a relatively bland, psychically speaking, target was located near a location or edifice that had a strong history associated with it, it was possible for the phenomenon of displacement to occur. Displacement is a shift in time or space. Sometimes it is to a time of the target more psychically interesting than the one you were investigating. Sometimes the displacement occurs in space, shifting the viewer's attention to a more interesting target nearby that has a more powerful history associated with it. There was no way to tell. Only practice and focus could minimize the chance that displacement would occur.

I had to hope that I was on target both space and time-wise.

In the distance there was a prominent peak or hill. I must have drifted off to sleep because the next thing I knew I returned to consciousness. Inwardly I smiled, thankful that the fourth of the Five Intentions brought me back to the zone. A moment of yogic breathing cleared away the mists and once again I was looking at the statue I had seen in the earlier session. It was round with a flared base and ebony in color.

It occurred to me that I had not seen any sign of Scott Speicher in the building. I shifted my focus of awareness to see if I could find any evidence of his proximity. As I did so I heard the sound of far-off music intruding on my awareness.

No! Not now! It was too late; the swirl of the Matrix descended on me and reluctantly I returned to Sanctuary and the classroom. Once firmly grounded I removed my eye-shield and wrote up my session. I could only trust in what several hundred sessions had proven before; that I was where I was supposed to be and the building was the correct target.

When I completed my session summary I took out the referenced paper that I was to use for the map dowsing. A referenced paper was simply a blank sheet with the coordinates of the target and a reference mark on it that would correspond to a mark on a map of the approximate area of our target. Hopefully this would hold the key to our missing person's whereabouts. We had no clue of the scale or where in Iraq the map was centered.

I was still fairly cooled down so only a moment of breathing exercises brought me to where I wanted to be. I ran my hand over the paper and waited for a feeling to surface, signaling that my unconscious had sensed my target. It took a while longer than I expected, but then this was only my second map dowsing. I had not had a chance to do another since the Masters class. I finally settled on the right-center of my reference sheet halfway to the edge. I made a mark that encompassed the area that I thought was significant and then got up. I walked over to Patty who was collecting the data sheets by the door and handed them to her. She took my results and smiled at me. I returned the smile and shrugged, indicating I hoped it had been a fruitful session.

I reminisced on my Master class and the Flight 800 map-dowsing target. Our results stunned us and Dave and Patty as well. Dave had said it was the best dowsing he had ever seen on such a complicated target. But I also remembered the results the previous year with the second Masters class. The outcome of that dowsing had been exactly the opposite, prompting Dave to remark that the results were closer to the results of a shotgun blast on a far target. The marks had been scattered randomly all over the map. The second Master class, though, had done an outstanding job with the pendulum exercise, far bettering our mediocre results. It was simply another commentary on the very personal aspect of remote viewing. Classes could be just as distinctive and idiosyncratic as the students were.

I walked outside to join several of our class for lunch. As I walked up on the group of classmates who were waiting for the rest of us to join them I overheard Taz commenting on his session. His statements stopped me in my tracks, "Yeah mate, it was two stories with a courtyard. In the middle of the courtyard there was a water fountain, round and black."

Shocked, I interrupted him, "Taz, are you talking about the location where Speicher might be located?"

Startled, Taz turned to face me, "Right John. I was in a courtyard that was surrounded by a two-story building. It had a second floor landing or balcony."

"That fountain; was it black as night?" I asked.

"Yeah mate. It really got my attention. Why, did you see it too?"

I caught my breath and nodded, speechless.

When we returned from lunch, our sessions were returned to us. Taz and I compared our sessions, marveling at the similarity of our independent experiences. His session looked like he had seen the same residence I had but from the viewpoint of someone standing within the courtyard, which of course he had been. I depicted that same building from an outside perspective. Our descriptions of the fountain were virtually identical.

I almost expected Scully and Mulder to walk through the classroom doors. There was only one word that seemed to fit as Taz and I compared our session summaries and drawings; spooky.

The feeling had not worn off the following night when I attended the closing party, a wonderfully catered affair put on by Dave and Patty to celebrate the first Explorer's class. It had been a week to remember; a week of discovery and new friends and adventures, and a week of hope. Hope that a lost sheep would be returned to the fold. The class had been dedicated to a true American hero, Michael Scott Speicher, and his return.

The following day Dave stood at the front of the room to address the class before the students departed. For me this was always the hardest part. We had shared a remarkable week. It had been the first class to realize Dave's dream. We had done some noteworthy investigations and all of us had shared a sense of community and friendship. This was what his classes were about. This was why I disliked being away so much and why I felt fulfilled and at peace when I was here.

This was my home. And now it was over.

"My friends, my heroes. I am so honored to have had the privilege of your company over the past week," Dave began. His eyes were shining and bright and it was obvious that he was filled with a combination of pride and humility.

"We have accomplished so much over the years and it fills me with pride to have shared that time with all of you. But what makes this moment so important is not so much what has been accomplished. What I remember that is so important are my friends, the great people such as you who have come into my life, who enrich it daily with your thoughts, your prayers, and your kindness. My life is perfect because of people like you.

"So much is ahead of you. Make each sunrise count for something, for someone. Make each sunset the close of a beautiful promise. You and your efforts will be the key to the promise and possibility awakening in the human condition. All of us, Patty and myself and the staff at RVT will miss you and are proud of you – proud to know you, and call you friends. We'll see all of you soon, and we all look forward to that day. Be safe going home, be happy and well, and may God watch over each and every one of you."

On the flight home I mused over the previous week. To take my mind off my sadness, I thought about the supernova target session. It had been an important target to Dave, part and parcel of his personal quest to understand the true nature of reality and the nature of life and death. That target had unwittingly fit into the week's events.

It wouldn't be until a year later that I would realize the connection that gave me the answer to the session that had eluded me. Appropriately, it came to me as I sat watching the sunset, enjoying my favorite time of the day, twilight, the coming of night.

THE EXPLORER GROUP
TARGET TASKING SHEET

TARGET SESSION #6

YOUR COORDINATES ARE:
2003
1352

I. SPECIAL INSTRUCTIONS TO VIEWERS:

a. Target is an event to be viewed in past time.

b. Target will have quantifiable feedback.

II. FOCUS QUESTIONS for this target session:

a. Describe what you see and feel.

*NOTE—how's that for no front loading information?

"JOURNEY THROUGH THE SANDS OF TIME"

THE EXPLORER GROUP
TARGET FEEDBACK SUPER NOVA SESSION

"Mankind will not remain on Earth forever, but in its quest for light and space will at first timidly penetrate beyond the confines of the atmosphere, and later will conquer for itself all the space near the Sun."

—Konstantin E. Tsiolkovsky

1. This target session sent you into the universe to a find and experience a collapsing sun, a super nova—the place you were sent was in the <u>direction</u> of the Eagle Nebulae and the Horse head Nebulae, although these <u>were not your targets</u>.

2. The concept of the target was simply the death of a star and the gestalt surrounding this event. Since this is the first time I have ever sent a class into such an event—I really have nothing to give you except the notes you brought back on your own. There is no telling what might really come from such an experience, perhaps nothing perhaps an overwhelming abundance of images and sensory data from surrounding worlds. Perhaps in the death of a star what is released is all of the knowledge contained in the life of the star—billions and trillions of years of life and remembrance cast back into the quantum foam of the Matrix field.

3. The fruit of the mind has been described as the 'consciousness of consciousness', I felt the death of a star was a direct reference to my soul, to my pursuit of knowledge my path to wisdom—I found this death to be an intellectual phenomenon rather than simply an act of physics played out in a violent fury. Why would the death of a star be any different that the passing of a human?

SESSION SUMMARY

MY IMPRESSIONS OF THE TARGET WAS FIRST A BRIGHT YELLOW FLASH OF LIGHT. UNUSUAL BUT NO SOUND ASSOCIATED.

SECOND IMPRESSION WAS OF A HIGH BRICK WALL MADE OF UNK BUILDING BLOCKS.

LAST IMPRESSION WAS OF A CAUCASIAN MALE AND FEMALE 25-35.

NO COHERANCE TO OBS - NOT SURE OF TARGET CONTACT.

SOUNDLESS BRIGHT YELLOW FLASH

WALL MADE OF BRICKS - BRICKS SMALL OR END ON

= MAN & WOMAN

CHAPTER SEVENTEEN

Confirmation

Be the change you want to see in the World.

— Gandhi

After the Explorer's class, I kept checking to see if any further developments occurred in the Speicher case. A book written by a former Naval Intelligence officer turned journalist, Amy Waters Yarsinske, titled *No One Left Behind*, was written in 2003, the same year as the Explorer's class. Her book suggested that Scott was still alive. She had been nominated for the Pulitzer Prize for her six part series on Speicher in The Virginian Pilot titled "Dead or Alive". The Explorer's class had come to an almost unanimous decision based on the results of our remote viewing sessions that he was, in fact, alive. The Pentagon, however, did not share that optimism. So at that time there was no feedback for the class.[37]

The fate of Scott Speicher still haunted me. I had bought an MIA bracelet from his family's website to help support ongoing efforts to locate his whereabouts and return him to America. There was anecdotal evidence that he was alive but the agency that was charged with the return of MIAs, JAPC/DPMO, seemed more interested in proving he had died in the crash of his F/A-18 than in following up the numerous sightings in Iraq. I hoped that I would see his safe return in spite of that lack of vision.

Later, in 2006, I received some really welcome news from Dave. A number of military personnel, attorneys, and investigators, including me, had petitioned the Inspector General of the U.S. Army on Dave's behalf to request that the IG review his case. We stated that the trial of then Major David A. Morehouse was seriously flawed and that testimony from a key witness was unreliable, based on court documents obtained by the FOI act. After six months of review, the IG's office agreed and reinstated Dave to his original rank and amended his resignation to reflect an honorable discharge. It was a tremendous victory for him and both he and Patty were overjoyed at the news.

Sadly, news of equal import but opposite result occurred in August of 2009. Scott Speicher had been found.

I watched with mounting dismay on the evening news when the Defense Department announced that the remains of Captain Michael Scott Speicher had been located in the desert not far from the wreck of his downed Hornet jet. He had apparently died in the crash back in 1991.

I was stunned. How could this be? How could the Explorer's class have been so far off? Forty experienced remote viewers, all graduates of Dave's Master level class. I could understand that a fraction of the class could have a bad session. Even up to a third of that many viewers could give data that could lead to a wrong conclusion. It had happened, especially to new viewers who had fallen out of structure and spiraled into AOL drive. But for most of us to have been so far off was hard to stomach.

For me to be that far off the mark was like a slap in the face. The things I had seen in session seemed to be right on target. I had the added insurance of Taz's session that had virtually duplicated my information, only from his point of view.

I shook my head in dejection. It was bad enough that Scott wouldn't be coming back to greet his family. Now all that I had learned, all that I had experienced, was called into question. Again. I felt humiliated.

There wasn't anything to say. I felt adrift once again with the specter of my doubts now reborn with more power to deny my experiences.

Over the next two years I put away the manuscript that I had written about my experiences in remote viewing. I stopped doing practice sessions and dust accumulated on my workbooks.

I still saw Dave occasionally. He was vice-president of operations for a company called Deployment Medicine International and I was one of their EMT assistants. We were teaching combat trauma management to the Special Operations Command personnel. We taught these techniques to the Army Special Forces and Rangers, Navy SEALs, Marine Recon and Special Ops teams, and Air Force Combat Controllers. It was fast paced and hard physical labor but very rewarding. I got to work alongside some of the finest combat medics and corpsmen in the service, some of them reservists, others on active duty between assignments. They were America's best and I was proud to know them and be associated with them.

This was real; this was reality. No more science fiction.

I was embarrassed enough by my failure in the Explorer's class that I never said anything to Dave about it. I'm sure he would have heard the news by now and I didn't know how he felt about the circumstances of Speicher's death. Even if I had wanted to ask we were both so busy that I never really had a chance. Besides, the deeper truth was that I no longer had any confidence in remote viewing.

In the years following the discovery of Capt. Scott Speicher's remains, there was a lingering doubt lurking in the back of my mind. Always the same thought ... how could I have been so wrong?

In the spring of 2011, I gave in to that nagging feeling, ostensibly to see if there was any further information regarding the Speicher case, and went on the Internet. Bringing up the name of Capt. Michael Scott Speicher on my search engine, I hit Enter.

Reading down through the entries, my heart skipped a beat. A number of the subject entries that ran down the page had in the title, "dispute the Pentagon's conclusion on Speicher's death." I started bringing up each of the web entries and reading them. After a dozen of the most pertinent stories, I sat back in my seat. Oh my God, I thought. It's Pat Tillman all over again.

Pat Tillman's story by all accounts is at the very least an indictment of the Defense Department and higher echelons of the U.S. military, and very possibly a conspiracy to cover up the murder of an American soldier.[38]

Tillman, a former NFL safety for the Cardinals, had given up a lucrative contract in order to join the US Army after the events of September 11, 2001. Serving first in the invasion of Iraq, he later became a Ranger assigned to the famed 75th Ranger Battalion and deployed to Afghanistan. On April 22, 2004, he was killed by overwhelming enemy fire, according to the Pentagon. Senior military officials lauded his heroic actions during the engagement and awarded him the Silver Star and the Purple Heart posthumously.

It was a lie.

Subsequent investigations proved that Pat Tillman was killed by friendly fire. It also showed that:

• There was no evidence of enemy fire at the scene.

• Soldiers at the scene were ordered to keep silent about the true nature of Tillman's death.

• Army attorneys congratulated each other in e-mails over obfuscating the investigations.

• Forensic examination of Tillman's body did not match the scenario as described.

There was more. Tillman, by all accounts, had become disillusioned with the Iraq war, which he now felt had been illegal. He also believed the American people were not being told the truth about the progress of the Afghan war. Friends had arranged a meeting upon his return to the states with Noam Chomsky, a noted government critic. This, plus the deliberate destruction of evidence by Tillman's platoon led Tillman's mother to ask Gen. Wesley Clark if her son could have been deliberately murdered. He replied that it was indeed possible. Tillman had no enemies and was popular with his men.

Several lower ranking officers and men were censured and transferred over the incident, but no officer of General rank nor Pentagon official suffered any consequences. No one was ever prosecuted.[39]

I wanted to know more. Several of the Internet entries mentioned a book entitled, An American in the Basement, on the truth about what really happened to Scott Speicher. The author, Amy Waters Yarsinske, was a former Naval Intelligence officer who wrote the aforementioned No One Left Behind. She would remove the veil of uncertainty that had surrounded me since the Explorer's class. I was able to contact her, first by e-mail, then by phone.

Amy confirmed the results of the remote viewing done on Speicher during our class.

We had been right all along.

At the time of the session in the spring of 2003, Speicher was still alive and in Iraqi custody. But what she told me next froze my blood. Speicher could have been rescued.

Lost on January 19, 1991, the Pentagon had asserted that Speicher was shot down by an Iraqi MiG-25 interceptor on the first night of the war and died in the crash of his F/A-18 Hornet fighter. In actuality, he was shot down by an AIM-7M Sparrow missile fired by a Navy F-14 Tomcat. This was due in part because of an error by a radar technician aboard an AWACS radar command and control aircraft. Speicher was able to successfully eject and survive the crash.

He was never picked up. Due to a combination of equipment failures, gross incompetence and indifference that extended all the way up to senior officials in the military, Scott Speicher was left for dead. Over the next three years, Speicher would leave messages in the desert using rocks and other means, yet the senior officials at the Department of Defense's Prisoner of War/Missing in Action office (DPMO), Defense Intelligence Agency, and the Office of the Secretary of Defense continued not only to insist he was dead but ran a disinformation campaign to promote that finding.

Finally Speicher, who had survived by staying in the desert with a friendly tribe of Bedouins who hated Saddam, ran out of luck. Putting together information gleaned from open sources and the interest the Americans had in the crashed Hornet, Iraqi intelligence, unlike the Americans, finally located him. The result was the capture of Scott Speicher and the deliberate slaughter of every man, woman, and child of the Bedouin tribe. He would be shuttled around Iraq for years, tortured and alone, until his death.[40]

I thanked Amy for taking the time to talk to me. We stayed in contact and eventually she and I, along with two remote viewers trained by Lyn Buchanan, and famed psychic detective Noreen Renier, would continue to use remote viewing to help locate other POWs and MIAs. Her investigation had restored my confidence in remote viewing, which had been lost due to the Pentagon's deception.

I couldn't help but remember what Dave had told me on my first day in his class. "Don't ever take the government's word at face value. Seek out the truth; become knowledge." I didn't think much of those words when I first heard them. I was that naïve about the government's duplicity.

Now I know.

TARGET SUBJECT:
COMMANDER MICHAEL SPEICHER, USN

BACKSTORY #1: WRECKAGE DISCOVERED IN 1994

Wreckage Of Missing Pilot's Plane Discovered

In 1994, three years after the end of the Gulf War, hunters in the Iraqi desert stumbled across the wreckage of Speicher's plane and informed U.S. officials of their discovery.

Top U.S. military and civilian officials considered whether to send a special team into Iraq to recover the wreckage, but Gen. John Shalikashvili, who then chaired the military Joint Chiefs of Staff, decided that he would not put U.S. soldiers at risk "for old bones." He decided instead to pursue diplomatic efforts with Iraq to excavate the site, officials said.

Two years later, Iraq allowed a Red Cross team, including Americans from the Defense Prisoner of War/Missing Personnel Office, to inspect the site. By then, the official said, the site had been picked over; no human remains were recovered, and there was not a great deal learned from the visit.

There are more than 2,000 U.S. military personnel listed as missing in action from the Vietnam War, more than 8,000 from the Korean War and more than 75,000 Americans listed as missing in action from World War II.

BACKSTORY #2: December 14, 1995

AVIATOR'S STATUS CHANGED FROM 'KILLED IN ACTION' TO 'MISSING IN ACTION'

BAGHDAD, Iraq (CNN) -- Baghdad on Saturday dismissed as a "lie" fresh U.S. claims that a fighter pilot shot down over Iraq during the 1991 Persian Gulf War might still be alive. "It is a new and cheap American lie," an Iraqi Ministry of Culture and Information spokesman said. "When the Iraqi Foreign Ministry reveals documents related to the subject, this lie will be an American scandal," the spokesman said in a statement carried by the official Iraqi News Agency.

The spokesman did not say when documents on the pilot would be made public.
On Friday, CNN learned that an Iraqi defector reported a U.S. pilot had been seen in an Iraqi hospital after the start of the war. Defense Department sources said Friday that the report by a defector contributed to Navy Secretary Richard Danzig's decision Thursday to change the status of Lt. Cmdr. Michael Scott Speicher from "killed in action" to "missing in action." But the report did not specifically say the pilot was Speicher. Navy officials say there were eight Navy and Marine Corps aviators captured during the Persian Gulf War.

Speicher was on his way to drop bombs on downtown Baghdad January 17, 1991, when the F/A-18 fighter jet he was piloting went down over the Iraqi desert. He was the first American lost in the conflict. It is unclear whether it was a surface to air missile or an Iraqi MiG that downed Speicher's plane. **He is officially listed as "the only air-to-air combat loss" of the war, since it is believed that he was in a dogfight with an Iraqi fighter jet when his plane went down.**

Earlier Friday, President Clinton said he had no hard evidence that a fighter pilot shot down over Iraq in the 1991 Persian Gulf War is alive and promised that the United States would do its best to find out. The president said that he didn't want to raise false hopes. "We do not have hard evidence that he is alive," Clinton told reporters Friday at the White House. "We have some evidence that what had been assumed to be the evidence air missile or if there was an accident. Results of the investigation will not be released for some time, according to the Pentagon.

BACKSTORY #3: March 12, 2002

U.S. OFFICIALS DOWNPLAY REPORT ON NAVY PILOT IN IRAQ

WASHINGTON (CNN) -- U.S. officials Monday downplayed a published report that a Navy pilot initially thought to have been killed in action during the Persian Gulf War might be alive and held in Iraq. The report in Monday's Washington Times said the CIA and Defense Intelligence Agency received new information several months ago from British intelligence about Cmdr. Michael Scott Speicher. A Pentagon source told CNN that new information came from a former Iraqi citizen who did not have firsthand knowledge of Speicher's fate. The Pentagon has an active investigation to determine what happened to the pilot, officials said. The Washington Times reported that U.S. intelligence officials said the British information came from someone who had been in Iraq and had learned that an American pilot was being held captive in Baghdad.

Last year, based on information from an Iraqi defector, the Navy changed Speicher's status from killed in action/body not recovered to missing in action, the newspaper reported. However, few U.S. officials are said to believe Speicher is alive, and several said the latest intelligence adds little to what is already known about his fate. Speicher's F/A-18 Hornet was shot down on January 17, 1991, the first day of the air war over Iraq. He was placed on MIA status the next day. Several U.S. officials who talked to CNN dismissed the Washington Times article. "We've had a number of leads over the years," one Pentagon official said. "This is among the slimmest." Another U.S. official said, "If Scott Speicher were still alive, Saddam Hussein would have brought him out for propaganda." He added, "We get reports all the time that we check out." The United States continues to seek a full accounting from Iraq about what happened to Speicher, but one official said the assumption is that he died shortly after the crash.

The official also said information provided by Iraq in the past had turned out to be wrong and said the classification was part of a renewed push to get Iraq to be more forthcoming. In 1990, Iraqi leader Saddam Hussein ordered an invasion of neighboring Kuwait, which eventually led to the United States-led attack on Iraq.

BACKSTORY #5 January 12, 2001

IRAQI DEFECTOR REPORTED U.S. PILOT IN IRAQI HOSPITAL

Aviator's status changed from 'killed in action' (KIA-BNR) to 'missing in action'

WASHINGTON (CNN) -- An Iraqi defector reported a U.S. pilot had been seen in a hospital in Iraq after the start of the 1991 Persian Gulf War, CNN has learned.

Defense Department sources said Friday that the report by a defector contributed to Navy Secretary Richard Danzig's decision Thursday to change the status of Lt. Cmdr. Michael Scott Speicher from "killed in action" to "missing in action." But the report did not specifically say the pilot was Speicher. Navy officials say there were eight Navy and Marine Corps aviators captured during the Persian Gulf War.

*NOTE: Speicher becomes the only casualty in the history of US warfare to ever have a status change from KIA BNR (killed in action-body not recovered) to MIA (missing in action). One presumes the information is just a tad bit more than hearsay or circumstantial

SUMMARY SYNOPSIS

The following information was extracted from the book "No One Left Behind" which is a code letter did not match the required code letter for that specific day—thus it was passed over as suspicious.

3. 12 hours after the attack on Baghdad began, then Secretary of the Army Donald Rumsfeld told reporters than Speicher was down and was in fact presumed dead. When asked by a reporter, "Was her sure that he was dead?" Secretary Rumsfeld replied, "Yes, we are sure." This began the shutdown of all further investigations and the disregarding of any further evidence in support of Speicher.

4. In the years that followed, numerous reports of sightings, locations of plane wreckage and attempts by Bedouin tribesman (desert nomads) who claimed they had Speicher in their possession were ignored or played off by Pentagon Officials. No one was interested in looking for a man who had been declared dead by the Secretary of the Army.

5. According to Bedouins who have since been questioned—Speicher was found by the tribesmen the day following his shoot down. According to reports he was badly injured with a broken back and severe injuries to his legs. The Bedouin's nursed him back to health, hid him from the Iraqi's and attempted repeatedly through the CIA to negotiate for his exchange using his "Blood Chit" (a piece of paper which is carried by select coalition military personnel—which is written in the native language and essentially offers to pay cash for the return of the bearer of the Bloot Chit back to friendly forces.). The Bedouins were trying to collect on the paper, but the US was not interested in exchanging money for a pilot who had already been declared as KIA-BNR (killed in action-body not recovered).

6. It was reported that the Iraqi's found out that Speicher was alive and that the Bedouins had him in their possession. The Iraqis reportedly took the Bedouin camp by force, capturing Speicher and then killed every man, woman and child that they could in the tribe's camp—some did escape

TARGET SUMMARY 2003 1627

TARGET IS MALE, OF MEDITERRANEAN DESCENT WITH DRK HAIR & MUSTACHE. HE APPEARS TO BE LOCATED IN A MULTISTORY BUILDING OF MODERN STONE EDIFICE WITH POSSIBLY A LARGE 3FT DIA SPHERE STATUE IN FRONT. SUBJECT APPEARS TO HAVE DISTINCT PROBLEM WITH HIS HEART, SUBJECT IS ALIVE BUT SICK.

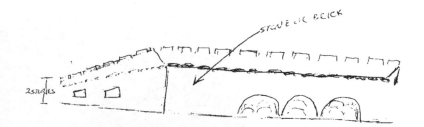

STONE OR BRICK

2 STORIES

LOW FLAT BUILDING, TAN COLORED WITH ELABORATE
UPPER WORKS, TAN COLORED, NEW CONSTRUCTION. HAS
CENTRAL COURT YARD SURROUNDED ON THREE SIDES BY
TWO LEVELS WITH EACH LEVEL HAVING STONE
ARCHES. ARCHITECTURE IS MIDDLE EASTERN, BUILDING
IS NEW AND OF EXPENSIVE WORKMANSHIP WITH A
DISTINCT FEELING OF MILITARY/GOVERNMENT PURPOSE.

IN THE COURTYARD SHOULD BE A STATUE OR
FOUNTAIN OF EITHER BLACK STONE OR METAL
WITH A SPHERICAL UPPER PORTION AND TRIANGULAR
LOWER SECTION.

FLAT
BLACK

CHAPTER EIGHTEEN

Paradigm Lost

*The universe is not only stranger than we imagine;
it is stranger than we can imagine*

−J.B.S. Haldane

Sorcerer's Apprentice is a personal journey that took place between 1999 and 2012. It is my testimony that we are more than our physical bodies. This experience changed my life forever and I will never look at the Universe the same way again.

It is not my intention to try and change the reader's belief in the existence or non-existence of psychic phenomena. As the popular TV show "The X-Files" so succinctly put it, *the truth is out there*. I was a skeptic, but with an open mind. After reading *Psychic Warrior* by David Morehouse, I did research into the reality of remote viewing and was intrigued enough to enter Dave's classes. As Dave sagely advised, the best way to introduce remote viewing to a skeptic is to have them *do* it and then let them make up their own mind. I leave it to the reader to do their homework. A cautionary note: remote viewing is best learned from a competent instructor fully trained in the intricacies of the protocols and methodologies. The original remote viewers were required to sign a Human-Use agreement stating that they understood the risks of a program that might challenge everything they believed. A person with a fragile psyche might be at risk in such a program.

In the 21st century, America is relying more and more on sophisticated technology to give our military an advantage, built around the concept of metricentric warfare. The main idea is that sophisticated sensors, communications and computers tie all of our assets together, whether located on the sea, air, or land. C3ISR-Command, Communications, Control, Intelligence, Surveillance and Reconnaissance are the foundations of metricentric warfare. We rely on highly mobile platforms that can take advantage of the opportunities that accrue from a sophisticated C3ISR to overwhelm our opponent. Our enemies know this. In this knowledge, are we actually showing a weakness that the antagonists of the future could exploit?

In 2007, Eric Sayers, a recent Master of Arts graduate from the University of Western Ontario, wrote a story for the *Weekly Standard* on Asymmetrical Warfare. In it, he discussed the fact that other countries have seen the success of asymmetric warfare against the United States and were advocating its incorporation into their own military planning. Sayers quoted military leaders and analysts from the People's Republic of China who are advocating asymmetric warfare should they face the forces of a technologically advanced nation in a regional conflict. These leaders are tailoring China's military weapon acquisitions with asymmetric warfare in mind.[41]

The successes that the Taliban and al-Queda enjoyed over the technologically superior military of the United States and its allies have not gone unnoticed. We face enemies who blend in with the local populace, espouse radical fundamentalist religious views, and strike with suicide bombers and kidnappers. They have the willpower to confront the world's most powerful nation, and back it up with suicidal determination. They strike not from established bases in established national boundaries, but from caves or condominiums located in countries around the world. They have taken advantage of our weaknesses and forced us to fight on their terms. This is asymmetrical warfare. We faced a similar situation in Vietnam, when we fought a technologically inferior enemy on his own ground using outmoded WW II tactics. The Vietnamese failed to win a single battle, but won the war. Sun Tzu, the author of *The Art of War,* would have been proud. The Vietnamese followed its tenets, which gave them the advantage that allowed them to force our withdrawal.[42]

One conclusion is inescapable. To win an asymmetrical war there is one element that is more important than firepower, mobility, or logistics. You need intelligence. One of the failures of the campaign against terrorism in the days before 9/11 was not the lack of intelligence, but the failure to disseminate and integrate that intelligence. That failure ran from the highest levels of government, through US intelligence agencies, to our front line units.

One would assume that with the devastation of 9/11 a coherent plan to address our shortcomings in the intelligence arena would have been the first thing on our government's mind. Instead of responsibility and culpability, we got recriminations, acrimony, and finger pointing. We still have not addressed our intelligence shortcomings. Satellite sensors backed up by highly mobile, heavily armed and electronically linked assets are useless if our enemies refuse to fight us on our technological high ground.

The terrorists are countering our reliance on those technologies. They are no longer using easily intercepted forms of communication. They use ambush and Improvised Explosive Devices, or IEDs, instead of pitched battles. They try to blend in with the local populace. They are adapting to attack us where we are vulnerable. What is the US relying more and more on than its vaunted intelligence technologies to combat these tactics? HumInt ... human intelligence; in other words, procuring tips from people in the area. Sometimes that intelligence is fruitful; other times it is not. However, some of the biggest victories in Iraq have come from human intelligence, which is considered the least reliable type of information. It was human intelligence that led to the end of Osama bin Laden.

This does not mean that technology has no place on the battlefield. It means that we need to evaluate where our weaknesses are and address those shortcomings. Asymmetrical warfare requires a different mindset from that which the military traditionally has been willing to accept. But, there are those in the military that are starting to look for new avenues of approach to the problem.

In 2001, Commander L.R. Bremseth, a Navy SEAL, wrote a paper as part of his studies at the Marine Corps War College. It was entitled "Unconventional Human Intelligence Support: Transcendent and Asymmetrical Warfare Implications of Remote Viewing." In it, the author discusses the idea of Transcendent Warfare; a new type of warfare characterized by technologies or techniques beyond all previously established paradigms. Development of a transcendental technology could enable a leap to a new dimension of warfare, incurring a perhaps insurmountable obstacle to an adversary. By the very nature of Transcendental Warfare, it might involve challenging earlier concepts or scientific dogma.

Commander Bremseth suggested that the remote viewing program, called by several different code names but most popularly known as Star Gate, utilized by US intelligence services between 1972 and 1995 was the first successful application of Transcendental Warfare. The author suggests there are other transcendent technologies beyond remote viewing. A nation-state with the mastery of such technologies could make present-day technologies either vulnerable or obsolete. Remote viewing may just be the first TW application. There is evidence of a second.[43]

In 1979, the Princeton Engineering Anomalies Research group, otherwise known as the PEAR group, performed an independent investigation into transcendental technologies. One was remote viewing. The other was psychokinesis, or the ability to influence material objects by the mind with no intervening physical contact. The creators of the project, Dr. Robert Jahn and Brenda Dunn, had heard anecdotal stories of large-scale events such as the bending of spoons or other large objects, called Macro-PK. However, they felt that it would be easier to perform experiments with the other form called Micro-PK. This is the ability of the mind to influence the outcome of a random process to a statistically significant degree. They did not choose subjects considered to have significant psychic ability, but rather just bright enthusiastic students who were interested in taking part. These "operators", as they were known, were to alter the output of electronic random number generators to a statistically significant level. They were to do this by the intention of their mind to change the output in a certain manner. The machines were isolated from the operators and standard scientific protocols observed.

The results of the experiments carried out over thousands of trials conclusively showed that the operators had an effect on the machines far beyond what is statistically significant. They were able to influence an electronic device to make it produce unexpected outputs.[44]

Consider an opponent who embraced Transcendent Warfare employing such a technology against an adversary that relied on electronic machines? Machines like computers, GPS receivers, and electronically integrated platforms. They could create havoc in a war-fighting machine that relies on electronic equipment that requires a stable correct result in order to function. If that stable output could be made unstable, our war-fighting machine effectively would be blind, deaf, and dumb.

There was an article in the January 3rd 2003 special issue of *US News & World Report* titled, "The History of American Spies." Part of the article focused on the Star Gate remote viewing program. The article questioned why US intelligence services still do not have an active remote viewing unit, even though from the mid-seventies to the mid-nineties remote viewing produced verifiable results repeatedly in situations where no other intelligence asset was able to.[45]

Why indeed?

The biggest argument that naysayers use is that it is not reliable. Satellites and signal intercepts can do it better.

However, reliability was never really the issue.

Major General Edmund R. Thompson stated, "I never liked getting into debates with the skeptics, because if you didn't believe that remote viewing was real, you hadn't done your homework." How could a classified program with congressional oversight last for twenty years if it was nothing more than pseudo-science?[46]

Dr. Jessica Utts, head of the statistics department at UC-Davis, stated in a report sponsored by the CIA that there is no question, mathematically speaking, that remote viewing works. Experiments originally conducted by Stanford Research Institute and then later replicated by another think tank, called SAIC, under the strictest scientific protocols showed there was no need for further replication. The results indicated it is time to change the emphasis to how and why it works.[47]

Is remote viewing perfect? No, but then neither are satellites or signal intercepts. Both require human interpretation. Human intelligence isn't perfect either, yet it has proved to be a valuable asset.

Satellites cannot see through steel, concrete, or rock. Signal intercepts cannot contribute if the enemy refuses to use electronic communications. Each of the various forms of intelligence has a role in providing a coherent strategic and tactical picture to provide the necessary data for a proper response. Remote viewing can make significant contributions to the intelligence picture. It has before, as shown in earlier chapters.

In 2004, large portions of the files of Project Star Gate were declassified. With these documents available, the true story of the success of Project Star Gate and remote viewing will be forthcoming.[48]

Jules Verne and H.G. Wells wrote science fiction at the turn of the 19th century. They talked of ships that could travel submerged around the world, killer machines, and death rays that could melt metal and kill people.

Nuclear submarines, armed remotely piloted vehicles, and laser weapons are an unpleasant fact in our century. What was fiction in an earlier age is now reality in ours.

Scientific beliefs once thought sacrosanct are being challenged as we enter the early twenty-first century. In the time of Newton, the universe was a giant machine based on scientific principles well understood in their time. Newtonian mechanics were the mathematics that held the key to the riddle of the universe.

That was the prevailing view in that era. However, as time and science advanced, cracks began to appear in the clockwork universe. Scientists with names like Heisenberg, Schrödinger, Planck, and Einstein found that the mechanistic universe was an illusion. The universe was anything but a giant machine ticking quietly and carefully away. They swept away the veil to reveal a universe of stunning sublime mystery. Not just a universe, a multiverse populated with spectacular phenomena such as black holes and quasars, wormholes and parallel universes. Dominated not by the clockwork of Newtonian mechanics, but ruled by the two greatest physical theories ever advanced by Man, Relativity and Quantum Mechanics.

These theories are counter-intuitive. Relativity says the Universe changes according to velocity and point of view. Space and time are no longer the Newtonian ideal but rather fluid, each changing based on what an observer experiences. Quantum mechanics eliminates the old view of atoms that follow the mechanistic mathematics of Newton's day and replaces it with a universe where atoms have a schizoid existence, both particulate and with wave manifestations. Until an observation by an observer is performed, information regarding a system is indeterminate. The particle's behavior follows statistical laws. A particle has a probability of being in many places at once and can tunnel through barriers that should prohibit any passage. Our knowledge of the basic properties of a particle, that of momentum and position, trade accuracy back and forth in a tug of war. The more you know about the position of a particle the less you know of its momentum and vice versa.

Even the matter and energy that composes our everyday existence we now find makes up only four percent of the mass-energy of the Universe. The light from the Sun and your tanning lamp, the atoms making up a cheeseburger and the hand holding it are made of material that barely registers in our universe. Ninety-six percent of the mass-energy of our universe is composed of a mysterious substance. We haven't the slightest clue as to its composition. Seventy-five percent is composed of what we call dark energy. The remaining twenty-one percent is what we characterize as dark matter.

We have no idea of what these two forms of mass/energy are composed. We do know that the dark energy seems to be a form of anti-gravity that is powering an accelerating expansion of this universe. Other than that, we have no clue to what the majority of our universe is composed of.

Scientists talk openly about wormholes and quantum teleportation. You can find papers in prestigious science journals by well-known scientists about faster-than-light propulsion. Articles that just ten years ago would have been deemed preposterous are now commonplace.[49]

Why should remote viewing be any different? Dr. Arthur C. Clark once said that any sufficiently advanced science is indistinguishable from magic. We can't explain remote viewing, so it seems like magic. Four hundred years ago, the belief that the Earth was not the center of the universe could get you a death sentence. Galileo narrowly escaped such a fate, doing so only by renouncing his discovery that the Earth revolved around the Sun. His compatriot Giordano Bruno wasn't as fortunate.[50]

Today that prejudice continues; fostered by people who suffer from what Dr. Arthur C. Clark characterized as either a failure of nerve or a failure of imagination. Scientists show a failure of nerve when they know a controversial assertion is true, but they don't want to risk their standing by acknowledging it. Or they suffer a failure of imagination when so wrapped up in their beliefs that they no longer have the ability to look beyond them.[51]

Debunkers will tell you that because scientists can't tell you how remote viewing works, it can't be a legitimate phenomenon. Yet not one of those debunkers have ever produced a peer reviewed and replicated series of experiments refuting remote viewing. In fact the Committee for the Scientific Investigation of the Claims of the Paranormal (CSICOP), now called The Committee for Scientific

Investigation, has expressly forbidden such experiments after one of there own, Dr. Ray Hyman, did such an experiment. He claimed the results were "short of scientific acceptability." It was never published or held to peer review.[52]

Ask any scientist how aspirin works in the body and he will be unable to give a precise mechanism. Ask a scientist how electricity moves through a wire or lightning moves through the atmosphere and he will admit that the exact mechanism is not yet fully understood. So does that mean aspirin is useless, or lightning a farce? Remote viewing lasted over twenty years in the intelligence community because it produced results. They didn't care that the physicists who created the program couldn't explain why it worked. They only cared that it produced verifiable results repeatedly when no other intelligence asset was able to.

They kept coming back for over twenty years.

The original military remote viewers always knew that the technology had applications beyond intelligence work. Questions like, how the Egyptians moved those massive stones for the pyramids. A physicist might ask what are the processes surrounding the supermassive black hole at the center of our galaxy? Perhaps your interest lies in the etiology of mutant AIDS virus strains or solving a twenty-year old crime. Remote viewing can offer both directions of investigation as well as answers, not by replacing standard investigative and scientific methodology, but as an equal partner in discovery.

A common misconception is that a remote viewer or a psychic found a missing person. They do nothing of the kind. They provide information to investigators who then go out and do the tedious legwork that leads to the discovery. The psychic gets the glory; the investigators get the body. Without the remote viewer, they probably wouldn't have the body. However, the viewers only provide leads for the investigators. This is a point that debunkers overlook when dealing with remote viewing; it is part of an overall investigative process, not a stand-alone effort. Remote viewing was never designed to replace other forms of investigation or intelligence gathering. It was meant to augment them.

Another common misconception is that psychics and remote viewers are the same. I wasn't born with my psychic "conduits" open. Very few people are. I had to learn how to use this innate gift we all share. I wasn't like a Mel Riley or Ingo Swann who was born with those conduits open and functioning. My ability came after long hours of training and practice, especially ceaseless, unrelenting practice. All remote viewers are psychic; not all psychics are remote viewers. To be a remote viewer you have to be trained as a remote viewer. Unlike natural psychics, remote viewing has a methodology and a protocol. If those are not followed, then it isn't remote viewing. A psychic does his thing as an event; he doesn't go through a process. A psychic is not constrained by the three laws of remote viewing nor by methodology or protocol. Does this mean a psychic has less legitimacy than a remote viewer?

I don't believe so. A psychic has lived with his ability most, if not all, of his life. All that experience and practice must prove some talent. Nevertheless, there is a difference. Remote viewers are trained in a protocol and methodology. They follow techniques born of the scientific method established through scientific inquiry, experiment, and peer review. All remote viewers follow those techniques or some variation of the original work done by Stanford Research Institute. The training makes the difference between a natural psychic and a remote viewer.

I started out as a skeptic, believing that remote viewing wasn't possible. Nevertheless, I kept an open mind and took Dave's courses to see for myself. I found that resolving the issues that learning remote viewing created was no small matter. I don't expect it will be for anyone else either.

The original military remote viewers maintained that the best way to find out if it works is to try it. Experience tends to overcome prejudice. Beliefs are stronger when backed up by experience. Belief then becomes truth.

It's hard when a belief falls. It's even harder to remain true to yourself and accept that truth. Some are never able to do that and will always remain a minion of the status quo. They remain a lifetime member of the "unconscious of the conscious."

I wrote this account not so much to change anyone's mind about whether or not remote viewing and other consciousness-related phenomena exist. Rather, it is aimed at others like myself who are skeptical but have an open mind. Those who haven't lost a child's curiosity about life, this universe, and our ultimate destiny.

This story is about the adventures and experiences that led to the discovery of my personal mythology, a personal mythology that culminated in the writing of this book. This story might never have happened but for the fact that I was lucky. I walked into a bookstore, and in doing so, walked into a new world of promise and possibility – a world introduced by someone who was once lost, very much like me.

There is a wonderful universe out there if you put aside ego and self-doubt. Voyage into darkness and learn a new way of seeing, and enjoy the journey inward and beyond.

CITATIONS

1. Rauscher, E.A. and Targ, R. (2001) The Speed of Thought: Investigation of a Complex Space-Time Metric to Describe Psychic Phenomena..

2. Morehouse, David A. PhD. Maj. US Army (ret.) Remote Viewing Sounds True (2008).

3. Atwater, F. H. Captain of My Ship, Master of my Soul Hampton Roads (2001).

4. Puthoff, H.E. and Targ, R. A Perceptual Channel for Information Transfer Over Kilometer Distances: Historical Perspective and Resent Research Proceedings IEEE, 64(3), 329-354.

5. Schnabel, J. Remote Viewers: The Secret History of America's Psychic Spies Dell (1997).

6. Schnabel ibid.

7. Schnabel ibid.

8. May, E.C. The AIR Review of the Dept. of Defense's Star Gate Program: A Commentary Journal of Parapsychology 60(1) 3-23.

9. Remote Viewing Instructional Services Inc. The Central Intelligence Agency's Star Gate Collection Archives Set of CDs (2006).

10. McMoneagle, J. Memoirs of a Psychic Spy Hampton Roads (2002)

11. Schnabel ibid.

12. Jung, C.G. Synchronicity: An Acausal Connecting Principal Princeton/Bollingen (1960).

13. Heckler, R.S. In Search of the Warrior's Spirit North Atlantic Books (1990).

14. Morehouse, David A. PhD. Maj. US Army (ret.) Psychic Warrior (1996).

15. Jahn, R. G. PhD and Dunne, B.J. Margins of Reality Harvest/HBJ (1987).

16. Strauss, W. and Howe, N. The Fourth Turning: An American Prophecy Broadway Books (1998).

17. Unsolicited customer review, Amazon Customer Review of Psychic Warrior By Morehouse, D.A. Maj. US Army (ret).

18. Pelligrino, C. Flying to Valhalla Avon Books (1993).

19. Everett, H. Theory of the Universal Wavefunction Thesis Princeton University (1956).

20. Sheldrake, R. The Presence of the Past Times Books (1988).

21. Schnabel ibid.

22. Mandelbrot, B. The Fractal Geometry of Nature Freeman (1977).

23. Smith, Paul H. Reading the Enemy's Mind Forge Books (2005).

24. Benford, G. Eater Eos (2001).

25. Dicke, R.H. and Wittke, J.P. Introduction to Quantum Mechanics Addison-Wesley (1960).

26. Schnabel ibid.

27. Targ, R. and Puthoff, H. Mind-Reach Hampton Roads (1977).

28. Jahn, R. G. PhD and Dunne, B.J. ibid.

29. Deutsch, D. and Ekert, A. Beyond the Quantum Horizon article in Scientific American magazine Summer 2013 vol. 22 no. 2 pp 107.

30. Everett ibid.

31. Bell, J.S. On the Einstein-Podolsky-Rosen (EPR) Paradox Physics 1 (3) pp 195-200 (1964).

32. Einstein, A. Relativity Tess Press (2005).

33. Marrs, J. Psi Spies Alien Zoo Publications (2000).

34. T'Hooft, G. Dimensional Reduction in Quantum Gravity arXiv:gr-gc/9310026 pp 10026 original paper.

35. Hameroff, S. and Penrose, R. (March 2014) Consciousness in the Universe: A review of ORCH-OR Theory. Physics of Life Review 11(1) 39-78.

36. Pribram, K. (1999) Quantum Holography: Is it relevant to brain function?Information Sciences 115(1-4) 97-102.

37. Yarsinske, A.W. No One Left Behind TrineDay (2012).

38. Wikipedia Encyclopedia Pat Tillman Wikipedia Foundation (2013).

39. Hansen, G.P. CSICOP and the Skeptics: An Overview Journal of the American Society for Psychical Research Vol. 86 no. 1 pp 18-63 (Jan 1992).

40. Yarsinske, A.W. An American in the Basement TrineDay (2013).

41. Sayers, E. China's Asymmetric Strategy paper FrontPageMag.com (2007).

42. Tzu, S. Art of War Tuttle Publishing (1996).

43. Bremseth, L.R. Commander US Navy Unconventional Human Intelligence Support: Transcendent and Asymmetric Warfare Implications of Remote Viewing Thesis Marine Corps War College (2001).

44. Jahn, R.G. and Dunne, B.J. ibid.

45. Szegedy-Maszak, M. and Fenyvesi, C. Enemies in the Mind's Eye article US News and World Report pp 64-65 Jan 27-Feb 3 (2003).

46. Schnabel, J. ibid.

47. Utts, J. An Assessment of the Evidence for Psychic Functioning Journal of Scientific Exploration 10 (1) pp 3-30.

48. Remote Viewing Instructional Services Inc ibid.

49. Davies, E. Teleportation Physics Study Special Report Air Force Research Laboratory (2004).

50. Clarke, A.C. Profiles of the Future Phoenix/Orion Publishing (2000).

51. Clarke ibid.

52. Hansen ibid.

RESOURCES

The following works are presented for those readers who wish to learn more about remote viewing and Project Star Gate. This list is not all-inclusive but these works presented herein are, in my humble opinion, some of the best.

Psychic Warrior by David Morehouse
Published: St. Martin's Press, Nov. 1996
ISBN-13: 978-0312147082
This is the work that started it all. It is an excellent account of David Morehouse's experience as a member of Project Star Gate. But it is also a highly personal account of what it was like to be a special operations warrior in the U.S. Army who rose through the ranks to become the youngest Ranger Company Commander in the Army. As one of his subordinates stated, "I would follow him anywhere!" I couldn't agree more.

David also has a website at David Morehouse Productions, where he offers a number of resources for interested parties. You can also find him at his David Morehouse Remote Viewing Group on Facebook where you can ask questions and find out more.

Remote Viewing by David Morehouse Ph.D
Published: Sounds True, Nov 2007
ISBN-13: 978-1604074369
This is the most comprehensive textbook on coordinate remote viewing that is available. It is not a casual read but is to be used in conjunction with an instructor to teach remote viewing. It is technical and detailed and designed to take the novice from beginner to intermediate remote viewer. To those who decide they wish to try their hand at becoming a remote viewer, this work is essential.

The Seventh Sense by Lyn Buchanan
Published: Gallery Books, Feb 2003
ISBN-13 978-0743462686
This is a fine introduction to coordinate remote viewing and remote viewing as done by the members of Star Gate, as Lyn was. Lyn trained a number of the members of Star Gate, and he discusses several of their successes. Lyn also runs a website at Problems Solutions Innovations where you can get more information.

Reading the Enemy's Mind by Paul H. Smith
Published: Forge Books Tom Doherty Associates, Jan 2005
ISBN-10: 0-312-87515-0

This is arguably the best history of Project Star Gate from an insider's perspective. Paul was one of the training officers in the program and writes from personal knowledge as well as a great deal of research into the history of the program and the people involved. Paul is a former officer of IRVA, the International Remote Viewer's Association. Their website is an excellent resource. Paul also runs his own remote viewing website at RVIS, Remote Viewing Instructional Services.

Mind Trek by Joe McMoneagle
Published- Hampton Roads, Sept 1992
ISBN-13: 978-1878901729
Joe is one of the original remote viewer's in Project Star Gate. His assigned remote viewer number was 001 and there are many stories of successful sessions attributed to him. This is his first book and although he never discusses the military program in it, he does an excellent job of writing about extended remote viewing. Joe never learned CRV and all of his sessions were in ERV. This was a great resource for me in the weeks leading up to my first ERV course in Carmel with David Morehouse. For those viewers who prefer ERV, this is excellent companion.

Remote Viewing Secrets by Joe McMoneagle
Published: Hampton Roads, May 2000
ISBN-13 978-1571741592
This is a companion work to Mind Trek and this one does discuss the Star Gate program. It is at present, the best work on extended remote viewing published. It, like the Morehouse book on CRV, is a technical work and not a casual read. But for those who have been taught or are considering a class in ERV, this book is an essential.

Remote Viewers by Jim Schnabel
Published: Dell Publishing, Jan 1997
ISBN-13 978-0440223061
I have included this work with a caveat. The author does occasionally write for the intelligence community, and although it turns out to be an excellent work by an outsider, well researched and with many personal interviews, it is a slanted view. He writes of the accomplishments of the Unit with a barely concealed skepticism that parroted the CIA's published position on the remote viewing program in 1995. It is, however, an excellent history by an outsider and read with that caveat in mind is a worthy read.

This represents only a small number of works on remote viewing out there in print or on the web. Once again I caution the reader about those unscrupulous types who would promise impossible results for your money. Do your research carefully. Caveat Emptor!

ACKNOWLEDGMENTS

No one writes a book all by themselves. Throughout the process there are usually many unsung heroes that help to create a finished work. I must mention the assistance of the following people who helped turn a rough stone into a polished jewel.

To my parents, John and Barbara, who regardless of where my journey took me, always supported me with love and encouragement.

To Meg Jernigan, my private editor, to whom the unenviable job of turning this work into something readable fell. She spent long hours reading and rereading, suggesting and cajoling, and pointing out where I either strayed off course, or actually fell. There were many times when her patience was tested. Her assistance was invaluable. And thanks as well to her daughter Katie Fuller, who did such a wonderful job on the design of my website.

My everlasting thanks to my publisher Kris Millegan, from TrineDay Press, who took a chance on a new author. He was always there with encouragement and enthusiasm. My thanks also to TrineDay who put the book together with additions and formatting the session summaries and pictures to the proper chapters. Kudos to Ed Bishop, who did such a wonderful job on the cover art. And kudos to my editor at TrineDay, Kelly Ray, who cleared out the last of the chaff and left behind a polished work.

To my good friend Joe Buff, an accomplished author in his own right, who helped a novice avoid the pitfalls of being new to the publishing field.

Thanks to my comrades from the Trojan Warrior II project. To Dru, Dr. Mike, Dr.s Susan and Sigfried, Dr. Barry, Norm, Lisa, Mark, and my buddies from SEAL Teams ONE and THREE; Keith, Shawn, Tom, and Jeff. And for their heartfelt assistance with the Project, my thanks and appreciation to the First Earth Battalion's Col. Jim Channon US Army (ret) and the original Trojan Warrior, Dr. Richard Strozzi Heckler.

To Patty Morehouse-DeMarco, Saundra Marsh, my classmates and the Barnacles, Mimi, Tina, Cynthia, and Ariane, who all helped me through some very rough times in my journey. Thank you for your trust and support.

Jason Hooper of RVT and Anita Luzinski, who read my first attempts and made numerous suggestions on how to make the manuscript more readable. Anita also provided the picture of the author on the back cover, taken while I was diving off Santa Catalina.

To Bill McDonald, former president of the Military Writer's Society of America, who believed in the manuscript and graciously volunteered to write the foreword. My deepest appreciation goes to Bill as well as to Paul H. Smith and Daz Smith. These three men graciously wrote reviews, offered encouragement, and selflessly helped to put the word out.

My thanks to Amy Waters Yarsinske, who not only saved the book by confirming the data from the Explorer's class and the truth about Capt. Spiecher, but who also opened my eyes about how our government has let down the very people sworn to protect it.

To military remote viewers Lyn Buchanan, Paul H. Smith, and Skip Atwater, who helped to teach me the art and science of military remote viewing. To Marty Rosenblatt, who helped me put aside my preconceived notions of what is possible in remote viewing. And a special thanks to the late Ingo Swann, creator of coordinate remote viewing and a true pioneer, a great teacher, and a good friend.

Finally and foremost, to Dave Morehouse. Teacher, mentor, and friend. Thank you, my brother, for taking a skeptic under your wing and opening a new world.